EDUCATION AND DIVINE REVELATION

by Herbert W. Byrne, Ed.D.

© 1998 ACTS MULTI-MINISTRIES

ISBN 0-9663098-1-2

LIBRARY OF CONGRESS CATALOG CARD NUMBER: 98-73209

Printed by:
EVANGEL PRESS
2000 Evangel Way
P.O. Box 189
Nappanee, IN 46550-0189

Published by:

ulti-
ACTS inistries
P.O. Box 11022
Fort Wayne, IN 46855
1-888-367-6647

Herbert W. Byrne, Ed.D.
Professor of Christian Education
Emeritus

Asbury Theological Seminary
Wilmore, Kentucky 40390

Other books by this author:

A Christian Approach to Education

Christian Education for the Local Church

Improving Church Education

Motivating Church Workers

Duties and Responsibilities of Church Workers

John Wesley and Learning

TO

My wife - Nelle

My son - Bert

My daughter - Betty

My son-in-law - Jim

TABLE OF CONTENTS

Chapter   Page

I.   THE SEARCH FOR MEANING AND UNITY 2
     A. The Situation 2
     B. The Search 3
     C. The Sources 16
     D. The Solution 20

II. DIVINE REVELATION, BIBLICAL EPISTEMOLOGY
     AND CHRISTIAN EDUCATION 25
     A. Revelation and Christian Education 25
     B. Biblical Epistemology 29
     C. Summary of Biblical Epistemology 34
     D. An Evangelical and Biblical Concept of Revelation 36

III. REVELATION AND CHRISTIAN EDUCATION
     THEORY 50
     A. The Need, Nature and Demand for Theory 50
     B. Revelation and Christian Education Theory 59
     C. Representative Evangelical Revelational
     Perspectives 70
     D. An Evangelical Proposal for Theory 75
     E. Revelation and Local Church Education 95
     F. Revelation and Other Christian Schools 104

IV. REVELATION AND GENERAL EDUCATION
     PRACTICE 112
     A. The Process of Education 112
     B. Objectives 119
     C. The Role of the Teacher 133
     D. The Role of the Learner 135
     E. The Learning Process 137
     F. The Teaching Process 160
     G. Curriculum 180

H. Authority, Freedom and Discipline........................ 197
I. Evaluation 200

V. REVELATION AND INSTITUTIONAL CHRISTIAN
    EDUCATION PRACTICE 208
    A. Local Church Practice.. 208
    B. Christian Day School Practice 218
    C. Christian Liberal Arts College Practice 224
    D. The Theological Seminary and
        Educational Practice 267

Preface

In recent years not a great deal of writing has been done in the field of Christian education theory. This seems to be true for both liberal and conservative thinkers. On the other hand an investigation of past writings will show some efforts on the part of educators in the field to find an integrating principle, some kind of <u>motif</u> or centralizing principle which would serve as the foundation for theory and guide for practice.

An attempt was made in this work to summarize such efforts and to throw them into a comparative light with an orthodox and evangelical position in Christian education. Thus, the comparative format of the work would appear evident. A search in first sources of these positions will be indicated in the references.

Chapter One was devoted to the subject of the search for an integrating principle. The current situation in the disciple itself, in the literature and on the field, was surveyed to point up the need for this principle. Section Two of this chapter surveyed the various evidences from the history, the scholars and practice on the field. This showed who is grappling with this problem. Section Three showed the sources utilized by various schools of thought and action. The last section made an attempt to resolve this problem by pointing up the advantages offered by a revelational approach.   Chapter Two focused exclusively on the concept and guidelines provided to Christian education theory and practice by divine revelation. The concept of revelation itself was defined. The chapter concluded with a statement on the crucial role that epistemology has in developing any Christian education theory, followed by a statement on an evangelical and biblical concept of revelation.

Chapter Three was designed to focus attention on the implications of divine revelation for building Christian education theory. A discussion was provided on the need, nature and demands for theory. An effort was made to show the place that revelation has in theory development. An evangelical position was compared to other theories and suggestions made whereby the construction of theory could take place based on the premises of divine revelation.

The implications such actions have for various types of Christian schools were indicated.

Chapter Four revealed the direct impact that divine revelation has on general Christian education practice. Definitions of the educational processes necessary to operate a Christian school were indicated.

Chapter Five gave attention to the implications that revelation has for institutional Christian education practice. Suggestions were made in this chapter on how to utilize the principles of revelation in the local church, Christian day schools, Christian liberal arts colleges, and the theological seminary.

A survey and comparative study of this nature makes it necessary to consult many sources. For suggestions and contributions made, the writer is grateful. For permission to use many quotations, I am grateful. For any mistakes and shortcomings, I take full responsibility.

Herbert W. Byrne

Some Definitions of Terms

Education is a broad term, referring to teaching and learning of almost anything and everything in one's life. Teaching sources are many.

Schooling, or school work, is the formal processes of teaching and learning, organized into an institutional setting for purposes of education.

Instruction is an educational process by which one is caused to learn, typically carried on in a classroom setting.

Christian education is that kind of education which focuses on the particular values we have in Jesus Christ, as well as our response to divine revelation. It is also used to describe that kind of education which takes place under the auspices of Christian people at any level of application.

Church education is that kind of Christian education that goes on in the setting of a local church.

Religious education is a term referring to that kind of education that goes on within a broad framework within which teaching and learning lead to individual commitment to general religious values. In contrast to Christian education it can refer to any kind of religion. It is not only used in this way in this work, but also is used to describe that kind of church education endorsed by the Religious Education Association in the past and those who follow in its tradition today.

Herbert W. Byrne
Asbury Theological Seminary

THE SEARCH FOR MEANING AND UNITY

A. The Situation
    1. In the Discipline
    2. In the Literature
    3. On the Field

B. The Search
    1. Evidences from History
    2. Evidences from the Scholars

C. The Sources
    1. Among Secular Educators
    2. Among Religious Educators
    3. Among Christian Educators

D. The Solution
    1. The Need
    2. The Task
    3. The Secret

CHAPTER 1

THE SEARCH FOR MEANING AND UNITY

A. The Situation

1. <u>In the Discipline</u>. An examination of the discipline of Christian education in general, and church education in particular, reveals the need for a unifying principle of thought and action. That a state of confusion exists becomes evident upon the most cursory examination of the state of these disciplines. If progress is to be made, if a sense of direction is to be given, and if proper foundations for theory and program are to be laid, Christian education needs a perspective based squarely on the demands of both the Christian faith and that kind of genuine education which is an outgrowth of Christianity. There is great need for the acceptance of a <u>motif</u> which will unify the thinking and practice of church educators.

2. <u>In the Literature</u>. The fact that some generally agreed upon principle of integration is needed for Christian education is nowhere revealed more readily than in the literature of the discipline. Scholars do not agree as to what such a unifying principle should be or where it can be found. The fact that we are now witnessing the passing of a period of time in Christian education characterized by confusion on the one hand and experimentation on the other is evidence of this.

In an article in the March-April, 1982, issue of <u>Religious Education</u>, page 123, Margaret Webster accurately described the current state of mind in religious education circles by saying:

> Today, I contend, there is an acutely serious separation of theory and practice in religious education. There is little or no resemblance between the theory of religious education explored and debated in the classroom of our seminaries and colleges of Christian education and the practice of religious education in the majority of our local churches and schools.

3. <u>On the Field</u>. A third evidence of the currently prevalent state of confusion in Christian education is to be found in actual field conditions. Publishers are searching for theoretical means by which

new and more relevant curriculum materials can be produced which will at the same time reflect the demands of true Christian education and cultural needs. At the local church level leaders and laymen are finding it difficult to apply new curriculum materials to their particular situation. This is seen, not only with reference to the place of the Bible in the curriculum, but also in the implementation of experimental curricula and educational theories in the church school.

B. The Search

1. <u>Evidences from History</u>. The mission of the church is to minister to the age in which it lives. As to what is the best method of doing this is a problem educational theorists have wrestled with throughout the years.

That history has something to say regarding a proper unifying principle for Christian educational theory on the surface is obvious. But one will search in vain for general agreement on what such a principle should be. A proper study of Old and New Testament histories should be profitable, revealing God's secrets in this regard. It appears, however, that man has imposed too much of his own thinking on holy writ and thus has failed to discover the principles of God's plan for Christian education. A study of Hebrew religious education would provide basic foundations and principles for building a system of Christian education which will stand the test of time. Here should be revealed basic content to be taught, acceptable methodologies, and a structure upon which to build a program. Most certainly in the life and teachings of Jesus, as well as in those of the early church, such principles should be found. Of course, this supposition is based on the acceptance of the premise that the Word of God essentially and inherently yields such guidelines.

As the church expanded it became necessary to adjust educational methods to the character and needs of the people. Catechetical, catechumenal and cathedral schools became prominent. It is possible that, in spite of the value of these schools, basic biblical insights were either lost or clouded. There is no doubt of this as the church moved into the Medieval Period. While it is true that monasteries provided refuge for educated churchmen and preserved what learning there was, outside among the laity and the common man illiteracy and ignorance of the Scriptures was rather universal.

In the great efforts to throw off the effects of medievalism, educators were divided largely into two camps: those advocating a return to the achievements of Greece and Rome, and others insisting on a return to true Christianity. There were compromising stances taken, of course. The Renaissance and Reformation, covered roughly by the fourteenth, fifteenth, and sixteenth centuries, illustrated the effectiveness of education in moral and religious activity. This period reveals the values of religious education as a means of social progress. The place of the Bible as a forerunner of the Great Awakening is not fully appreciated, however, in some circles. While it may be said in general that the church dominated educational circles during these periods, one can see a two-track system of education clearly emerging. One track emphasized religious values and the other track followed Greco-Roman patterns of education, deeply affected by secular philosophies prominent among which were humanism, rationalism, realism, idealism, and naturalism. The latter removed many from biblical and evangelical influences in education.

In the eighteenth and nineteenth centuries, the Bible became prominent in an effort to fight off the inroads of secularism. Efforts to use Scripture as an integrating factor were largely limited to the use of the Bible message for evangelism and instruction. While these two factors served to vitalize church education, they were largely neglected in educational circles outside the church.

The pragmatic philosophy of John Dewey with its consequent issuance in the Progressive Education Movement dominated secular education. His philosophy of instrumentalism and relativism was given wide acceptance. He sought to integrate educational theory and practice by emphasizing biological and social factors, primarily in a democratic setting, as the means of unifying educational thought and practice. He was opposed by conservative educators who sought to perpetuate indoctrination in the fundamental principles of American democracy and the "three R's." Dewey's philosophy deeply affected more liberal advocates of religious education who sought to popularize

4

Progressive Education in the church. The chief exponent of this view was George A. Coe.

Early advocates of theological liberalism in the twentieth century attempted to achieve integration for Christian education by rejecting orthodox theology and supplanting it with a reinterpretation of the Gospel in social terms. At the same time historical and critical scholars broke with the traditional view of the Bible as the inspired Word of God. Psychology became supremely important to these people. The advocates of the Religious Education Association turned to this kind of theological liberalism for the premises of their work. This whole movement came to its height in the organization of the National Council of Churches of Christ in America. During the period between World War I and 1960 a marked decline in Christian education took place. Among reasons for such a decline were the neglect of biblical truth, the effects of secularistic philosophies, the spirit of professionalism among the leaders, the prominence of ecclesiasticism, and weaknesses in leadership training. Among evangelicals, during this period, a lack of unity no doubt was part of the problem.

In reaction to this movement and to theological liberalism, the National Association of Evangelicals, representing some twenty million evangelicals, was organized in 1942. They sought to restore traditional and conservative theological values. For some twenty years they were successful in reviving the Sunday School Movement with its emphasis on evangelism and Bible instruction. Upon the development of stronger denominational programs and publishing houses this movement waned in the past two or three decades.

A movement known as neo-orthodoxy was launched to make an attempt at rediscovering theology as the unifying factor in faith and practice in the church. The movement was traced by Cully who described it as a "search for Christian education since 1940."

J. Donald Butler assesses the present theological situation on the field when he says:

It yet remains for this generation or its successors to explore thoroughly the possible continuity between theology and nurture, building responsible theory in the light of such a

5

continuum and putting it to work in effective practice.[1]
Wyckoff identifies "two outstanding needs":

The need for the building of theory by which these commitments (theological and educational) may be both checked and implemented, and the need for the communication of theory to those who are doing various aspects of the job.[2]

How does one assess the present situation? Among liberals the camp is split between old line liberals and neo-orthodox adherents as far as theology is concerned. Here, however, neo-orthodox believers are beginning to doubt the sufficiency of their position. The encounter with God has not really come. While much has been said about the Word of God, many have failed to make it as relevant as they claimed it was. Some have felt that the emphasis on the sovereignty and majesty of God has led to the belief that God is too far away to be related to us today. Perhaps this was at the root of the "God is Dead" movement. In the curriculum world the situation may be characterized by experimentalism but confusion.

Among evangelicals, goals of church education still appear to be hazy. While loyalty to Bible teaching appears to be strong, in some circles concern with the matter of relevancy in content is evident. Some recognize that a good balance is needed but that this is hard to achieve. While the Sunday school is being critically examined, it still remains the primary school of the church. Many churches, however, no longer restrict the school of the church to the Sunday school. Publishers inside and outside denominational circles, along with liberal advocates, are revising and restructuring curriculum materials, in an effort to update and upgrade them and make them more functional and relevant for the times. Large sums of money for new buildings and equipment have been raised and expended in recent years.

Evangelism continues to be the primary thrust of evangelical Christian education. Spiritual needs are always kept in the forefront. Nurture is considered to be important, as reflected in books and curriculum materials. Great needs center in the demand for more and better trained leaders, teachers and workers. Involvement of the family in the program is considered imperative.

Looking back, one is impressed with the gains noted and has much for which to be thankful. It is evident, however, that a new day is here and much needs to be done. Opportunities are great and the prospects are bright. Much confusion, however, regarding theory remains, and this is a major concern.

A recent phenomenon in the educational world is that of the Christian Day School Movement. Many Christian parents and educators have become dissatisfied with the modern public school system. The aims of the public schools are considered too humanistic and secularistic to satisfy these people so they have started their own schools where Christian principles and practices are integrated with subjects of study. While in the beginning public schools in this country were characterized by religious emphasis, in time secular and civic control of education became dominant, with both aims and curricula predominantly nonreligious. In fact, the philosophy of education in public schools today is at odds with revealed Christian faith. In an effort to restore some of the original Christian emphasis in education, Christian day schools have been started and maintained. As increased enrollments take place in these schools and as continuous upgrading in curriculum materials and facilities is made, this educational movement will continue to make a great impact on education in this country.

Another educational development at the higher level of education focuses our attention on the Bible Institute and Bible College movement. This movement has made great contributions to evangelism at home and abroad, trained hundreds of missionaries, and helped shape the lives of prominent Christian leaders in America. Some denominations depend on these schools to prepare people for Christian leadership. Bible institutes have specialized in English Bible instruction and the practical skills of Christian witness and service. Since about 1947, when the Accrediting Association of Bible Colleges was organized, and in the face of increasing concern for academic excellence, Bible colleges were developed. Such schools are devoted to a program designed at the college level to produce people for Christian ministries and Church vocations through a combination of

7

biblical, general and professional studies. These schools are similar to theological seminaries but operate on the undergraduate level, whereas seminaries operate on the post-college level. While Bible colleges have developed a wide variety of programs for specialized ministries, seminaries have majored in the production of pastors.

Bible colleges and Christian liberal arts colleges are similar in philosophy of education and the Christian development of students. However, where Christian liberal arts colleges build their curricula on the foundations of general education in the humanities and sciences to prepare students through liberal arts majors for many professions and vocations, Bible colleges are more specialized in that they largely restrict their purpose to training people for Christian ministries and church vocations, also combining a major in Bible with general and professional education.

The need for Christian colleges was seen early in the history of this country. Harvard College, for example, was started in 1636 to train ministers. Many others followed, largely sponsored by Christian people and motivated to prepare good citizens with Christian and general education. Even state universities stressed religious values. Surveys of Christian leaders in America show that a large percentage were educated in Christian colleges. Thousands have been trained through the years at the college level.

Problems soon arose. In all the mass of literature on Christian colleges, much is said about "atmosphere," Bible courses, religious activities and chapel, but very little is said about how to get the Christian faith with its presuppositions into classroom teaching. Instead, the philosophy, program and products of Christian colleges are all dealt with in a "secular spirit."

Few have been the efforts among leaders in Christian higher education to make suggestions on how to integrate the Christian faith with higher education practice. Between 1950-52 the Hazen Foundation published a series of pamphlets entitled "Religious Perspectives of College Teaching" in which they suggested that religious facts, issues, and implications should be dealt with in every division, department, and course when they arise naturally. But no suggestions on "how" to do this were successfully made.

The need for a Christian integrating factor is recognized in the light of the complete secularization of American culture. God has been pushed out and this has denied the true source of truth. Christianity is largely ignored, opposed or treated with condescension. Many professedly Christian colleges are in fact secular. Religion is a sideshow and the curriculum is essentially secular.

Secularism took over in time and this deeply affected Christian colleges. Factors which fostered secularism in Christian colleges include:

1. The pressures of accrediting agencies and standardization
2. The seeking of finances and resources from secular sources
3. The influence of graduate schools where the university spirit prevails among leaders
4. Academic pride
5. Narrow-minded church boards
6. Lack of a clearly articulated philosophy of Christian higher education
7. Secularism within the church itself
8. Reactions against sectarianism and fear of indoctrination
9. The secularism of the culture and influence of materialism
10. The rise of humanism and naturalism which issued in the dominance of a scientific world view

Such factors which currently exist all call for the revival of religious values at the college level and for the development of a Christian philosophy of life and education.

2. Evidences from the Scholars. One of the first late scholars to discuss modern religious education theory and practice was Horace Bushnell. His work along with that of George Coe gave impetus to the Religious Education Association. This organization created considerable discussion on the problems of church education within a liberal theological context.

As a reaction against this movement, some new developments took place among liberals. In 1940 Harrison Elliott sprang to the defense of liberal religious education with his book, Can Religious

Education Be Christian?[3] He sought to answer his own question by concluding that religious education can be Christian but on terms which he himself identified and defined as Christian. He rejected our revelation, stating that, to be Christian, religious education must rest upon human experience through which Christianity is interpreted to people today.

In 1941 H. Shelton Smith published a book, Faith and Nurture,[4] in which he attacked liberal religious education and revealed the errors of this movement. He showed conclusively that the theological assumptions of liberal religious education were not Christian as measured by New Testament standards. The book is historic, for it represents the first major effort to express discontent with the lack of theology in Christian education as well as to reveal the errors and weaknesses of liberal theology.

While Shelton Smith's book was not a direct answer to Elliott's, he did deal with the same issues. He pointed out the four marks of classical liberalism as (1) divine immanence, (2) growth, (3) essential goodness of man, and (4) the historical Jesus. He showed that such views were derived from secular philosophical sources, not the Bible and New Testament Christianity.

In 1944, the International Council of Religious Education, in the face of the new emphasis on theology and noting the attack on liberalism, authorized a Study Committee to produce a statement on the place of theology in Christian education. The Committee reported in 1947 in the book edited by Paul Vieth entitled The Church and Christian Education.[5] This report noted the importance of theology in Christian education, gave new emphasis to the church as the context for Christian education, reaffirmed the importance of the family and expressed a new concern for evangelism. While this book neglected the issues of the theological controversy then in progress, it did represent a definite move away from liberalism. It is significant also that the term "Christian Education" had now replaced the term "religious education."

This concern was followed with that of Randolph C. Miller's in his The Clue to Christian Education[6] in 1950. While Miller failed also to identify the existing clash of theologies already at work, often implicit in statements of Christian education, he did point up the importance of theology for Christian education. In this work he did not stress theological content so much as the use of theology as a means of properly relating pupils to God. The "clue" was that theology would be used as a bridge between content and method. He goes on later to show how the various doctrines of the church should be taught at the different age levels in his book Biblical Theology and Christian Education,[7] stressing that such teaching should be related now to the understanding of the learner.

In 1954 James Smart published a book entitled The Teaching Ministry of the Church,[8] in which he makes the case for a return to theology in Christian education much stronger, stressing that Christian education should be a discipline of theology. Thus, the period known as the rediscovery of theology was launched, dominated by the advocates of neo-orthodoxy and representing a strong reaction against the Religious Education Movement with its liberal theology.

Evangelicals were not inactive. The National Sunday School Association and certain independent publishers, such as Gospel Light Publications, Scripture Press, and others, published revised lesson materials. Certain denominations within the evangelical tradition produced materials, such as the Aldersgate Series published by the Free Methodist Publishing House, Nazarenes and others.

Certain authors have influenced evangelical thinking in Christian education. In 1958 Dr. Lois Lebar published her book Education That Is Christian,[9] in which she advocated a completely Christ-centered and Word-centered approach to Christian education. Frank E. Gabelein has stressed integration of truth in Christ and the Scriptures. He edited Christian Education in a Democracy[10] in 1951, and wrote Pattern of God's Truth.[11] Following in this school of thought, H. W. Byrne wrote A Christian Approach to Education[12] in 1961, stressing the thesis of Revelation as the key to education and emphasizing the importance of the Bible as the integrating factor in the curriculum, calling this a biblio-centric and theocentric approach. Previous to this Cornelius Jaarsma edited the volume Fundamentals in Christian Education: Theory and Practice,[13] representing the philosophy of certain Calvinistic groups. In 1964 a symposium appeared, published by Moody Press and edited by J. Edward Hakes entitled <u>An Introduction to Evangelical Christian Education</u>.[14]

In recent years two more books have appeared which deal with the subject of a Christian philosophy of education. With particular attention being given to the problem of integrating the Christian faith and educational theory and practice, in his work <u>Education in the Truth</u>[15] Norman De Jong has made an attempt to structure educational thought upon the Christian biblical basis of principle. He made an effort to show how the tenets of biblical faith are directly relevant to educational matters. Likewise, Ronald P. Chadwick, in his work <u>Teaching and Learning</u>[16] has done essentially the same thing except that he focuses more on how biblical principles directly affect the teaching-learning process. He gives particular attention to the problem of integration. It is encouraging to see educators beginning to explore the implications of biblical faith for education. The author completed a manuscript in which an attempt has been made to study the English Bible text to determine what the Scriptures have to say about education in general and teaching and learning in particular.

A group of Christian educators met at Trinity Christian College, Palos Heights, Illinois on November 11, 1983, for a conference on Christian approaches to learning theory. Offering new insights into the integration of faith and learning, the contributors to the volume <u>Christian Approaches to Learning Theory: A Symposium</u>, edited by Norman De Jong, asserted that the learning theory cannot be adequately understood within the limitations imposed by secular, contemporary psychology. Instead, the learning process is multidimensional in character.

In recent years one can see an upsurge of educational emphasis among Roman Catholics. Definite attempts are being made to return the church to an emphasis on the importance of teaching and learning. As in other groups one can see two general camps: that of the conservative, representing a catechetical approach, and that of the more liberal. James Lee, for example, while conservative in theology, is advocating an outright social science approach to Christian education. Thus, a review of the literature reveals that the search is still on for a <u>motif</u>, some centralizing and unifying principle upon which to base both theory and practice.

A fairly recent book written by a Roman Catholic addressed directly the question of the relation that revelation has to religious education. The book is entitled <u>Above or Within?</u> and was written by Ian Knox (Religious Education Press, 1976). Knox surveys three theoretical approaches to religious education in terms of the relation of revelation to religious education. He calls them (1) transcendist, (2) immanentist, and (3) integrationist. He likens the first to traditional views which emphasize the "aboveness" of God, as stressed by both Protestant and Catholic educators. The second view parallels the liberal theological movement as developed in the early part of this century. Emphasis is here laid on the "withinness" of God. The third view attempts a compromise between the first two. Knox does not attempt to formulate a personal position of his own in this work but he does see in the third view the most fruitful theological perspective for religious education.

The search for meaning in education has not been neglected among secular scholars and educators. Recognizing the need for a directive and motivating force for education which would result in integrating educational theory and practice, and thereby providing the instrumental power for achieving unity and coherence in education, the Harvard Report,[17] given in the mid-forties, sought for a possible means for integration. Four possible means by which integration could be attained were suggested: Religion; Western Culture with Change; Contemporary Problems; and Pragmatism and Natural Science. The conclusion was that these means were either impracticable, too narrow, or intrinsically deficient. Thus the search goes on for some unifying principle which will achieve the goal of integrating theory and practice which is most meaningful and useful.

Perhaps it is possible from the foregoing survey to summarize trends and efforts to find an integrating factor for Christian education. In the 1930's and early 1940's religious educators seemed to rely more upon the psychology and philosophy of modern education to build educational theory.

In the 1950's there was a shift to build theory on theology.

Between 1940 and 1960 the issue was whether or not theology should or could be the basis for religious education. The "liberals" maintained that "biblical theology" could not function adequately because the approach was contrary to the fundamental principles of education. Neo-orthodox advocates rejected experimental grounds and sought a return to theology. They insisted that religious education must first of all be "Christian." To them the crucial issue was the kind of education to be developed. Thus, a choice needed to be made between education based on educational principles or one based on theology. It soon became apparent, however, that religious education must be both "Christian" and "education."

Thus, before 1940 the emphasis was more heavily on educational soundness whereas since then the emphasis has been more heavily on theological soundness. Miller's view that theology is the clue to Christian education became popular, so that in the late 1950's and 1960's there was an awareness and agreement that theology plays a basic role in Christian education theory.

During this period, however, there were noticeable changes in the kind of theology and the kind of education to be stressed. There was the clash between "content-centered" versus "experience-centered" education and "revealed" versus "natural" theology, respectively. These differences produced conflict.

Since then the trend has been toward some resolution of the conflict by a modification of approaches in both theology and the educational principles adopted by theorists. Theology has currently seemed to move away from an emphasis on "doctrine" toward one that views theology as a "dynamic process," a view loosely defined as a biblical picture of God, man and the universe. Educational principles have shifted from the progressive individualism of an earlier day to a group-oriented approach focusing on the central importance of membership in the religious fellowship of the church.

In spite of the trend toward using theology as the integrating factor for Christian education, a number of issues and questions arise which have not been adequately solved, such as:

1. *Which theology?*
2. *What is the function of theology?*

14

3. *How does theology* <u>*guide*</u> *educational processes?*
4. *How can theology and education* <u>*work*</u> *together?*
5. *What is one's source of authority?*

This short review of the history of efforts to discover an integrating factor for Christian education reveals little evidence that Christian people have solved the question of the presence of this factor, one which will unify and give direction to theory and practice for Christian education. Current trends include a rediscovery of deep faith, a growing critical examination of our ministry, the importance of social responsibility, greater respect and concern for the individual in an age of the impersonal, and the importance of teachers who will love and model the faith they proclaim.

Some of the important issues facing Christian education include the following:

1. *Clarification of the foundations of the field, particularly the relation of theology to the findings of philosophical, and artistic insights and modes of thought;*
2. *Clarification of the nature of human development;*
3. *Clarification of the nature of the educative process;*
4. *Clarification of institutional settings and structures within which Christian education will operate;*
5. *The need for greater emphasis on the place and importance of Christian education in theological education and other institutions, placing particular stress on the place of ministers in education.*

C. The Sources

1. <u>Among Secular Educators</u>. To achieve the construction of educational theory the philosopher and educator must have sources of information and authority from which to draw. Such sources have frequently served to enable the philosopher to develop a philosophy of life. From the resulting philosophy of life have come guidelines for the development of a philosophy of education. The assumptions of the general philosophy thus serve as the assumptions for the philosophy of education.

The history of western philosophy reveals four primary assumptions upon which philosophies have been formulated. a) Scientific naturalism works on the assumption that truth is obtained by means of inductive inquiry. No place is found here for the spiritual or the supernatural. Generally, the source of authority is found either in the State or parents, at least legally. More specifically it is found in the revelations of science. The function of education in this view is virtually nothing more than to afford man an adjustment to his environment. The end of education is found either in the individual or the group. The method employed is that of experimentalism. The basic weakness of this view to the Christian is that it denies the reality of the spiritual and supernatural.

Closely allied to this position, rationalism assumes that a philosophy of life can be formulated through the use of pure reason. Educational humanism has been built largely on this premise. It is claimed that reason rises above thinking and attaches itself to principles of eternal truth which never change. This eternal truth forms both the core and criteria for knowledge. Human values are central in this view. This leaves God out or places Him on the periphery, thus making this view unacceptable to the Christian.

b) Similar to the above position is that of the social concept of educational authority, where authority is posited in society itself. Schools are set up by society to prepare pupils to live in society. Thus authority is found in the fundamental moral and intellectual commitments constituting the core of society. The democratic tradition is said to best represent this view. Again, while the Christian can find commendable features in such a position, objection is made on grounds that this view is fragmentary. Society does not tell the whole story, for man is more than a social being. The spiritual aspects of man's nature are paramount.

c) Idealism claims that reality is mental in character and can be demonstrated by coherence. Coherence is arrived at through the use of the experimental method but probability is the limit of this method. While there are commendable features about this view, to the Christian it needs to be supplemented by the tenets of Christian theism to become acceptable. Thus, to the Christian these approaches fall short of capturing the secret for unifying truth and practice.

d) The fourth source is that of the Christian. Here the basis of authority is to be found in the revealed will of God. Divine Self-Revelation yields the guidelines and assumptions for building educational philosophy and theory. This view will be more fully explored later on in this work.

2. Among Religious Educators. Nowhere can the impact of secular philosophies, even non-Christian philosophies, be seen more clearly than among the advocates of the Religious Education Association and those who embrace theological liberalism.

A great deal of writing by these people is at our disposal. A careful analysis of their views shows how much, in some cases, and how little, in other cases, religious educators have relied on secular philosophies. Naturalistic liberalism and social liberalism are almost devoid of Christian rootage and exclusively philosophical. Neo-liberalism, Neo-orthodoxy, the Psychological School and Relationship Theology draw from both secular and Christian sources. Only the advocates of Church Emphasis and Evangelicalism reveal efforts to utilize completely biblical and Christian sources of information.

A very recent book, Contemporary Approaches to Christian Education, edited by Jack L. Seymour and Donald Miller, Abingdon, 1982, recorded the efforts of selected current Christian educators to find an integrating factor for theory and practice. Five writers described five ways in which primary metaphors are utilized to understand the task of Christian education. Readers of this work may be encouraged by these attempts to show that an understanding of the various perspectives by which Christian education is being organized will contribute to shaping a comprehensive and coherent theory and practice of Christian education. It is evident, however, that no general agreement can be found among these writers, with the possible exception of their emphasis on the place that theology has. Their views will be dealt with at greater length in Chapter Four. It is interesting to note that Seymour and Miller conclude that "none of these approaches offers the final answer to the identity for Christian education, but they do provide movement toward it." The overall conclusion left is to leave room for more dialogue. A study of recent literature shows efforts to integrate theory and practice around such theological concepts as commitment, faith, ethics and spiritual formation.

      3. <u>Among Christian Educators</u>. Christian educational philosophy, like all others, must be built on philosophical premises. Among advocates of the orthodox and traditional positions in Christianity the basic assumption is that God exists and has revealed Himself to mankind. Authority, therefore, is to be found in the revealed will of God. Such revelation provides the basis upon which an adequate philosophy of life and education can be built. As a part of this general framework, Christian education draws likewise upon this primary source. The Scriptures provide the guidelines for the establishment of educational theory and practice.

      Advocates of church education have been traditionally divided into two camps: Roman Catholicism and Protestantism. For Catholics, the source of church authority is to be found in the decrees of church councils, and papal encyclicals. Man belongs to two orders, natural and supernatural. Authority for teaching him lies in the church which is infallible in matters of faith and morals. The norms of Catholic philosophy of education are laid in the traditions of the church. The task is to transmit church tradition, to enable pupils to define church doctrines and usages with exactness, distinguish these from errors and defend them against objections, to help them understand and accept the duties of church discipline.

      Among representatives of so-called sectarian theology who find themselves within the framework of ecclesiastical circles one finds diverse systems of biblical interpretation. The claim is made that this has impeded the development of a philosophy of church education because of insistence on holding to a specific theology. The findings of behavioral sciences on personality and learning have provided many insights that are now being used instead of traditional sources, such as Bible and theology, and while helpful, this has caused a cleavage in the ranks. The weaknesses of liberalism have already been pointed out.

The advocates of Protestant Evangelicalism find their source of authority in the Bible which is conceived to be the supernatural Word of God. It is the avenue of God's primary revelation. It adequately describes man's nature and needs. Man is a sinner and in need of salvation through regeneration. The aim of education in the church is salvation and nurture in faith. The Bible is the main textbook but other educational media can be useful but they must be evaluated by scriptural criteria. Science is accepted or rejected in accordance with its agreement with scriptural principles.

Perhaps it is now possible to summarize the process of constructing Christian educational theory, as a result of the previous discussion, in the following manner:

The Concept of Christianity

The Concept of the Church and of Faith

Acceptable Supplementary Sources

Concept of Christian Educational Theory

Concept of Christian Educational Practice

D. The Solution

1. <u>The Need</u>. Man's greatest longing is to find purpose and meaning in life. This is seen as a universal expression of man's nature and is generally recognized. In an atomic age fraught with its inherent dangers of world conflict and destruction, the hour is so desperate that man must not play with surface issues. Man must turn away from himself to find a higher source of help to meet the needs of the present time. Man needs to find a life-principle by which to live, one which gives his life and educational activities real depth of meaning and satisfaction. The source of meeting this need is to be found in a God-centered approach to life and education. The need incorporates the necessity of seeing all things from God's point of view.

Either God or man is the center of the universe. There is no other alternative. The crux of all our problems lies in the fact that man has made all things to revolve around himself. But when the center is wrong, then all other things are wrong. Man needs a new center -- God. He gives us the correct perspective. When man changes from man-consciousness to God-consciousness, all of life becomes new and God is the center from which all truth is revealed and understood.

In modern education, religion, science and philosophy the attitude is one of relativism. There are no absolutes. Evangelical Christians believe, however, that we can find a secure base for living and operating our educational systems based on God's revelation and will. The lack of this leads to fragmentation and distortion of truth. The Scriptures show us that God has provided mankind with a basic philosophy of all life and truth by which basic life issues and questions are adequately answered (I Corinthians 1:30).

2. <u>The Task</u>. It is imperative that Christian educators at all levels assist all Christian believers to develop a God-centered philosophy of life and a God-centered philosophy of education. Only in this way can man develop a proper outlook and sense of destiny.

There are only three possible sources that man can refer to in building his philosophy of life and philosophy of education: nature, man, or God. If man does not start at the right place, he has no proper point of reference and coordination. But we find in God and His viewpoint the place to start. It is God Who gives us the right perspective, the correct point of reference, and the integrating factors for life and thought. The Fall of man into sin blinded man and caused man to center all things in himself.

3. The Secret. The secret is to secure God's viewpoint through divine revelation. This starting point helps us to determine all basic concepts for life and education. Paul expressed this secret in Romans 11:36, *"For of Him, and through Him, and to Him, are all things: to whom be the glory forever. Amen."* "Of God" implies origin and revelation. "Through God" shows that all things are sustained by Him. "Unto God" shows that all things find their proper relatedness and true meaning because they reflect His divine will.

Through the work of the Saviour and the Cross man can move from self-centeredness to God-centeredness (2 Corinthians 5:14-15). All things become new (2 Corinthians 5:17). We have a new view-point-revelation (2 Corinthians 5:16); a new relationship - sons (2 Corinthians 5:18); a new occupation - ambassadors (2 Corinthians 5:20), and a new yardstick - measurement (John 14:6). *"I am the Way, the Truth, and the Life."*

21

Notes

1. Butler, J. Donald. Religious Education, Harper and Rowe, 1962, p. 121.

2. Wyckoff, D. Campbell. The Gospel and Christian Education, Westminster, 1959, p. 70.

3. Macmillan, 1940.

4. Charles Scribners' Sons, 1941.

5. Bethany Press, 1947.

6. Charles Scribners' Sons, 1950.

7. Ibid., 1956.

8. Westminster, 1954.

9. Revell, 1958.

10. Oxford University Press, 1951.

11. Ibid., 1954.

12. Zondervan, 1961. Later revised and published by Mott Media, 1977.

13. Eerdmans, 1953.

14. Moody Press, 1964.

15. Presbyterian and Reformed Publishing Company, 1979.

16. Fleming H. Revell, 1982.

17. General Education in a Free Society, 1950.

OUTLINE FOR

CHAPTER TWO

DIVINE REVELATION, BIBLICAL EPISTEMOLOGY AND
CHRISTIAN EDUCATION

A. Revelation and Christian Education
    1. Three Basic Positions
    2. The Primacy of Revelation for Evangelicals
    3. The Implications of Revelation
    4. The Values and Application of Revelation

B. Biblical Epistemology
    1. Biblical Concepts of Knowledge
    2. Biblical Concepts of Wisdom
    3. Biblical Concepts of Truth

C. An Evangelical and Biblical Concept of Revelation
    1. The Origin of Revelation
    2. The Character of Revelation
    3. The Purpose of Revelation
    4. Revelation and Language
    5. The Process of Revelation
    6. The Methods of Revelation
    7. The Means of Revelation
    8. The Credentials of Revelation
    9. The Types of Revelation
    10. Revelation and Relationships
    11. The Place of Scripture in Revelation
    12. The Climax of Revelation
    13. Education and Revelation

CHAPTER TWO

DIVINE REVELATION, BIBLICAL EPISTEMOLOGY, AND CHRISTIAN EDUCATION

A. Revelation and Christian Education

1. Three Basic Positions on Revelation. The effect that revelation has on Christian education is quite evident. Positions on this matter are widely divergent, often as numerous as the individuals who espouse them. A study of the literature, however, reveals at least three basic positions: (1) liberal, (2) integral, and (3) traditional.

In the liberal view revelation is a natural part of life. Great stress is laid on the immanence of God. Revelation comes from God to man through God manifesting Himself in man's experiences, both personal and social. Great emphasis is laid on man, human values, and the human condition.

Regarding Special Revelation, the Bible is only a partial expression of God's revelation, or, as others put it, the Bible is nothing more than religious literature. Revelation for the individual becomes an existential experience with God. Transformation takes place primarily in social relationships guided by Christian principles. In this view the church is a human society or community of believers concerned with the improvement of society.

Views of liberalism differ rather widely from those of traditional and integral views on the questions of whether Jesus was the final revelation, or whether there have been other lesser revelations before and subsequent to His life and work on earth. Are there other revelations which have validity for the faith, or was Christ the final and unique revelation for all times? Liberalism has generally held that, though Jesus was a unique revelation, He was so only to a degree and thus was not a final revelation. Liberal thinkers further maintain that there were revelations before Jesus, and that there have been revelations subsequent to His time. Though these revelations have been lesser than He, they have served, nevertheless, to heighten appreciation of Jesus and to disclose God, making them more meaningful for the world of experience.

Centers of revelation, found in both nature and the social order, have supplemented as well as complemented the revelation which was unique in Jesus and have helped man to reach a better understanding of His meaning for the human race. Liberal thinkers also contend that, in and through these sources, God is at work more fully to disclose Himself to mankind. Such an argument makes it possible for the liberals to insist that God is immanent in all aspects of the historical process and, therefore, in the educative process. The chief advocate of this position among Protestants has been George Coe and among Roman Catholics Gabriel Moran.

On the other hand, a number of traditional and integral leaders have asserted that Jesus was the unique and final revelation of God to the world; that it is Jesus alone who makes life and history meaningful for mankind. In making Jesus the final revelation, these writers differ from the liberal position in that they consider the uniqueness of Jesus one of kind rather than of degree, and revelation is in that sense final. In thus making Jesus the final and unique revelation, these writers think of other sources derived from the natural order or from social intercourse as secondary, or from General Revelation.

In the integrationist view an attempt is made to combine the values of traditional and liberal views of revelation into a synthesis. Both transcendence and immanence are integrated. Attempts are made to focus on human situations but using those situations to discover the revelation of God. The view of revelation here is one which sees it as the action of God in the events of history and thus in human experience. Thus, revelation is a dynamic process as interpreted in the light of the Bible, but it is not merely information. Its purpose is to help man experience a personal relation to God through communion with Him. Man uses his reasoning powers to appropriate God's revelation in human events. The church becomes the focus of revelation and the instrument used by God to interpret revelation. Thus, integrationists see God as both transcendent and immanent in human affairs. Randolph C. Miller, who stressed the importance of theology as a God/man relationship, is a chief advocate of this view among Protestants. Among Roman Catholics Marcel van Caster is prominent.

In the traditional view revelation comes to man from outside himself, from God who chooses to make Himself known to man. It is a supernatural gift from a transcendent God.

Revelation is a body of truth, a message from God. It is Special, focusing on Jesus Christ as Son of God and Logos, and the Bible. It is also general, focusing on God's revelation in nature, providence, and the conscience of man. The purpose here is to show God revealed and to help man reveal God in character and work. The message is received by man in faith and practiced in personal and social experiences with the help of the Holy Spirit. The church, as the body of Christ, provides the framework for Christian education ministry.

Adherents of this view are to be found among Protestants, such as James D. Smart, and most evangelicals. Among Roman Catholics are Joseph Jungman and Johannes Hofinger.

To summarize this discussion it is apparent that the traditionalists emphasize predominantly Special Revelation. The liberals emphasize General Revelation primarily, and the integrationists attempt to synthesize both. We turn now to the implications of revelation from a traditional and evangelical point of view.

2. The Primacy of Revelation for Evangelicals. No thinker can devoid himself of an absolute. Either he will give allegiance to some man-projected absolute or he will begin his philosophy with a revelational absolute. The Christian philosopher begins with the latter, for he believes that God has chosen to reveal Himself to man. All truth to the Christian is the reflection into the soul of the truth that is in God. Since all truth belongs to God, the related truths of all human concerns will be measured in terms of revelation. This does not mean that theology will dictate the findings of any subject matter discipline. It does mean that the interpretations will be found there.

Since God is the source of all truth and since He has not left Himself without witness everywhere, all knowledge is revealed knowledge. Thus, philosophy reveals ideas; revelation reveals divine actions; aesthetics reveals appreciation, etc.

The special disclosure of God's grace in providing His revelation came not as an inner obligation nor did it rise primarily from the transcendent power of God. It came rather as a display of His unmerited favor and because of the Fall of men into sin.

Special Revelation in the Bible and in Jesus Christ does not comprehend the entirety of God's revelation. Christianity does not deny that God is everywhere revealed in the space-time universe and internally in the very mind and conscience of man as well. This is called General Revelation. The actual revelation of God in nature, history, and man, therefore, is a central biblical affirmation.

3. The Implications of Revelation. One direct implication of revelation points up the nature of education itself. Where God is central, the Creator of the universe, and has made Himself known through revelation, it naturally follows that education must be defined as a reinterpretation of God's revelation. Education is seeing things as God sees them; it is thinking God's thoughts after Him.

A second implication concerns the purpose and objective of education. The purpose of education is to show God revealed. The immediate objective is to qualify men to reveal God. This involves the total person in his total environment. The ultimate objective is the King of God to come.

A third implication involves the curriculum. Where all truth proceeds from God, it becomes clear that revelation becomes the very heart of the curriculum. All curricula content is related to God.

4. The Values and Application of Revelation. Christian education concepts are derived from divine revelational sources provided in Christian theology, Bible and Christian philosophy. From these synoptic studies it is possible to develop and organize a World View of Christian Theism. From this world view it is possible further to develop a Philosophy of Christian Education. This philosophy will serve education in several ways:

(1) By providing a world view which gives unity
(2) By providing a philosophy of life which gives meaning

(3) By emphasizing values and objectives which give purpose, direction and evaluation

(4) By providing an integrative means for the total educative process

(5) By providing systematization of content by showing relations and interrelations in the totality of truth which provide, in turn, a workable pattern for the curriculum

(6) By providing clues for the interpretation of truth in the teaching-learning process, and

(7) By providing guidance in the use of personnel, resources and facilities

B. Biblical Epistemology

1. Biblical Concepts of Knowledge. There are several Old Testament terms for the word knowledge:

YADA - to know, discern - Gen. 3:5,7,32
This is not knowledge through reasoning but knowledge through personal experience
Not "knowledge of God" but "acquaintance with" Him - Gen. 4:1,17,25
This term is used in a wide variety of ways to refer to man's knowledge, skills in hunting, sailing, playing an instrument, and sexual intercourse

BIN - to understand - Job 38:20
Personal - Prov. 24:5; discernment - Psalm 119:66
To know by experience - Job 15:1,2

DEA - knowledge - Job 36:4

NAKAR - to perceive - Gen. 37:33; 42:7,8

The prophets were concerned about knowledge (Isaiah 1:3; Hosea 4:1; 6:6; Jer. 22:15-16), but they also recognized that man's knowledge is limited (Job 11:7; 26:8-14; Isaiah 55:9). The highest knowledge is to know God (Job 11:7,9; Hosea 6:6). Such knowledge is to be sought (Prov. 1:2; 2:3-6) and communicated (Deut. 4:9; 6:7; Psalm 78:4; 119:13).

New Testament terms and teachings reveal the importance of knowledge:

GINOSKO - to know (by experience), to cause to know - John 17:3; Eph. 3:19

GINOSKEIN - to know - Mark 5:29; Luke 8:46
Means to detect, to note, to recognize, to confirm, to be aware, to understand, and to learn (Mark 5:43; Luke 9:11; John 11:57)

EPIGINOSKO - to know fully - Gal. 4:9; Romans 8:29

EPIGNOSIS - Knowledge of God through conversion - I Tim. 2:4; II Tim. 2:25 and mediated by Jesus Christ - Matt. 11:27; Col. 1:19; John 1:18

KNOSIS - Obedient acknowledgment of the will of God - Luke 1:77; Romans 2:20; 11:33

The New Testament reveals that God is the Source of Knowledge (Romans 11:34) and has made Himself known (Romans 9:22,23; Eph. 1:9; 3:10). But men lost a thorough knowledge of God by sinning (Gal. 4:8-9; Titus 1:16). The highest knowledge is the essence of redemption (2 Peter 1:2; John 17:3). This knowledge is to be sought (James 1:5) and communicated (Matthew 10:27).

Much more is said in the New Testament about God as the giver of knowledge and what this knowledge is. In fact the Bible reveals the vastness of God's knowledge by relating it to everything within the experience of human beings.

Man was created by God with the power to know (John 8:32) and experience truth (John 7:6,17) but by the Fall of man into sin man has lost most of this knowledge. But God set about to help man recover this knowledge through redemption and the work of the Holy Spirit. Natural knowledge comes to man by means of discovery and reason. Spiritual knowledge comes by the Spirit of God (I John 4:2,6,13; 5:10-17), and leads to eternal life (John 17:3). Christians need to constantly deepen their knowledge of God (2 Peter 3:18; Phil. 3:10). Such knowledge, according to Scripture, will touch all aspects of devotional life, Christian living and service.

2. Biblical Concepts of Wisdom. Perhaps the most common Old Testament term for wisdom is the Hebrew term, HOKHAM, which means to be wise, to act wisely (Psalm 105:22). Other terms include:

BIN - to perceive
BINAH - understanding - Proverbs 4:5,7
TEBHUNAH - reason - Job 6:13
SEKHAL - intelligence
SAKHAL - prudent
HOKHMAH - simple skill
LEBH - heart
LABHABH - be wise

In the New Testament there are two Greek words expressing wisdom, SOPHIA, the wisdom of God (Luke 11:49; Matthew 23:34) and PHRONESIS, understanding (Luke 1:17).

Two kinds of wisdom are revealed in New Testament teachings: the wisdom of God (I Cor. 2:7) and the wisdom of the world (I Cor. 1:20-21; 2:6-7). They are contrasted in Scripture. Godly wisdom is not the wisdom of words (I Cor. 1:17), nor of the orator (I Cor. 1:26), nor is it the result of blue blood or high birth (I Cor. 1:26).

Earthly wisdom is described by James as earthly, sensual, and devilish (James 3:15). It is worldly wisdom (I Cor. 2:6). It comes from the spirit of the world (I Cor. 2:12).

Heavenly wisdom is the wisdom of God (I Cor. 2:7). It is dispensational wisdom (I Cor. 2:8,9) and unintelligible wisdom (I Cor. 2:8,9). It is found in Jesus Christ (I Cor. 1:24) and has been prepared for those who love God (I Cor. 2:9).

Spiritual wisdom is revealed by the Holy Spirit (I Cor. 2:10-16) and by God's Son (I Cor. 1:30) and manifested through the saints of God (I Cor. 2:12,13; James 3:12-18).

True wisdom starts with God (Prov. 15:33; 19:20f), centers

in God (Prov. 1:7; 9:10) and ends with Him (Prov. 2:5). Such wisdom is equated with life itself (Prov. 8:35) and is a gift from God to man (Prov. 2:6). This kind of wisdom is revealed in revelation (Eph. 1:9,18) and is described as pure, peaceful, considerate and sincere (James 3:17,18). It is revealed also in God's redemption and forgiveness (Eph. 1:7,8) and made available to man through the Holy Spirit (I Cor. 2:13).

For man, wisdom is a healthy quality (Isaiah 10:13; Ezek. 28:3-5). Man is urged in Scripture to seek it (Prov. 15:14), to accept it (Prov. 21:11) and to store it (Prov. 10:14).

The secret of wisdom is fearing and hearing God (Prov. 15:33). The writer of Proverbs characterizes the wise man as one who hears, increases learning, and seeks wise counsel (Prov. 1:5). It is to be found in serving God (Psalm 2:10-12), studying nature (Psalm 19:1), and prayer (James 1:5,6). Some wisdom comes from experience (Job 12:12; Prov. 16:21) but is found primarily in Jesus Christ (Col. 2:3). In relation to knowledge, wisdom is first (Prov. 3:12-18; 4:5-9), and it leads to knowledge (Eccles. 1:13).

A study of the Book of Proverbs reveals many attributes of wisdom, including prudence, temperance, chastity, diligence, and many others. The practice of this kind of wisdom causes one to depart from evil (Prov. 14:16), listen to counsel and correction (Prov. 12:15; 15:10,31), exercise restraint (Prov. 12:23), maintain self-control (Prov. 12:16), restrain the tongue (Prov. 16:23) and stay ready for the Second Coming of Christ (Matt. 25:2,4,9,13). It leads to wealth (Prov. 8:18), health (Prov. 3:7,8), long life (Prov. 4:10,13) and heavenly reward (Daniel 12:3ff).

3. <u>Biblical Concepts of Truth</u>. There are three prominent Hebrew words to show the Old Testament concept of truth:

EMETH-EMUNAH
       Firmness, stability (Exodus 17:2; Psalm 31:5)
       Constancy, faithfulness (Deut. 32:4; Psalm 33:4;
                     Prov. 12:22)
EMUN - steadfastness (Isaiah 26:2)

Several Greek words reveal the nature of truth:

ALETHEIA - reality (Romans 3:7)
ALETHOS - (Luke 21:3; John 6:14)
ONTOS - (I Corinthians 14:25)
PISTIS - (Romans 3:3)
PISTOS - faithful (I Timothy 3:1)

This word finds broad usage in the English to refer to such qualities as loyalty, honesty, fidelity, justice, faith, confidence, veracity and reality.

As used in Scripture the word - - truth - - is associated with behavior (Gen. 24:49), promises (2 Sam. 7:28), kindness (Gen. 47:29), justice (Neh. 9:13; Isaiah 59:14) and sincerity (Joshua 24:14).

Truth is a chief element in God (Psalm 36:5; 119:30). The Holy Spirit is the Spirit of Truth (John 14:17). All God's works are done in truth (Psalm 33:4). This shows how truth is connected to what God does.

God wants all men to have truth (I Tim. 2:4; I Peter 2:2). To obtain truth man must listen to God's Word (John 18:37; I John 2:20) and walk in His truth (Eph. 4:24; 3 John 3,4). His truth endures forever (Psalm 117:2).

Scriptures reveal several types and concepts of truth:

Ontological truth - John 18:38
    Trueness - John 1:9; 4:23; 6:32
    God is Personal Truth - Deut. 32:4;
        John 1:14,17; 14:6
    His Word is truth - John 17:17
    His moral law is truth - Psalm 119:142,151
    Truth gives the true meaning of life -
        Proverbs 23:23
Cognitive truth - Job 28:20-26; 38; 39; Mark 5:33
Logical truth - facts - John 8:26,28,32,38,40
Moral truth
    Shown in God - Psalm 89; Hosea 2:19-23

Shown in man
     By honesty (Psalm 15:2)
     By civil justice (Isaiah 59:4,14,15)
     By truthfulness (Ex. 18:21; Joshua 24:14)
     From the heart (I Sam. 12:24; Ps. 15:2; 51:6)
Biblical truth
     Comes by God speaking (Genesis 1)
     Comes by creation (Psalm 33:6,9; Hebrews 11:3)
     Comes by God's command (Genesis 1:28)
     Comes by man listening (Genesis 1:29)
     Comes by prohibition (Genesis 2:17)
     Comes by promise (Genesis 3:15-20)

The foundation of Christian education is found in the God of Truth. The framework for Christian education is the Word of Truth. The function of Christian education is centered in a workman with truth (2 Tim. 2:15). The practice of truth in Christian education touches everything and everyone engaged in it.

C. Summary of Biblical Epistemology

1. Old Testament concepts
   a. God is the God of all knowledge - Job 36:4;
      I Sam. 2:3
   b. To know God is personal knowledge rather than
      mere facts about God.
   c. Knowledge of God is not merely abstract
      knowledge but awareness of and obedience
      to God - Deut. 11:1ff
   d. Spiritual knowledge and the fear of God are one
      - Isaiah 8:13
   e. Old Testament Law is not merely a legal code
      but teaching about the character of God and
      man's response - the Law is a schoolmaster -
      Gal. 3:24
   f. Sin gave men a knowledge apart from God -
      Psalm 103:14   Stubbornness and hardness

of heart - Deut. 29:18

    g. The forbidden knowledge acquired in the Garden of Eden was not merely factual knowledge but a knowledge of pride which caused man to want to be like God

        (1) Eating of forbidden fruit caused men to lose the knowledge of God and acquire a knowledge of sin

        (2) Man was given dominance over the rest of God's creation (Gen. 1:28) but sought knowledge to do this and made himself independent of God. Man sought to use creation for his own ends rather than for the will of God

    h. In the Fall man turned his back on the knowledge of God and became engrossed in "this world"

        "Let us make a name" - Genesis 11:4

    i. A new self-consciousness with guilt resulted

        Now man seeks self-fulfillment through "earthly wisdom" and thus perverted his true knowledge of God

    j. Through a covenant relationship God extended His love, grace and forgiveness. This opened the door to reestablishing true knowledge. It made restoration of personal knowledge of God possible

    k. A new heart is needed to get restored knowledge of God

2. New Testament concepts

    a. God is the Source of Knowledge - Acts 17:28; Phil. 2:12,13

    b. Knowledge is a gift of grace - I Cor. 1:5; 12:8; II Cor. 8:7

        This comes through obedience and love

    c. True knowledge is found in Christ - Phil 3:8,9

        A living faith through the Holy Spirit

d. To know God is to have His life - John 17:3
   And His love - I John 4:7f
e. But sin interferes - John 1:9,10; 3:19-21;
   Gal. 4:8-9
f. Sin has affected man's mind
   (1) Blindness - II Cor. 4:3,4
   (2) Rationalistic - I Cor. 1:20,21
   (3) Heart defiled - Mark 7:21-23
g. True knowledge of God comes through
   conversion - I Tim. 2:4; II Tim. 2:25; 3:7;
   Titus 1:1
h. Worldly wisdom is foolishness - I Cor. 3:19,20
i. True wisdom is in God - James 1:5,6; I Cor. 2:7
j. Spiritual wisdom is revealed by the Holy Spirit -
   I Cor. 2:10-16
k. God's Word is truth - John 17:17
l. In Christ are the treasures of wisdom and
   knowledge - Col. 2:3; I Cor. 1:24

D. An Evangelical and Biblical Concept of Revelation

1. Origin of Revelation. Revelation originated in the Trinity. God, the Father, is Light and Truth. The Psalmist said, "With Thee is the fountain of life; in Thy light shall we see light" (Psalm 36:9). The Son is the revelation of truth (John 1:14,17; 14:6). Truth is thus a Person. The Spirit interprets truth (John 15:26; 16:13; I Cor. 2:10).

This kind of revelation is God's Self-revelation (I Cor. 2:9-11; John 3:27; Gal. 1:12). God enters the process of revelation personally through inspiration (2 Tim. 3:16). This personal aspect of revelation is also seen in the teachings of Jesus Christ (Gal. 1:11,12). God's speech is another personal method God used (Hebrews 1:1-3).

2. The Character of Revelation. Revelation is more than investigation and observation; it is a divine activity (Hebrews 1:1). It is both personal and inspired activity (I Kings 20:13,28; John 1:8; 8:23-34; 2 Peter 1:20). It becomes directly relevant to Christian education because it is a method of teaching (Gal. 1:12). Such

35

revelation is both unified and progressive (Heb. 1:1-4; Romans 3:29-30; I Cor. 1:16-18). Progressive means "not from error to truth" but rather "from truth to more truth." Revelation is both rational and written (John 14:10; Matt. 4:4; Rev. 1:19) and thereby intelligible in conceptual verbal form. It thus becomes a very necessary rule (2 Cor. 10:12,13). Revelation is supernatural in character and not of man's wisdom (I Cor. 2:1-2,6,10-12). As such it is distinctive and final - note the "once for all" in Romans 6:10; I Peter 3:18; Jude 3; Hebrews 7:27; 9:28; and 10:10. But not all of God's revelation is made known to man -- it is partial (I Cor. 13:12; 15:51; Deut. 29:29; Isaiah 55:9). In relation to education revelation is a method of teaching (Gal. 1:12).

Revelation is <u>heilgeschichte</u>, the story of salvation and the plan of God for the whole world. In this sense, it is a revelation of divine reality. By making Himself known, God gives man a complete picture of true reality, one that was hidden but now has been revealed to us by His Word and Spirit (I Cor. 2:10-14). In this context revelation becomes both propositional and personal. It is the story of God in His relation to man and the universe. As previously noted, a study of the biblical terms for knowledge and wisdom shows that these terms do not refer exclusively to cognitive or factual knowledge but rather to the knowledge which comes through experience and reality.

Lawrence Richards has spoken of Scripture as a revelation of reality.[1] He points out that the Bible should be perceived, not primarily as propositional revelation, but as a revelation of reality, as affirmation about God, man, and life in the world. He goes on to point out, further, that the reality of Scripture is to be experienced in terms of a life to be lived so that a person may experience the truth of scriptural reality personally. The implication of this for Christian education, he says, is clear. Christian educators must not be satisfied with merely transmitting information only but rather to help believers experience truth personally, to help them learn to walk daily in the revelational reality of scriptural truth. The great themes of Scripture need to be related directly to life experiences at all developmental age levels so that life and truth are directly connected. Richards concludes also that revelational reality is experienced more fully in the context of

Christian community. The sharing of common life and experiences in the fellowship of the church adds a corporate facet to revelational reality. In Christian community Christian education can both experience and teach the concepts and practices of revelational reality. It is here that believers together are committed to giving living expression to God's revealed perception of reality.

3. The Purpose of Revelation. The primary purpose of revelation is to reveal God as central (Psalm 97:6,8; 19:1; Isaiah 6:3; II Cor. 4:6; John 5:39; Hebrews 1:3). By this divine wisdom is revealed (Jer. 32:17; Eph. 1:8) and blindness is removed (John 6:68,69; 8:12). Revelation shows the goal of salvation (I Tim. 1:15). It yields benefits to mankind: the friendship of God (Gen. 3:8; John 4:23), removes blindness and gives life (through Christ) (John 6:68,69; 8:12) and guidance (Psalm 119:105).

The cause of revelation is to be found in God's grace (Gen. 12:3; Ex. 19:5-6; Deut. 7:7-8; Titus 2:11; 3:5). It removes man's ignorance (I Cor. 1:21; Gal. 4:8; I Thess. 4:5). The touch of Jesus drives away blindness and ignorance (John 9:25). The very essence of revelation is light and life (John 14:6). It gives personal experience in the knowledge of Christ (John 4:42).

According to II Timothy 3:16 revelation is inspired of God, God-breathed. Its threefold purpose is (1) instruction, (2) profit, and (3) maturity. This is consistent with the nature of the Revealer. God's attributes are the attributes of the Word. But it is incomplete. It is truth but not exhaustive truth. It is true communication but not exhaustive communication. It is unified and progressive (Isaiah 28:13). The fact of revelation by God assures the comprehensive unity of divine revelation.

While there is fresh illumination, essentially there is no new revelation. God perfectly revealed Himself in His Son and in the Bible. In the light of this, revelation becomes a method of teaching (Gal. 1:12). In summary, one may say, then, that the purpose of revelation is "to get the mind of God into the actions of men" and "to communicate God's being, word and will to fallen men."

4. Revelation and Language. Scriptures reveal many instances of the direct relation that revelation has to language. In the

beginning God spoke (Gen. 1:3-29; Heb. 1:1,2). Many passages point up the significance of revelation and language. God spoke audibly, intelligently and orderly. He used words as symbols, to speak directly to people, and to evaluate. Words were created to make communication possible. They were used in the Fall of man into sin. God's revelation about redemption was shaped in written form (I John 5:13).

Language is the divine link between God and man. It is the means by which man's ignorance and darkness are turned into knowledge and light. As the Divine Word the Lord spoke and man heard Who it was and from Whom all words have proceeded and of Whose voice all words should be the echo. Words, therefore, are not arbitrary signs which have been created by man to describe his own thoughts but are dependable symbols of reality since they are expressions of the nature of God.

5. The Process of Revelation. God has revealed Himself to all men (Psalm 19:7-8; Isaiah 40:22; Romans 1:20). He took the initiative in doing this (Gen. 3:9; 12:1,7; 6:3; Luke 19:10). For example, He called to Adam and Eve (Gen. 3:9); He made His name and nature known to Moses (Ex. 6:3); He appeared to Abraham (Gen. 12:1,7); and Jesus came to seek and save the lost (Luke 19:10). Thus, revelation comes as a result of God's personal determination (Romans 1:19,20; Acts 14:17,26; John 1:9; Hebrews 1:1). It is mediated by Jesus Christ as the Divine Agent (John 1:5) the eternal Logos, preexistent, incarnate, now glorified, and is inspired and supervised by Jesus Christ also through the work of the Holy Spirit (2 Tim. 3:14-16; 2 Peter 1:19-21). Revelation is progressive (Hebrews 1:2; 7:22,26,19; 9:8; 10:19ff). It finds its climax in Jesus Christ (John 1:14; Col. 1:15; John 5:23) and will be complete in the future (John 13:7; 16:13; Rev. 4:1). This revelation came from God's life, to Bible truth, then to knowledge and wisdom for man (Psalm 36:9).

The process of revelation continues to man in a variety of ways: (1) through the Bible (John 5:39,46-47), (2) through redemption (Acts 17:31; John 3:16), (3) through the church (Matt. 11:5; Acts 2), (4) through individuals regenerated by the Spirit of God (2 Cor. 4:6; 5:17; John 1:12), (5) through the Gospel (Romans 1:16,17), (6) through spiritual realities (Romans 1:20) and (7) will be ultimately revealed in the consummation of all things (Isaiah 45:23; John 14:6; Rev. 4:11; 5:13; Eph. 1:10). What a rich resource of truth for Christian education!

6. The Methods of Revelation. God has chosen to reveal Himself in many ways (Heb. 1:1). Following is a list of some of these ways:

(1) He appealed personally (Gen. 12:7)
(2) He spoke (Ex. 20:1,5; Isaiah 45:19; Matt. 3:17;
2 Peter 1:17)
(3) He revealed Himself in His works
In the heavens - Psalm 19:1; 102:25;
Isaiah 40:26-28
In maintaining the world - Amos 5:8
In helping people - Ex. 18:10; I Kings 18:17-20
(4) He used words - John 15:20-27; 17:17-20
(5) He used visions - Numbers 12:8; Isaiah 6:1-9
(6) He used dreams - Genesis 20:3; 28:12,13
(7) He used the Shekinah Glory - Ex. 40:35; Lev. 16:2
(8) He used theophanies - Genesis 18; 32:25-30
(9) He used supernatural writing - Exodus 31:18;
Daniel 5:5
(10) He used the Law - Deut. 6:24; 31:10-13; Neh. 8:18
(11) He used acts in history - Ex. 7:5; 16:6; 18:11; Isaiah 45:3
(12) Through the prophets - Heb. 1:1,2; Amos 1:3-5;
Jer. 1:5-9
(13) Through individuals
To Adam and Eve personally - Gen. 4:5,6
To Noah - Genesis 9:1
To Patriarchs - Gen. 12:4; 17:1; 18:19
To Moses - Exodus 3:6,16; 34:29f
(14) Through His wrath - Psalm 76:10
(15) To the nation of Israel - Ex. 6:7; Lev. 26:12; Deut. 29:12
(16) Through representatives
The Ark - Joshua 3:3-8,13 (29 times)

Messengers - Zech. 1:11ff; 3:1,5,6; 12:8
The Face of God - Hosea 5:15; Psalm 24:6
The Glory of God - Luke 2:9; Rev. 21:23; Isaiah 6:3
(17) Through special manifestations - Ex. 3:2; Acts 2:3
(18) Through the Spirit - Isaiah 44:3-5; I Cor. 2:9,10;
Luke 12:12; John 14:26
(19) Through His Son - Heb. 1:1-3; Gal. 4:4-6; John 15:15;
II Cor. 4:6

7. The Means of Revelation. God used a wide variety of means through which He has revealed Himself to mankind:

(1) Through the Bible - John 5:39; 46-47; Luke 16:31
(2) Through redemption - Acts 17:31; John 3:16; 5:24,25
(3) Through the church - Matt. 11:5; Acts 2
(4) Through Christian individuals - II Cor. 4:6; 5:17;
John 1:12
(5) Through the Gospel - Romans 1:16,17
(6) Through spiritual realities - Romans 1:20
(7) Through the ultimate consummation of all things -
Isaiah 45:23; John 14:6; Rev. 4:11; 5:13; Eph. 1:10

8. The Credentials of Revelation. Divine revelation has within itself inherent credentials which give it high priority and standing. Among these are:

(1) Miracles - Mark 2:1-12
(2) Prophecy - John 14:29
(3) Christ - Matthew 28:18
(4) Work of the Holy Spirit - Acts 2:32,33; 5:32
(5) The Word - II Timothy 3:15,16

9. The Types of Revelation. The Bible teaches that God has revealed Himself to man in two ways: (1) through General Revelation in nature (Psalm 19:1) and man's conscience (Romans 2:14-16), and (2) through Special Revelation in the Bible and His Son Jesus Christ

(Hebrews 1:1,2). The terms, "general" and "special revelation," reveal the extent and purpose of God's revelation. God has revealed Himself both in what He has created and what He has spoken. Christians are expected to be diligent in understanding both of these sources of revelation. Biblical revelation does not pretend to answer all questions but theology does provide one with a guide to the understanding of all other channels of revelation.

We see Personal Self-Revelation in the Son (John 1:1,2,14; Romans 11:36). He is the Light of the World (Isaiah 9:2; John 1:4; 8:12). He is the Revelation of God (John 14:9). He turns darkness into light (John 9:25,39). He is the secret of all wisdom and knowledge (Eph. 1:17-19; I Cor. 1:5). He provides grace and truth (John 1:17). He is the basis of all revelation (John 1:18).

General Self-Revelation is shown in the natural world (Gen. 1:1; Psalm 19:1,2; 8:1,9; 24:1; Romans 1:20), in maintaining that world (Amos 5:8) and in helping people (Ex. 18:10; I Kings 18:37-39). We see it in the conscience of man (Romans 2:14-16). We see it in history (Eph. 1:10; Acts 14:17; Romans 2:9,10; Psalm 103:7), and as God works among the nations (Acts 10:34,35; 14:15-17). General revelation is the source of the enlightenment of every man (John 1:9; Romans 1:20; 2:12-16; Acts 14:17; II Cor. 4:6; Gal. 4:8-10) and the expression of God's goodness to man in general (John 3:16; Acts 14:17; Matt. 5:45). But it has been affected negatively by the Fall of man into sin (Gen. 3:8-24; chapters 7-8). Its ultimate climax is in Jesus Christ (John 1:14; Col. 1:15; John 5:23), and will be completed in the future (John 13:7; 16:13; Rev. 4:1).

While one may speak of two general types of revelation, one must also not lose sight of the fact that truth is unified, one whole, because God is the Author. In a sense, therefore, all reality reveals God. One may speak of the "sacred" on the one hand or the "secular" on the other hand, but essentially there is no such thing. These two terms speak of seeing reality from two different perspectives. They are complementary points of view, not mutually exclusive blocks of knowledge and subject matter. The "sacred" deals with specific religious ways God shows Himself to man. For example, the Sacraments are sacred because they are touchstones of the divine reality, showing a self-giving God; God is directly revealed. Miracles are signs of God's presence; the church is the mystical body of Christ.

On the other hand, all social and political affairs, spoken of as secular, are "sacred" to the extent that they reveal God, and show His love for man mediated through the gift of human relationships. Through participating in and observing the manifold aspects of secular life, by experience in society, and observation of the natural world, man can be led to see the divine unity that supports every facet of life. This depends, of course, upon proper interpretation led by the Spirit of God whereby sin and self-centeredness are ruled out. By identifying social and religious action in the Sermon of the Mount Jesus showed that social relations can be instruments for mediating God's will.

The love of God should be used as the social ideal for all mankind. In family life the primary function of the parent is through love for the children to convey the reality of God's love for them. As such the family is the human microcosm of the larger divine family of God.

Since Jesus Christ is the Lord of History, man can learn lessons from history by observing the power of God and His will as the prevailing one. From historical events man must seek to learn the lessons in them as we open ourselves to the Holy Spirit as our Divine Teacher.

Correctly observed, science has the power to reveal the stability and order, the beauty and creativeness of God. It is the instrument by which the reality of Christ as Logos is communicated. As Creator He shows, not only the attributes of God, but the very nature and orderliness or reality.

God, as Lord of Creation, gives life and direction to all the processes of nature. Creation is one of the ways in which God's nature is revealed. The principles of His righteousness, orderliness and permanence are clearly revealed in His works. Thus, matter is revelatory of spiritual realities and, therefore, this gives scientific knowledge a genuine and not an idolatrous role in revelation. True science, therefore, is rooted in the doctrine of God which ensures both direction and freedom to scientific investigation. The order and law of God is revealed in the laws of the natural world. Thus, true science and true religion are not in conflict because they deal with a God-created reality which cannot be in conflict.

If the structure of the natural world testifies to the harmony and order of God the Creator, the means by which students perceive the world is a witness to the divine light. The method of the scientist requires trust and openness to truth. Thus, the scientific method can be viewed as emanating from God. The honest search for truth is pleasing to God. The true scientist, therefore, is a man of faith and must be open to the guidance of the Holy Spirit.

10. <u>Revelation and Relationships</u>. The relationships of revelation are seen in three categories: (1) faith and reason; (2) man and revelation; and (3) teaching and revelation. Faith and reason go together in the discovery of truth (I Peter 3:15; I John 4:1; I Thess. 5:21; Isaiah 1:18; 41:21; I Sam. 12:7). With relation to man, revelation is available to men (Deut. 29:29; 30:14). Truth and knowledge are classified thereby. There is earthly wisdom (I Cor. 1-2; James 3:15) and there is spiritual wisdom (I Cor. 1:30; 2:10-16; James 3:13-17). Both wisdom and knowledge are gifts from God (Eph. 1:17-19). Knowledge of Christ is the most precious knowledge (Phil. 3:8; Col. 2:2,3). Man is to experience and walk in truth (II John 3, 4; Psalm 51:6; John 8:32).

Revelation has something to say about teaching. Early teaching has been described (I Cor. 12:8). It is the world of wisdom - <u>logos sophia</u> - truth arrived at by the teacher's powers of observation and reason. It is the word of knowledge - <u>logos gnoseos</u> - truth bestowed as the gift of the Spirit. The first enables teachers to explain truth; the second qualifies them to interpret it.

11. <u>The Place of Scripture in Revelation</u>. One form of revelation has been given in writing (II Peter 1:21). The purpose of this writing was revelation -- to know (I John 5:13). Scriptures speak to the church (Acts 28:25; Heb. 10:15) and preserve revelation for it (Isaiah 30:8). Written revelation was authenticated by Jesus Christ (John 10:35) and its purpose is identical with the purpose of revelation itself -- to witness to Jesus Christ (2 Tim. 3:15; Acts 17:2-3; 28:23; Luke 24:27). Jesus stressed its authority (Matthew 5; 7:18).

43

Scripture is the Word of God (Heb. 4:12; 8:8-10; Acts 28:25; Gal. 3:8) and as such, is inspired (II Tim. 3:16). Scripture is the voice of the Spirit (Heb. 3:7; 10:15) because God is the Author of it (II Peter 1:20,21). The properties of Scripture are authority (Isaiah 1:2); sufficiency (II Tim. 3:15); clarity (Psalm 119:105) and efficacy (Heb. 4:12) and cannot be broken (John 10:35).

As God's revelation, revelation is Special Revelation through the Word (Heb. 1:1,2). The terms "God spake," or "God said" are used over 2000 times in the Bible. The characteristics of this Special Revelation are revealed clearly in Psalm 19:7-10. The law of God is perfect -- it converts (vs. 7); the statutes of the Lord are right -- rejoicing the heart (vs. 8). The fear of the Lord is clean -- enduring (vs. 9). The judgments of the Lord are true -- righteous (vs. 9). They are more valuable than wealth (vs. 10), and there are great rewards for obeying them (vs. 11). The Word of God is Special Revelation (II Peter 1:19; Rev. 1:1; 22:18f; Heb. 1:1,2; Psalm 119:105,130). It issues in the Gospel (Romans 1:17).

12. <u>The Climax of Revelation</u>. The climax of God's special revelation is in Jesus Christ. He was the personal incarnation of God in the flesh. In Him both the source and content of revelation wholly coincide. He is not simply a proclaimer of a divinely given word but on the basis of His inherent authority Himself stipulates and determines the Word of God.

The Holy Spirit has communicated the intelligible content of divine revelation through prophetic-apostolic inspiration and He remains the authoritative interpreter of His Scripturally given Word of God. He is the bestower of spiritual life and He enables us to appropriate God's revelation efficaciously and thereby attest the redemptive power of revealed truth in the personal experience of reborn sinners.

The Church is the Kingdom of God on earth and as such it appropriates and passes along to successive generations the realities of divine revelation. This is done through personal witness, worship and acts of love and mercy extended to fellow men.

The ultimate climax of revelation will take place when Jesus Christ returns to unveil the glory of God and to consummate the

44

plans of God in the eradication of evil and the establishment of a new heaven and earth. This end-time revelation will reveal God fully to His children and will continue throughout eternity to come.

13. <u>Education and Revelation</u>. It should be obvious from the above discussion that education and revelation are directly related. The term "revelation" itself means to make known, to draw back the veil, and education is concerned with the same thing -- making truth known. More will be said about this matter in Chapter Three.

Notes

1. Lawrence Richards, "Experiencing Reality Together: Toward the Impossible Dream," in Norma H. Thompson, ed., <u>Religious Education and Theology</u>, Religious Education Press, 1982, C

OUTLINE FOR

CHAPTER THREE

REVELATION AND CHRISTIAN EDUCATION THEORY

A. The Need, Nature and Demand for Theory
    1. A Crucial Need
    2. The Relation of Theory and Practice
    3. The Place, Demands and Criteria of Theory
    4. The Approach to Theory
    5. The Source of Theory
    6. The Construction of Theory

B. Revelation and Christian Education Theory
    1. The Case for Revelation
    2. Revelation in Christian Education Theory
    3. Implications of Revelation for Integration
    4. Implications of Revelation for Evangelical Christian Education Theory
    5. Implications of Revelation for the Construction of Theory

C. Representative Evangelical Revelational Perspectives
    1. An Early View
    2. The Current Situation
    3. Frank E. Gabelein
    4. Mark Fakkema
    5. Lois Lebar
    6. Lawrence Richards
    7. Summary

D. An Evangelical Proposal for Theory
    1. A Revelational Approach
    2. God as Teacher
    3. Christian Epistemology

4. The Life Principle
5. The Light Principle
6. The Master Teacher
7. The Church
8. The Marks of a Christian Educational System

E. Revelation and Local Church Education
   1. Focus of Attention
   2. Traditional Approaches
   3. Contemporary Theological Approaches
   4. Representative Theological Approaches
   5. Representative Evangelical Approaches
   6. Implications of Theocentic Revelation for the Local
      Church Program

F. Revelation and Other Christian Schools
   1. Types of Christian Schools
   2. A Common Foundation Needed
   3. The Christian Liberal Arts College

CHAPTER THREE

REVELATION AND CHRISTIAN EDUCATION THEORY

A. The Need, Nature and Demand for Theory

1. A Crucial Need. One of the great needs prevalent in Christian education circles at all levels is that of an adequate theory to direct practices. When one thinks of the vast amount of resources poured into Christian education, such as money, facilities, equipment, etc., this becomes more evident. If education is to meet the needs of people then a clear theory is necessary to provide guidelines for this task.

2. The Relation of Theory and Practice. If educational administrators attempt practice not based on sound theory, results take place rather haphazardly without too much reference to reasons for practice. Such practice as this yields little or no possibility of evaluation or improvement. Without adequate theory educational practice is in danger of operating without the guidelines provided by aims, goals, purposes and objectives. If any educational practice is to be fruitful and effective it demands a definite base in theory.

3. The Place, Demands and Criteria of Theory. One's theory of education determines practice. Based upon a proper philosophy of education, theory becomes the bridge between principle and practice or program. An adequate theory of education for Christian education must meet the demands placed upon it by being philosophically acceptable, theologically valid, and educationally sound.

To be philosophically acceptable, evangelical Christian educators believe that educational theory needs to draw from and build upon the presuppositions of Christian theism. This points up the importance of foundational principles. Content of theory consists of principles derived from biblical and theological sources. Such principles provide working hypotheses derived from a Christian philosophy of life. They direct the operation of the total program. They guide in the selection and utilization of objectives, curriculum and administrative procedures. They serve as basis for evaluation. They will be modified only as Christian educators come to greater under-standing of the Christian philosophy of life as it is related to God, man's need and to the culture.

To be theologically valid theory must conform to both biblical teachings and the particular theological premises acceptable to a particular denominational frame of reference.

To be educationally sound, Christian education theory must point up the distinctive thrust that Christian education has in the educational world. At the same time it will provide an integrating factor which will unify all educational efforts. Most certainly it will help meet the demands of quality teaching and learning. Overall, adequate theory will provide the means by which educational, philosophical and theological insights are translated into practice.

4. <u>The Approach to Theory</u>. The many efforts to develop educational theory both inside and outside Christian circles reveal ineffectiveness and confusion. This is nowhere revealed more clearly than in the various approaches in the field of secular education. One approach is advocated by Butler in his <u>Four Philosophies and Their Practice in Education and Philosophy</u> in which he makes a systematic study of philosophy by systems of thought. A second approach advocates study of schools of thought within a particular philosophy. This is illustrated by Brameld's <u>Philosophies of Education in Cultural Perspective</u> in which he compares the influences of progressivism, essentialism, perennialism and others. A third approach makes a study of the basic issues of education in the light of what the various philosophies have to say about such issues. Brubacher's <u>Modern Philosophies of Education</u> surveys aims, curriculum, methods, etc., and shows how various philosophical positions on these matters compare. A fourth approach is illustrated by Hansen's <u>Philosophy of American Education</u> in which he takes concrete practices in education and examines them in the light of history, the nature of man, society, and learning. In all of this wealth of information one becomes confused. Obviously, an integrating principle is lacking in these approaches.

A more recent review of integration possibilities was offered by James McDonald.[1] He recommends that education can be integrated by showing the relationship that people have to culture, that relationship which exists between inner experience and outer experience. He lists four alternative models. The romantic model emphasizes inner experience and focuses on developing the capacities of the individual. The cultural transmission model is grounded on external experience, of injecting cultural values into the learner. The developmental model emphasizes the person's internal structures which are developed by external experience. The praxis model stresses the structures of social life and the function of education is to enhance the learner's awareness of cultural and value transmission. McDonald then proposes what he calls a revisionist model entitled a transcendental development ideology. Both inner and outer experiences are equally emphasized in this model.

In the field of Christian education one finds hardly any difference in results. On the one hand one can find some approaches representing the church, some form of theology, or the Bible. On the other hand, an emphasis on scientific method, social theories, or humanism can be found. One is left in the same predicament of confusion on the Christian side of education. Some of these latter views will be dealt with later on under the discussion of the place of an integrating principle in the development of educational theory.

5. The Source of Theory. In view of the confusion mentioned above, it is important to lay out precisely what is required in terms of constructing a theory of Christian education. First in consideration is the matter of the source of information which serves as the major premise upon which the superstructure of theory is built. There are really only three sources of information available to man -- God, man himself, and nature. The starting points of all philosophies are found in one or more of these three.

The advocates of naturalism place great confidence in nature and its orderliness. They deny supernaturalism and place faith in the inductive method of the natural sciences to secure their information. Such findings along with the methods of experimentalism provide the basis for educational theory. Naturalistic liberals in church education use this approach.

Rationalism emphasizes human sources of information. Great

51

faith is placed in man's powers of reason. Liberal Christian educators have leaned heavily on these resources as well. Reason, however, is only a part of experience and rather arbitrary at that.

Idealism combines the two approaches above by stressing both inductive methods and reasoning in building theories. Probability, however, is as far as one can go with this philosophy.

There is a definite, intrinsic correlation between existentialism and religious education. The philosophies of both are uniquely synonymous. One might say that existentialism presents a challenge to liberal religious faith, not with a set of religious or philosophical doctrines, but with a series of questions, doubts, and desperate hopes. Similarities between the two doctrinally can be found in a denial of the meaning of the Crucifixion and of the fact of the Resurrection. Existentialism also denies the fact of the Incarnation, saying it is unreasonable. In fact, existentialism opposes all forms of Christian dogmatism making man less than absolute authority.

Educationally considered existentialism is essentially humanistic in emphasis. It deals with the primary concerns of man, life and death and makes these the center of the philosophy. As philosophy, it is concerned with the actual character of human existence and the calling of men to a realization of their essential freedom. It overemphasizes personal freedom and self-expression. It demands that the educative process take its major direction from the principle of freedom. It ignores quantitative aspects in education and instead looks at the inner being of the individual and society. It dwells upon values and continually examines new explorations; it is concerned with creativity. It regards formal standards as hindrances in the achievement of real wisdom. It believes that subject matter is meaningful when the student relates it to his own ideas and purposes and when it gives him a sense of discovery. It looks upon children as creative beings who are intent upon finding a more permanent meaning in life.

Existentialism recommends a rebellion against conformity, and thus it holds in common with pragmatism the idea that education is a process of continuous reconstruction of experience with the purpose of widening and deepening its social content, while, at the same time, the individual gains control of the methods involved. Both pragmatism and existentialism are concerned with growth and change; both are concerned with experience.

Some advocates of religious education have adopted the suggested methods of existentialism. The first is participation as a form of learning for people of all ages. The second is recognition, involving an awareness that comes through participation, but which is a personal response on the part of the learner. The third is communication, as illustrated in symbols. Pupils communicate with one another through conversation, discussion, witnessing, questioning, and in the classroom.

The existentialist is always in a state of tension, derived from his uncertainty about any absolute education foundation or source of truth from which he can determine goals to be realized. It thus becomes an unending quest with no definite formulas. It is filled with uncertainty, stressing subjective, problematic situations, not absolute answers.

There is little or nothing in contemporary religious existentialism that indicates how the school might be reformed. There are no absolutes, no Sovereignty or determination of God. All rests in man. Education, therefore, rests upon the learner's inner motivations and responses. Whatever the stimuli, it must produce a desirable response. Nothing negative can infringe upon his personal freedom or desire. Any regulation, dogma, or restriction must be eliminated. The learner is the final source of truth. All existent truth is consolidated and subjected to the approval of the individual. Truth, as revealed in the Word of God, is truth accepted only when the individual declares it truth. The serious risks of existentialism in religious education occur in its tendency to corrode faith in sustaining institutions, thus producing cultural and religious emptiness. The excessively critical mind may be a human disguise or substitute for a biblically oriented educational philosophy that is Christian.

In contrast to all of the above views the true <u>Christian educator</u> looks to a source of truth completely different from all the rest. The main source is to be found in the presuppositions of Christian theism.

Among the advocates of religious education and Christian education one finds, from a survey of the literature, a wide variety of theory sources. The chart which follows summarizes the various schools of thought, showing basic aims, goals, the philosophical rootage from which the views come, along with the basic theological/ revelational sources of information. The schools are arranged according to the following classification: (1) liberal, (2) traditional, and (3) integral.

School - <u>Naturalistic Liberalism</u>
Aim - Personal creativity; natural growth; religious sensitivity
Goal - Social adjustment
Philosophical Rootage - Naturalism; humanism; realism;
        naturalistic idealism
Basic Theological Rootage - Immanence; anthropocentric; liberal
Advocates - Sophia Fahs and Ernest J. Chave, 1952 and 1947

School - <u>Social Liberalism Existentialism</u>
Aim - Spiritual growth
Goal - Democracy of God; self-realization
Philosophical Rootage - Naturalism; humanism; pragmatism;
        realism
Basic Theological Rootage - Immanence; anthropocentric; liberal
Advocates - John Dewey, George Coe, Harry Monroe, William
        Bower, Harrison Elliot, 1920's to 1940's

School - <u>Neo-liberalism</u>
Aim - Growth in grace
Goal - Faith relationship; social reconstruction
Philosophical Rootage - Humanism; realism; Christian theism
Basic Theological Rootage - Immanence; anthropocentric; liberal
Advocate - L. Harold De Wolf, 1963

School - <u>Neo-orthodox</u>
Aim - Conversion; growth in grace; nurture
Goal - Christian discipleship

Philosophical Rootage - Christian theism; humanism; realism
Basic Theological Rootage - Transcendental; theocentric;
     traditional
Advocates - Iris Cully, D. Campbell Wyckoff, 1950's

School - <u>Church Emphasis Protestant and Catholic</u>
Aim - Transmission of culture and spiritual heritage;
     growth in grace
Goal - Realize the authority and fellowship of the church
Philosophical Rootage - Christian theism; realism
Basic Theological Rootage - Transcendental; theocentric;
     traditional
Advocates - Jacques Maritain, Wesner Fallaw, Howard Grimes,
     Donald Butler and Dora Chaplin, 1940 - 1960's

School - <u>Evangelicalism</u>
Aim - Revelation; conversion; growth in grace
Goal - Christlikeness; the Church; Kingdom of God
Philosophical Rootage - Christian Theism; Christian; realism
Basic Theological Rootage - Transcendental; theocentric;
     traditional
Advocates - Frank Gabelein, Lois Lebar, Larry Richards, Harold
     Burgess, and H.W. Byrne, 1950's and 1960's

School - <u>Psychological School</u>
Aim - Nurture; encounter
Goal - Acceptance; changes in self
Philosophical Rootage - Christian theism; pragmatism; humanism
Basic Theological Rootage - Transcendental; theocentric; integral
Advocates - Ruell Howe, Lewis J. Sherill, 1950's

School - <u>Relationship Theology</u>
Aim - I-Thou relationship; nurture; engagement
Goal - Christian character in conversion; Christian living;
     commitment
Philosophical Rootage - Christian theism; humanism; pragmatism

Basic Theological Rootage - Transcendental; theocentric; integral
Advocates - David Hunter, Martin Buber, Randolph Miller, 1950's

School - <u>Social Science</u>
Aim - Christian understanding, action, and love
Goal - Christian service to God and man based on love;
      Christian living
Philosophical Rootage - Christian theism; social science theory;
      humanism; pragmatism
Basic Theological Rootage - Transcendent and Immanent; integral
Advocate - James Michael Lee

     The chart above shows that there is a wide diversity of opinion on sources of information from which the knowledge necessary for the building of theory can be drawn. Furthermore, it is not too clear from most of these schools of thought just exactly what integrating principle is available for the construction of Christian education theory.

     6. <u>The Construction of Theory</u>. Theory consists of those principles and guides to practice which on the one hand reflect one's basic philosophy of life, and on the other hand provide guidance for practice. From a Christian standpoint, immediate responsibility for such construction of theory lies with the church and its educational arms.

     To accomplish the demands of theory it is necessary to identify and use some ordering principle or integrating factor which will form the practical basis for using theory and guiding practice. It will enable Christian educators to use the knowledge available in Bible, theology, philosophy, education, and other acceptable sources to reach the standards of practice in the field. Furthermore, it will help laymen in the church who are generally untrained and widely unskilled in theological and educational matters. In other words the <u>function</u> of an integrating principle is to <u>guide</u> the whole process of theory and practice. On the one hand it will identify and uphold the distinctives of Christian education as a discipline and on the other hand be the central power in making operative all the principles demanded. The <u>values</u> of such a principle can be seen as follows in providing:

1. Motivation - yielding objectives
2. Integration - providing unity
3. Correlation - showing relationships
4. Direction - giving guidance
5. Supervision - stressing improvement
6. Evaluation - identifying achievement

Such an integrating principle must meet certain criteria. It must be scriptural and thoroughly compatible with the nature of the Christian faith. Thus it must be theologically valid, but it must also be educationally sound. It must be adequate to guide all educational processes, simple and clear enough to be used by untrained laymen in the church. It must assure good balance in the program and be the means whereby evaluation of results is made effective and possible.

As one surveys the various schools of thought for Christian education the following summary shows the core ideas which are advocated as integrating factors for theory construction:

School of Thought	Integrating Factor
Experimental - Humanist	Religious Humanism & Science
Religious Naturalism	Natural Growth
Liberal - Rationalist	Liberal Theology
Thomist	Roman Catholic Doctrine, Ideals
Neo-orthodoxy	Dialogue, Encounter
Religious Psychology	Engagement, Relationship
Relationship Theology	Confrontation
Church Thought	Fellowship (Koinonia)
Social Science	Theology/Social Science
Social Liberalism	Social Values and Democracy
Evangelicalism	Christian Theism and Revelation (Personal and written)

Certain individuals have proposed plans for integration:

Individual	Integrating Factor
Lawrence Little[2]	Synthesis of behavioral science, Christian theology and experience
J. Gordon Chamberlin[3]	Responsible freedom
Kendig B. Cully[4]	History
D. Campbell Wyckoff[5]	The Gospel

Some have drawn sources from past views, such as the Greek and Roman emphasis on good citizenship, the Renaissance stress on reason, or the scientific emphases giving preeminence to reason, inductive methods and democracy.

B. Revelation and Christian Education Theory

1. The Case for Revelation. As previously noted, the many efforts surveyed, which point to an integrating principle of some kind, have revealed confusion, uncertainty and downright disagreement over the exact character of the required integrating principle. The writer submits the case for the utilization of divine revelation to meet this need.

This case has been stated by others. A chief advocate is Huston Smith in his work Beyond the Post Modern Mind (New York, The Crossroads, Pub. Co., 1982). Smith maintains that the basic problem faced today in education is the loss of transcendence. This, he says, has led to a "decline in the sense of the sacred and a fading of the belief that we live in an ordered universe." Modern higher education has little or no sense of a value framework. A complete devotion to the scientific method, which cannot provide a value system, has led to complete reliance on empirically derived data and a humanistic philosophy of life largely devoid of the presence of God. Modern universities, therefore, have contributed directly to the decline of religious belief and actually encouraged a skeptical attitude toward everything that cannot be empirically verified. While no one would question the valid contribution of science we must not at the same time blind ourselves to its limitations. But modern science cannot deal with values and purposes, for they are beyond the possibilities of discovery by science. Thus, important values are overlooked, transcendence wanes, religious belief ceases, human beings are depreciated, and alienation results. Modern science, therefore, rejects transcendence because it is beyond its control. The inevitable result is a reductionistic naturalism which emphasizes that nothing that lacks a material component exists.

To the Christian, truth goes beyond such unwarranted and unsubstantiated claims. The writer contends that education must get beyond empiricism to an epistemology that is based on the very nature of reality as created by God, Who chooses to reveal Himself to man. Such epistemology goes beyond intuitive discernment, as advocated by Smith, to one based on an objective revelation of a Personal God such as the Scriptures set forth.

A revelation claim always evokes among some the fear of indoctrination. But the same people do not seem timid in indoctrinating one against indoctrination. Others propose a rather nebulous approach to what is termed "Christian values" but a careful reading of the literature fails to reveal just exactly what those values are, and, more importantly, just how they affect the educational process.

The force of argument for an epistemology and education based on divine revelation lies in its authoritative character. Truth comes from God as Creator Who knows. It is our responsibility to hear, heed, be what He wants us to be through Christ, and then behave accordingly. Then we can build educational theory and practice on an authoritative and successful basis.

A strong case for revelation can also be based on the very practical values for education of biblical revelation. In a special study of this matter in 1970 the Calvin College faculty pointed out several of these practical values. First, Scripture speaks of total reality -- about man, God and the world. While obviously the Bible is not a textbook on these matters, it does provide a Christian perspective on total reality, a framework for basic convictions. Christian educators should strive to show reality from this perspective. Biblical revelation helps to overcome distorted perceptions of God, man, and the world and provides a correct understanding of reality.

Second, biblical revelation often speaks to the conceptual schemes, methodologies, and presuppositions employed in an academic discipline as well as to indicate what is to be accepted as fact or not. Subjects such as human sin and behaviorism are dealt with differently in Scripture from that in humanistic disciplines.

Third, biblical revelation shows the place and limits of academic disciplines. It shows that no one discipline dominates truth in the field. It shows that no single facet of reality encompasses the whole.

Fourth, biblical revelation gives direction to research and conclusions to be drawn from it. It requires honesty and scrupulous loyalty to the findings of research.

Fifth, biblical revelation provides assistance in evaluating truth in the disciplines. It can help shape those evaluations.

Sixth, biblical revelation helps determine the purposes of knowledge and the use to which it is put.

Another prominent voice to champion the cause of a revelation perspective for education is that of George A. Buttrick. In his brilliant work <u>Biblical Thought and the Secular University</u> (Louisiana State University Press, 1960) he proposed biblical thought as the integrating factor for education. By biblical thought he meant "the thinking and faith set forth in the Bible." He contended that American culture rests on it. The contribution, he said, that biblical thought makes to education is the gift of faith. On page 56 he goes on to say:

The Biblical view of nature is largely taken for granted by education, and the word "taken" is accurate; it is taken from its Biblical source. The faith that the cosmos is one and worthy of study is Biblical faith, against the view that would make matter a fetter, and flesh the evil work of some demiurge. Thus all science rests on Biblical faith. The faith that time is not a treadmill fate, but a straight line of purposeful change (not of man's purposes only), is Biblical faith; and the histographer lives and labors within it. The faith that things are not merely things but hieroglyphics is Biblical; the whole world is both instrumental and revelatory; and in that faith, art, such as architecture, lives its life, stricken by radiance yet serving man's daily needs. The faith that the body is precious, an inescapable term in personhood, twin of the psyche, not a burden nor the prison of some imaginary "soul", is Biblical faith; and therein medicine finds both warrant and ordination. Western culture in its myriad boons lives by legacy of a faith which now it tries to disown. The destructive heresies of our time are heresies against Biblical thought. So the church, or God's purposes through the church, has already given to higher education the ground-of-faith on which it lives and moves -- and which it often forgets.

2. Revelation in Christian Education Theory. Obviously, one's view of revelation determines largely his view of theory and likewise this determines the function that revelation has in theory. In the case of those who subscribe to liberal views revelation is largely anthropocentric in character and stresses the immanence of God in human life and affairs. Traditionalists hold to a transcendental view of God and would see revelation theocentrically. Those who hold to an integral view would seek to stress both the transcendence and immanence of God and stress a divine/human relationship in Christian education.

In the case of the liberal view, God enters human affairs in the events of history and human activities. Traditionalists would say that God invades life from above and gives a supernatural dimension to education. In the integral view both of these matters are expressed equally.

Views of revelation impact directly positions to be taken regarding God, the nature of man and education, and the concept of the curriculum. Education to liberals differs rather widely from the views of others because their view is based on another frame of reference which in turn leads to different aims and objectives. Some liberals make hardly any distinction between general education and religious education.

Most liberals stand together in their emphasis on an experience-centered approach to religious education. A person, to them, becomes religious or religiously mature through the processes of experiences which are religious. These experiences are social. It is the by-product of the meeting of persons, the interaction between persons and the world of nature, and the interaction with a God who is conceived as immanent in all phases of this total dynamic process of interaction.

Liberals tend to make man continuous with nature. Man is

conceived as being progressively a part of the evolutionary process of becoming. Here they interpret religious education in terms of processes. They take their educational cue from the personality principle; they view man as both a biological and a spiritual being. Man is viewed as a product of the processes of evolution and has arrived on the scale of development where he now is by means of creative intelligence and the ambitions which he possesses. From his birth man possesses the ability to change, which cannot be measured at any stage of human growth. By his creative endeavor man is able to overcome difficulties, to achieve superior selfhood, and to discover peerless values, spiritual insights, and the workings of God Himself.

To the liberal, revelation is little more than man finding God like any other discovery. He knows God better as he fulfills the highest demands of personal adjustment placed upon him by the conditions of his environment.

Liberals are not too clear on their concept of God because they are so consumed with the importance of the human situation. To some, God may be no more than a creation of minds which are in relationship. Thus, God can only be known through His manifestations in this world and in human nature. Knowledge of God is derived out of experiences which are social and religious. God is in and above the educative process, but they do not make clear just who and what God is. All matters, such as sin, salvation, redemption, the church, etc., are treated from the point of view of human experience, leaving the extra-human aspects of these concepts implicit but not explicit. Social values and social ends are emphasized without fully explaining spiritual values and spiritual ends in their system of religious education.

Most liberals are committed to the methods of science to the exclusion of much needed theological support for their educational concepts. In their concentration on growth and what man can do for himself rather than on what God can do for man, there is little room for a strong faith in God and His redemptive powers. God seems more of a passive symbol than a dynamic reality in the educative process.

All of these views are in marked contrast to those of

traditionalists and integrationists who emphasize the supernatural aspects of God and the work of His Spirit in Christian education. Christian education, to them, becomes a matter of working with God toward the transformation of the human spirit and bringing in the Kingdom of God on earth.

3. <u>Implications of Revelation for Integration</u>. Integration simply stated is unity. Revelation makes it possible in Christian education to find this unity in at least two phases of the program: (1) at the philosophical level in terms of its relation to a philosophy of education, and (2) at the level of teaching and learning in the classroom.

The philosophy of education as derived from revelation is based on three basic presuppositions. First, education is a unifying process. This can be viewed in a narrow sense in terms of intellectual unity. Christian thought is dependent on the unifying thought in the mind of God. To be correct, therefore, the mind of man must be patterned after the mind of God because His thinking is correct. Man's thought life as a creature of God must reflect the mind of the Creator. "In thy light do we see light." (Psalm 36:9)

In secular education, education is a mental unifying process also, but it seeks to be independent of Divine thought. It assumes that the unifying process is purely a subjective experience. It ignores God.

Education is more than a unifying process of the intellect. It involves the totality of life. For Christian education the whole life of the student should be God-determined, God-motivated, and God-centered. On the other hand in secular thought the pupil is viewed as man-made.

Revelation provides next a unifying objective in a God-glorifying life. All subject matter originates in God. All subjects in the curriculum are expressive of the ideas of God. All of these truths are God-glorifying. They not only help the student but provide a source of God-revealing truth. Truth best helps the student when it reveals God. Conversely, in secular education subject matter does not reveal God but exists in and of itself. But the true aim of Christian education is that the subject matter will help the student to self-consciously glorify God in his life.

In leaving God out of education secular education tends to produce practical atheists. It cannot truly educate, therefore, because God is the Fact of all facts. To ignore God, the Source of truth, is to present facts abstractly-detached from their source. Without this, truth is meaningless to the Christian. A loss of objective moral standards makes morality virtually unteachable. Without its center in God, knowledge is cut off from its roots and thus disintegrates.

Unity is also to be found in the redemptive work of God through Jesus Christ. True education must have His work as its basis. Otherwise education must work on the assumption that man can lift himself up by his own bootstraps.

The second way in which revelation contributes to integration is by providing clues essential to the handling of truth in the classroom. It provides guidelines for handling subject matter in terms of how the disciplines are related and interpreted.

Some refer to this function as "structured" integration. Where informal integration takes place through the lives and general program of the school, structured integration is realized through the creation of definite curriculum objectives designed to show how the Christian philosophy of life, as reflected in biblical and theological points of view, directly impacts the planning and teaching of subject matter. This requires unity on the part of the faculty as a whole who are committed to seeing that Christian and secular truth are unified in the curriculum. Each individual teacher will also be required to set up teaching-learning objectives in handling subject materials which will bring about integration of truth in each discipline taught. Still further, students should be made aware that this process is actually taking place in the classroom. This will help the student to develop his own Christian world view and evaluate all curriculum materials to this end.

Suggested themes for the integration of the Christian faith with secular subject matter will be provided in a chapter to follow. Suggestions will also be made on how to achieve integration.

4. Implications of Revelation for Evangelical Educational Theory. The basic premise of Christian Theism provides for the

existence of a Personal God, such as the Bible sets forth and Who was revealed in His Son the Lord Jesus Christ, and Who has chosen to reveal Himself to man. "The fear of the Lord is the beginning of knowledge" (Prov. 1:7; 9:10). God's Self-revelation, therefore, provides the fundamental source of truth to the evangelical. The nature of this revelation is twofold, being both natural or general, and special. The secrets of education, therefore, are to be found in Divine Revelation. Direct relevance for Christian education is the category of special revelation, which in turn upon examination can be divided into three disciplines which form the complete unity of God's special Self-revelation, namely, Bible, Christian Theology, and Christian Philosophy. The relationships are revealed in the chart which follows:

A term used to describe these disciplines is that of "Biblical Studies." As a whole they provide the thought structures for all Christian education and from them principles are derived whereby all truth is recognized and evaluated. Furthermore, these studies are conceived as synoptic studies which provide a perspective of viewing reality in connected wholes. They function also in providing the Christian educator with the source and basis for formulating a Christian world view which in turn yields guidelines for educational theory and practice.

We are able to see now the implications of divine revelation as the basic source of truth for the Christian educator. A working principle is revealed. God is the Source of all life and truth and He has revealed Himself to mankind. This revelation yields the possibility of developing the World View of Christian Theism which encompasses the church and education within its scope. Thus, the guidelines are supplied for implementing the work of the church in all of its educational responsibilities at all levels of educational practice. These relationships are revealed in chart form below.

THE WORKING PRINCIPLE

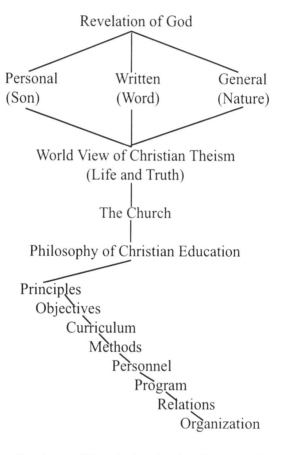

Revelation of God

| Personal | Written | General |
| (Son) | (Word) | (Nature) |

World View of Christian Theism
(Life and Truth)

The Church

Philosophy of Christian Education

Principles
Objectives
Curriculum
Methods
Personnel
Program
Relations
Organization

5. <u>Implications of Revelation for the Construction of Theory</u>. Theory consists of those principles and guides to practice which on the one hand reflect one's basic philosophy of life, and on the other hand provide guidance for the organization and administration of a

program of Christian education. Its function, therefore, is to provide the connecting link between the sources of information provided in Special Revelation, particularly the Biblical Studies, and practice as it takes place in the program of Christian education. Biblical Studies focus on principles, basic issues, and resources, whereas practice focuses on the operational aspects involving responsibilities, duties, and problems.

Ultimate responsibility on earth for the construction of theory lies with the church, the body of Christ, for it has a <u>mission</u> to perform in the world, that is to carry out the mission of its Head. In the light of this mission there are <u>ministries</u> to be performed, one of which is the ministry of teaching and education, therefore there is a <u>manner</u> in getting the job done. This process may be pictured as follows:

GOD
|
REVELATION
|
THE CHURCH
|
Mission
|
Ministry
|
Manner

Christian education at all levels is a part of and supports the church in all of this work for God in the world. To assist the church in this work, God has made available His revelation. Primary Sources from Special Revelation are the Bible, Christian Theology, and Christian Philosophy, as we have noted previously. In addition to these sources, however, and drawn from General Revelation, are what might be termed Secondary Sources. Primary Sources provide thought structures, principles, and norms which are formative and directive. Secondary Sources supplement the information provided in the Primary Sources.

Among Secondary Sources are church history and life which reveal the organization and administration of church affairs throughout history and of which education has been a part. Psychology supplements the biblical knowledge of man, stressing personality development, mental development and behavior, all of which directly affect and involve education. Educational Psychology focuses on the teaching-learning process. Sociology emphasizes the importance of the institutional frame of reference within which man lives and works as well as the effects of social groupings. Educational sociology studies the effects of these emphases in education. Science makes its contributions also. The new discipline of communications studies the transmission and appropriation of attitudes and ideas, both of which are directly relevant to Christian education.

From the contributions of knowledge and guidelines supplied by both Primary and Secondary sources of information, Christian educators are able to develop the Christian theistic world view and to formulate both theory and practice for Christian education. Thus, at least theoretically, Christian educators are enabled to develop a Christian education system for the church and its educational institutions which is both theologically valid and educationally sound.

C. Representative Evangelical Revelational Perspectives
     1. An Early View. One of the earliest attempts to suggest an integrating factor for education was made by St. Augustine. His basic premise was that Christ is the first principle of knowledge. Man, however, cannot appreciate this fact fully because of the presence of the carnal mind. The unregenerate mind cannot reason adequately and therefore needs assistance. As a result of the rebellion of Adam against God his mind became unregenerate and carnal. This was a turning of the mind away from God to a contemplation of creation and led ultimately to making man himself the center of the world.

     Augustine listed several results of the unregenerate mind as follows:

1. It does not take faith seriously.
2. It does not see God as the Source of all truth.
3. It does not see all of life as a gift from God.
4. It does not see faith beyond reason.
5. It is not able to bring experience into an integral whole

The solution of these problems lies in God who must communicate Himself to man and persuade him to turn from self to God. God reveals Himself to man through the gift of faith by which the unregenerate mind is transformed.

Christ is the first principle of knowledge because He delivers man from ignorance about God and his own nature as a sinner created in the image of God. God cleanses the carnal mind and through communion with Him the reason of man is used clearly and properly to see truth and see it whole. God illuminates the mind. Faith supplies the clues to interpretation by which all truth can be understood. All truth is one, and all truth is God's truth, for God is the God of Truth.

The study of the arts and sciences and disciplines of human culture should take place under the light of revelation which gives unity and synthesis to the entire curriculum. This gives them a Christian purpose. While their content will remain largely the same as received, they will serve the needs and progress of civilized life on earth. They are to contribute to the building of a Christian social order, theocentric, tuned to God. To accomplish this end all the arts and sciences are to be taught in the light of the Bible.

To Augustine the Bible served a twofold function. First, it gives us <u>content</u> of itself to be studied, and second, it <u>guides</u> us in teaching what we have understood.

To bridge the gap between God and man and to erase the blindness of ignorance requires two things. There must first be a process of illumination and second, an experience of purification in man to accomplish the full purpose of Christian education. The way to this grand design is through Jesus Christ, the transforming and enlightening power of the Word of God Incarnate.

Perhaps Augustine's greatest contribution to education in general was his concept of integration. The purpose of all education, in his view, was to bring about an integrated view of knowledge and life in the light of revealed wisdom and divine revelation, a world view centering in God.

2. <u>The Current Situation</u>. Not a great deal of writing on the subject of integration is to be found among evangelical Christian educators. Frank Gabelein, Lois Lebar, Mark Fakkema, Lawrence

Richards, certain writers of the Dutch school of thought, and the writer have published materials. Dr. Gabelein has not written specifically for church education. Dr. Fakkema specialized in the Christian day school movement, as have the Dutch writers. Lois Lebar's philosophy of Christian education for the local church can be examined in her Education That Is Christian where she applies it to teaching. The writer's Christian Approach to Education was an attempt to produce a theory which could be applicable in Christian higher education, but it was based on a general philosophy of Christian education which theoretically could be applied at any level of Christian education.

3. Frank E. Gabelein. Frank E. Gabelein has written brilliantly on the basic philosophy of Christian education in his The Pattern of God's Truth. He stated his basic premise as "all truth is God's truth."[6] Integration in Christian education at all levels is thus made possible. Here is where all Christian philosophy of Christian education begins. Integration is found on this basis not only in subject matter but also in the teacher.

4. Mark Fakkema. Mark Fakkema built a philosophy of Christian education based on God's Self-revelation. Central to his viewpoint was his "image" concept which provides the ordering principle for Christian education. All things reflect God's attributes. Man and all other creatures are images of God. Whatever exists reveals God (Rom. 11:36; Acts 17:28). The purpose of Christian education is to show God revealed; the goal is to reveal God. Man is to be the image of God. All truth is God's truth and reveals His attributes. The whole school system, both subject matter and its teaching together with its structure and administration, is to reflect as in a mirror the character and conduct of God. In this, Dr. Fakkema has developed a theory which is theologically valid and educationally sound. It is consistent and clear throughout its structure and development.[7] This same major premise is carried through by advocates of the Dutch school of thought.[8]

5. Lois Lebar. Lois Lebar has developed a God-centered approach to Christian education. The core idea in her viewpoint might be termed "the Word-centered" approach. In explaining this concept she says:

*" . . . only a God-centered curriculum can be Christian.
Can we put the Word of God in the center and yet have a dynamic
curriculum? We can, for no other book is comparable to God's
Revelation. God means His words to be more than facts, even eternal
facts. He means them to reveal Himself and His Son. He never
meant us to separate the Written Word from the Living Word. The
Living Word is contacted only through the Written record. Therefore
Christians have a curriculum that is Word-centered rather than Bible-
centered.*[9]

With the help of the Holy Spirit both Living and Written Word are
made parts of the pupil's personal Christian experience through which
his needs are met and his life situations changed. Christian maturity
is the goal with Christlikeness the characteristic. Dr. Lebar applied
this philosophy to teaching-learning processes in church education.

    6. <u>Lawrence Richards</u>. Lawrence Richards also takes his
stance within a divine revelational framework. His views are
expressed in his work entitled <u>A Theology of Christian Education</u>.[10]
His basic assumption is that those concerned with Christian education
must build and rebuild on the principles laid out in the Word of God.
Richards insists that basic reality is to be found in "the divine
perception of total creation." As expressed in the Bible the Scriptures
are "in fullest harmony with reality." In the light of this premise it
becomes the function of education to process Scripture "as reality to
be lived and reality to be seen," not merely to be believed.

    Based on a scriptural premise Christian education functions
within the context of the church as the Body of Christ. The primary
purpose is to develop the "life of God" in the body through a process
of discipleship. The goal is to set up contextual factors, including
teaching and learning, which will result in the realization of Godlike and Christ-like disciples. This requires both transformation and
growth. It goes on in the context of the socialized character of the
church as the Body of Christ which models Christlikeness.

    The role of the teacher is that of one who models genuine
Christianity, subject to the authority of God through Scripture, a
fellow-learner, an example of biblical truth and living. All

71

relationships are based on Christian love. The whole teaching-learning process also goes on in a context of love, faith, and obedience.

To accomplish the true goals of the church, all workers should think of themselves as educators, teaching both by precept and example. To bring this to pass greatest emphasis should be placed on non-formal learning settings. Formal learning should focus on cognitive development but total discipleship development depends most on non-formal teaching settings, on life-related experiences. Most certainly the supernatural affects of the Word of God and the person and work of the Holy Spirit must be present to make the whole educational enterprise succeed.

7. <u>Summary</u>. Perhaps it is possible to summarize the main concepts of the evangelical writers just surveyed by indicating points of common agreement.

1. A philosophy which stresses God's transcendency, His creation and providence
2. A theology which stresses God's immanence, His presence in the Person of the Holy Spirit
3. God has chosen to make Himself known through divine Self-revelation, in nature, in His Son, in the Scripture, and through redemption
4. All truth is God's truth
5. Christian education should be God-centered
6. The purpose is to show God revealed; the character goal is Christlikeness; the ultimate goal is the Kingdom of God
7. The Bible is God's written Revelation, and as such is inspired of God, serving as a means to an end, and pointing men to the Living Word. It functions as the basic authority for curriculum construction
8. Christian education is dynamic rather than static in character
9. Revelation provides the integrating factor for Christian educational theory
10. The Person of the Holy Spirit and His work provides the power to achieve the goals of Christian education.

While it is perhaps true that some fundamentalists have been guilty of overstressing Bible memory work, have been somewhat authoritarian in spirit, also literalistic and legalistic in their educational approach, the concepts above, and others not mentioned, currently reflect the best in evangelical thought and are a far cry from the "fundamentalist stereotypes" held by liberal thinkers in the past.

The writer classifies himself in the evangelical school of thought. An attempt will be made in the section which follows to offer an evangelical theory of Christian education for all educational levels. In this theory a core idea, or integrating element, will be indicated with the hope that the theory submitted will be philosophically accepted, theologically valid, and educationally sound.

D. An Evangelical Proposal for Theory

1. A Revelational Approach. The approach to theory which follows might be termed a "revelational approach," in which both the God-centered concept and biblical authority are integrated. Thus, we shall follow in the school of thought sponsored by Augustine, Gabelein, Fakkema, Richards and Lebar. The theory is developed according to the scheme of the "working principle" previously mentioned in this chapter.

Christian education like all other forms of true education must look to its Source for a beginning. This source is God. Other forms of education look either to nature or to man for a beginning. The Apostle Paul warned of this in II Corinthians 10:12,13, where he pointed out that men commend themselves or measure themselves by themselves or other men, but the Christian takes the rule which God supplies.

The major presupposition of Christian education is that God exists, has created all things, and has made Himself known through Self-revelation. The chart which follows shows this clearly.

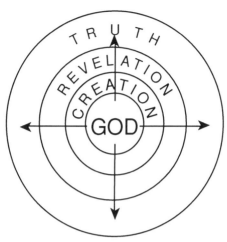

All life and truth come from God. Christian education, therefore, will find all of life and truth in Him. All Christian education finds its source, content and meaning in the God of Creation (Gen. 1:1; Rom. 11:36). This provides the basis of the world view of Christian Theism which gives the Christian his philosophy of total reality. Truth is made available to man in both propositional and personal forms. It is at once apparent that such a philosophy can serve Christian education at all levels in several ways: (1) by providing a world view which gives unity, (2) a philosophy of life which gives meaning, (3) emphasis on true values and objectives which give purpose and direction, (4) systematization of truth-content which provides the basis for the curriculum, (5) clues regarding methodologies and procedures to be employed, and (6) a means of evaluation.

     2. God as Teacher. A direct implication of the fact of the existence of the God of Truth is that He is Teacher. He alone unites knowledge and life, means and goal. As Teacher, God "unveils" truth to the student. He reaches out to the student. The Trinity is totally involved in revelation and teaching. Truth is the chief element in God (Psalm 31:5; 119:30; John 3:33; 7:28; 8:26). All the works of God are done in truth (Psalm 33:4).

     The love of the Father provides the motivation for education; the Son as the Word, the Logos, provides the link; and the Holy Spirit provides the interpretation. Christ, as Logos, provides structure for education. He does this by making language a dependable form of communication. He brings rationality to knowledge. He provides meaning to observable facts. He has opened the world to all men to be observed and known. All subject matter disciplines, therefore, reveal the rationality of the world and of God Himself so that students can be led into truth.

The Logos, however, is not merely the basis for rationality. As the Word "made flesh" and as Person, He gives unity to human personality and joins together intellect and spirit.

Since Christ as Logos precedes time and creation, He is present in all truth. The Word is not only the structural basis for language, He is the creative inspiration that moved the prophets, gave courage to Joshua and wisdom to Solomon. Furthermore, He is continuously active in fulfilling His function as Creator and Revealer.

As Logos, Christ Jesus is the key to knowledge. He said, "I am the way, the truth, and the life" (John 14:6). As Creator, he provides the basis and motivation for all reality. He is the way to the Father (John 14:6); He reveals the Father as God (John 14:9). He is the way to heaven (John 14:1-3). He is the way to successful living (John 14:1-14; 15:1-8).

As Truth, Jesus Himself is Truth (John 14:6). As Creator, He provides truth (John 1:3). As Mediator, He interprets truth through the work of His Spirit (John 14:26).

As Life, Jesus Himself is life. He gives life, sustains life and gives it an abundant quality (John 10:10). He gives us personal fellowship (John 14:18). He provides hope for eternal life and victory over death and the grave (John 14:19). This results in peace (John 14:26,27).

Education that is Christian centers, therefore, in Jesus Christ the Son of God. God was in Christ as Creator, Designer and Preserver of all things (Col. 1:16,17; Rom. 11:36). The whole process of creation as conducted by Jesus Christ was an educational process, for this process was accomplished by the wisdom of God (Prov. 3:19a), by understanding (Prov. 3:19b), by knowledge (Prov. 3:20), and by the spoken Word of God ("And God said" - Genesis 1; Psalm 33:6; Hebrews 1:3). As Divine Prophet, Jesus Christ was the Revealer of divine truth.

Christian education, therefore, is education that is Christ-dependent in its responsibility. God is Creator (Genesis 1:1) but man is creature (Genesis 1:26,27). He was made dependent upon God and therefore responsible to Him (Genesis 1:28). Man's need, therefore, is to know God (John 17:3). In fact, man's whole life is held accountable to God (I Tim. 5:24; Rom. 14:10,12). If man is to overcome the presence, power and penalty of sin, he must depend on Jesus Christ for deliverance (Matt. 6:13; II Cor. 1:10; Gal. 1:4; Matt. 11:27; II Peter 2:9). As applied to the field of Christian education, all mankind is dependent upon Jesus Christ for life and truth (Acts 17:28; I Cor. 1:24,30).

Christian education is education that is Holy Spirit controlled. A God-centered education is accomplished through the superintendency of the Third Person of the Trinity -- the Holy Spirit. He is the Control factor in church work and Christian education. Jesus said, "I am the Truth" (John 14:6). He communicates His truth through the Spirit of Truth (John 14:17; I John 2:27; 5:6) Who also is the Author of Truth (John 15:26; 16:13; I John 4:6).

In a very real sense the Holy Spirit is Teacher. He interprets truth (John 14:26). He helps man to know (John 16:13).

The Holy Spirit controls the educational process of character development. He convicts the sinner (John 16:8-10); He implants new spiritual life (John 1:4; 3:3,7,8); He provides a new heart (Ezek. 36:26-27; I Cor. 3:16). He witnesses to new life in Christ (Rom. 8:15,16); He guides, develops and educates the saint (John 16:13-14). The Spirit sanctifies the child of God (Titus 3:5; I Peter 1:2; II Thess. 2:13).

The Holy Spirit overcomes the debilitating effects of sin in the human personality. The human spirit is given eternal life (I John 5:11,12). He renews the mind (Eph. 4:23; Rom. 8:6). The heart is purified (Col. 3:2; Acts 15:8,9), the will is energized (Heb. 13:21; Phil. 2:13), and the body becomes the habitation of God (Rom. 12:1; 6:13; I Cor. 6:16-20).

By overseeing the work and leadership of God's people the Holy Spirit has supervisory control (I Pet. 1:2; I Thess. 5:23; Acts 13:2). By anointing teachers and educational leaders He energizes and anoints them for service (Eph. 3:16-20; Titus 2:14; 3:8; II Tim. 3:17; Rom. 12:1).

3. Christian Epistemology. The means by which the Christian philosophy of life is translated into educational processes is through the application of Christian epistemology, the theory of knowledge. The biblical view of knowledge presupposes a source of all knowledge, for knowledge is dependent upon truth and truth in turn is dependent upon God. The Bible pictures God as the source of all life and truth. "In the beginning God created the heavens and the earth" (Genesis 1:1). He is a God of truth. It follows naturally, therefore, that any truth which comes to man must be an expression of the nature of God.

Truth is ascribed to the Trinity -- the Triune God is a God of truth. God the Father is the source of truth, God the Son is the manifestation of truth, and God the Spirit is the interpreter of truth. In outline form the biblical theory of knowledge is as follows:

The Trinity (God) and Truth
    The Father is light and truth -- Psalm 36:9;
      I John 1:5
    The Son is a revelation of truth --
      John 1:14,17; 14:6 (Truth is a Person)
    The Spirit interprets truth -- John 15:26; 16:13
General Revelation
    Through creation -- Gen. 1:1; Ps. 19:1,2; Rom. 1:20
    Through conscience of man -- Romans 2:14-16
Special Revelation
    In the Scriptures -- Hebrews 1:1,2;
      Psalm 119:105,130
    In the Son -- Colossians 2:3,9; John 14:9; 8:12
Man and Truth
    There is earthly wisdom -- I Corinthians 1,2;
      James 3:15
    There is spiritual wisdom -- I Cor. 1:30; 2:10-16;
      James 3:13, 17
    Wisdom, revelation, and knowledge are gifts
      from God -- Ephesians 1:17-19

Knowledge of Christ is most precious knowledge
    to man -- Philippians 3:8; Colossians 2:2,3
Man is to experience and walk in His truth --
    II John 3,4; Psalm 51:6; John 8:32
School and Truth
    There is propositional truth -- academic content
      and program
    There is personal truth -- through regeneration by
      the Spirit of God and Jesus Christ, the Truth

In diagram form the Christian theory of knowledge might appear as follows:

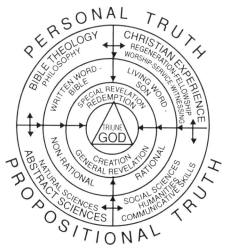

CHRISTIAN THEORY OF KNOWLEDGE AND LIFE

In the diagram above it becomes evident that God has chosen to reveal truth through two phases of His activity: creation and redemption. The truths of redemption have been transmitted through God's Special-revelation in the Written Word -- the Bible, and through the Living Word -- the Son. In creation, God's General Revelation is evident through both the rational and non-rational creations. It is to be expected, therefore, that all curriculum content will be related to these phases of revelation and that subject matter areas will be abstractions from them. Thus, subjects incorporate records of God's nature and works as man is able to develop them into organized form. They are "lesson-books."

The inner circles of the diagram suggest the objective pattern and source of all truth centering in God. The outer circle takes us to man -- his experience of truth and his organization of knowledge into a curricular pattern. Here emerges the broad pattern of Christian education -- Bible, theology, ethics; Christian experience in worship and service; the social sciences and the humanities; and the natural and abstract sciences.

Local church education emphasizes primarily <u>personal truth</u>, that truth which centers in God Himself as a Person, revealing His work in redemption and <u>special</u> revelation. Other forms of Christian education are based on Special Revelation likewise, but the thrust of the curriculum for other forms of education is in the category of <u>general</u> revelation. The thrust of the curriculum in church education concerns the implications of redemption as seen in the revelation of the Written Word and salvation provided through the redeeming work of the Living Word -- the Son.

The core idea and integrating factor for Christian education at all levels is revelation, both Written and Personal, an education under the mastery and control of Jesus Christ through the work of the Holy Spirit. The following diagrams reveal this.

No. 1

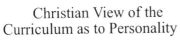

No. 2

Christian View of the
Curriculum as to Personality

Christian View of the
Curriculum as to Program

Like any other type of education, Christian education is concerned with people as well as subject matter. Christ should be in the center of both, controlling and directing them to the outcome of His will. In diagram No. 1 above we see this principle as it is related to <u>personality development</u>. Christ, the Living Word, controls such development through the work of the Holy Spirit and the revelation of the Written Word -- the Bible. As a revelation of His will the Bible becomes an integrating factor for building the curriculum to accomplish Christlike character; it is a blueprint. Both Life and Truth are then focused on the pupil and related to his needs and development; then all is applied to the social structure as a manifestation of light and truth.

In diagram No. 2 above we see the "Christ controlled" principle as it is applied to the <u>program</u> in the Christian school. Christ is Life, the Bible provides divine wisdom, general education supplements biblical knowledge in the development of Christian culture, and skills are provided for life vocations and service to God. The school in the church, or the church school, does not concern itself with general education, but it is concerned with placing Christ at the center as the controlling Power of its program, using the Bible as its textbook, and seeking to develop skills for church work and service to God in society.

From all of this it can be seen that it is the power and life of Christ sublimating and integrating all of life and expressed in the fruit of the Spirit. The work of the Holy Spirit provides the structure or frame of reference within which the curriculum processes operate. It might be pictured in chart form as follows:

WORK OF THE SPIRIT

STRUCTURE OR FRAMEWORK
FOR THE CURRICULUM

In the preceding diagram, it is evident that the curriculum or total program is operated within an atmosphere which provides the frame of reference or the structure for the curriculum. The presence and power of the Holy Spirit should be felt and seen in the manifestation of the fruit of the Spirit, all of which affects the teaching-learning process. The three cardinal and dominating aspects of this work are Christian love, faith and obedience. All workers who manifest the presence of the Spirit are able through example to teach through their lives the great truths of the Christian faith and thus enable the pupil to assimilate the Spirit of Jesus Christ as they see Him manifested in the total atmosphere of the school. Thus, Christ the Son and the Paraclete, the Holy Spirit, provide the dynamic power for making God's life and truth a present reality in the world, in the Church, and in the heart and life of the redeemed individual.

4. <u>The Life Principle</u>. The epistemology of the Christian educator is based on a life-view which rejects sense experience as the only medium of knowledge. It stresses rather that experience is more fundamentally based on supernatural reality. The supernatural world is just as real, and perhaps more so, as the natural world.

Based squarely upon the Christian epistemology described above Christian education at all levels has involved at its very heart a <u>life principle</u>. The life of God has not only been made available <u>to</u> man, that life works <u>in</u> man. The life of God the Father is eternal and active, not passive, but also creative, life-giving, and inherently communicative. The Scriptures tell us that to <u>know</u> God is the very essence of wisdom and knowledge (Prov. 1:7; 9:10). God's life is truth and therefore inherently educational. The Psalmist said, "With thee is the fountain of life; in thy light shall we see light (Psalm 36:9).

The Son of God is both life and truth. He said, "I am the way, the truth, and the life" (John 14:6). John tells us that "grace (life) and truth came by Jesus Christ (John 1:17). Still further he said, "In him was life and the life was the light of men" (John 1:4). Note that both life and light have come to us in Jesus Christ, the direct relationship between these two elements. The life that Jesus lived was revelational and educational in value. The death that He died was likewise. In fact all that was involved in the birth, life, death, resurrection and teachings of Jesus Christ was fused with divine life and light for man.

The Holy Spirit of God is life and truth. It is His business to make the life of God the Son available to mankind based on the redemptive provision of the Son. The very impartation of that life involves an educational process. This is seen in the very terms used to describe the person and work of the Holy Spirit, for He is pictured in Scripture as one who convicts, convinces, leads, guides, rebukes, corrects, enlightens, anoints -- all of which have educational connotations.

Furthermore, the work of the Holy Spirit in the reconstruction of fallen and sinful human personality shows how instructional divine life really is. To receive divine life the sinner must know his need and condition and turn to the source and hope of his salvation, and Christian development. The Holy Spirit guides the sinner through enlightenment and conviction through the conditional aspects of redemption necessary to his restoration and regeneration. Thus the very act of being "born again" is an educational process. It is evident also that the carnal mind in the unregenerate person is illuminated and changed to a spiritual one. Still further in the maturation process divine life is progressively developed in the child of God through a discipling process which maintains the new Christian in a divine-human relationship and fellowship in which the Christian is constantly educated regarding the quality of life expected of him. We also see as well that the whole process of sanctification for the Christian through which he is made holy constantly involves the maturing Christian in a never-ending educational process.

Some Evangelicals, like Lois Lebar for example, feel that the Written Word and the Living Word are so closely related the Life principle shines through the Written Word. Perhaps Jesus Christ had this in mind when He said, "The words that I speak unto you they are spirit and they are life (John 6:63).

On the basis of the revelational aspects of God's life, therefore, it is not hard for one to conclude that the life of God in its very essence is educational. The further fact that man through divine creation has been made receptive to this process reveals how much man finds it possible to participate in the educational aspects of that life.

All this points up the place that evangelism has in general in the life of the church and specifically in the educational program at all levels. To make the life-principle available to mankind, Christian education in all its phases of work needs to begin its work in the practice of evangelism and continue all of its work in the spirit of evangelism.

In some circles, even evangelical ones, it has gone largely unrecognized that the very essence of Christian teaching is to be evangelistic. When one teaches the gospel he should expect to get the same results as when one preaches the gospel. A Christian teacher must be evangelistic if he expects to get Christian results. The writer fails to see at what point the work of a teacher ends and that of an evangelist begins. How can one teach a sinner to be more Christian! Christian teaching demands the creation of a Christian to be educated and this requires evangelism. One may find it possible to do "religious education" without evangelism, but most certainly not find it possible to do Christian education, for it is in evangelism that the life of God comes into the hearts and lives of sinners.

Christian education and evangelism at all educational levels are inseparable, for Christian education which is not evangelistic is simply not Christian. The work of evangelism is the work of the teacher because he is both a Christian and a witness. So many teachers in Christian education often fail to be Christian teachers because they do not serve as evangelists. So often they see their task as one which involves the transmission of facts about God as revealed in Jesus Christ and not as one which helps persons find a meaningful personal relationship to Jesus Christ as Savior and Lord. No wonder then that so much Bible teaching is dry and dull!

Teachers in Christian education do not teach lessons merely, but people, and these people need to know Jesus Christ personally. Therefore, it requires an evangelistic process to bring this about. Facts and materials are means to this end.

Jesus Christ brings to life and renders concrete the functions of God as Logos and God as Light. It is Christ as Person Who gives meaning to all persons. In Scripture, God is revealed as One concerned with small and ordinary people. Because Jesus Christ, the Universal Light, became man, all men are important in God's sight and the recipients of His love.

The development of personhood, the true realization of the person as "I" is fully dealt with through Christ as Life. The purpose of God is to educate man for eternal life and in this way bring man to the fullest realization of his personhood. Through response to the "grace of the Lord Jesus Christ" man becomes a true person.

The revelation of the "I" of the burning bush is confirmed by Christ. God the "invisible guide" has become God the "visible teacher." The Incarnation and the particularity of Christ as Jesus of Nazareth presents man with the type, the model, the tangible realization of the "image of God." Without Christ as Person truth would remain an impersonal, shadowy abstraction. Through Christ God's love for man is concretely displayed; it moves from principle into practical reality.

5. The Light Principle. The very nature of God is to be a God of revelation. God is Spirit (John 4:24) and as Spirit He is Life (John 5:25; 14:6) and Light (I John 1:5). The Father is Light (Psalm 27:1; I John 1:5; Rev. 22:5); the Son is Light (Isaiah 9:2; John 1:4; 8:12; 12:35) and Spirit is Light (John 14:17,26; 16:13). The purpose of the creation by God was to show His power and wisdom (Genesis 1:31), to show His excellence (Psalm 104:31; 19:1,2) and to show His glory (Rev. 1:11; Psalm 103:20-22; 107:15,21,31; 111:2,4; 148:2-13).

Christian epistemology, therefore, yields the light principle. God is truth. Jesus the Son said, "I am the truth." The Holy Spirit is the Spirit of Truth. God makes Himself known. All aspects of His creation tell us something about God. "The heavens declare the glories of God and the firmament showeth His handiwork" (Psalm 19:1).

Truth is neither a human invention or discovery. It has entered the human sphere in Jesus Christ. It is a "given" from God. In social science circles there is no "giveness" other than the orderly sequences implied in causality and controlled experiments. In Christian circles knowledge can also be gained through the "giveness" of revelation.

Jesus said, "Ye shall know the truth and the truth shall make you free" (John 8:32). Man's life finds, therefore, its fullest and richest meaning through divine truth. By coming to know God, man is educated in the fullest sense of that word. The carnal mind is transformed by God's truth.

The Scriptures also say that "no one teacheth like God" (Job 36:22). God is Teacher, an Educator, a Communicator. He not only provides the substantive content of truth but reveals also the processes of teaching and learning in His revelation. The life that He lived and the work that Jesus did revealed God in operation. The way God does things yields, therefore, principles and practices inherent in a Christian theory of education. Furthermore, the Scriptures, while primarily yielding knowledge regarding the redemptive plan and activities of God, also reveal the ways of God's workings, including the processes of communication and education. Still further, Jesus Himself was the very epitome of the Master Teacher. An analysis of His teaching procedures and ways of dealing with people will show teaching and learning at their very best. Many books have been written devoted to studies of what and how Jesus taught, yielding valuable implications for curriculum development.

The Scriptures themselves yield marvelous educational principles and practices. The total range of elements for the establishment of an educational system from objectives to methods of teaching and learning is to be found in the Bible. The consecrated application of Christian reasoning to an analysis of scriptural content makes it possible to see the implications of the Written Word for educational purposes. It must be admitted, however, that no formal system of educational psychology and educational administration can be found there, but the principles for such systems are to be found.

The Scriptures are self-authenticating and exist objectively for man's enlightenment and guidance. This places the Bible at the very heart of the educational process, because the God of Scripture tells us in Scripture to go to Scripture.

Because God is light, knowledge that man acquires comes from God. It is not the mere gathering of information but the insight into truth. From an educational point of view light is associated with the transition from ignorance to knowledge. It creates the possibility for discernment. This is illustrated in our speech when we say, "I see," when we mean "I understand." The light creates unity -- moral, social and intellectual. Inasmuch as it enables an individual to see his relationship to others, it overcomes isolation.

Light not only makes it possible to see others; it enables us to distinguish fact from fantasy. Furthermore, the image of light is a felicitous one for understanding the fallacy of man's self-centeredness. Light, as such, is not a possession but an illumination from an outside source. When man thinks of illumination as a personal possession, this is the very darkness that man brings upon himself.

Not only theological knowledge but all knowledge must be understood as illumination, as the humble reception of truth rather than as acquisition and private possession. In this sense discovery and revelation are virtually synonymous. For this reason the Christian, or any man, should not be afraid of a diversity of experiences and ideas. We can support intellectual freedom, because all truth, whatever its source and no matter how inconvenient its specific limitations might at first appear to be, must be listened to because it comes from God.

God's children receive His Light by revelation and thus become children of the light (John 12:36; Eph. 5:8; I Thess. 5:5; Matt. 5:14). Light is promised to the obedient (Psalm 97:11), to the upright (Psalm 112:4), to the benevolent (Isaiah 58:8) to the church (Isaiah 60:20), and to all followers of Christ (John 8:12). The duties of believers, therefore, are performed in His light: worshipping (II Chron. 5:13,14), working (John 9:4), walking (Eph. 5:8), witnessing (Phil. 2:15), and watching (I Thess. 5:5,6).

A major premise of Christian education, therefore, is that God has made Himself known (Rom. 9:22,23; Eph. 3:10; 1:9; Col. 1:27). Because knowledge is in God (Acts 17:28; Phil. 2:12,13), its very essence is found in redemption (II Peter 1:2; John 17:3). The highest knowledge that can come to man, therefore, is to know God (Rom. 11:33; Eph. 1:17; 4:13; Phil. 1:9; 3:8; Col. 1:9,10).

What does it mean to know God? Biblical terms help us with

this question. Several Old Testament terms point up the character of knowledge. The term "YADA" means to know, discern (Genesis 3:5,7,22). This is not knowledge which comes as a result of reasoning but rather through personal experience. It means "acquaintance with," not knowledge about God (Genesis 4:1,17,25). The term "BIN" means to understand (Job 38:20), to know by experience (Job 15:1,2).

This meaning is confirmed by New Testament terms. The Greek "GINOSKO" means to know, to cause to know, by experience. Knowledge of God through conversion is highlighted by the term "EPIGNOSIS" (I Tim. 2:4; II Tim. 2:25; 3:7; Titus 1:1). Such knowledge is mediated by Jesus Christ (Matt. 11:27; Col. 1:19; John 1:18; 14:8-10).

This kind of knowledge comes by way of revelation from God to man in several ways: (1) by direct revelation (Col. 2:2,3), (2) by intuition (Matt. 16:17; John 20:26-29; Rom. 8:15-16), (3) by rational effort and reflection (Acts 17:16-34) and (4) by practical demonstration (John 1:1,9,12; 3:21; 7:17). Upon achievement of these things wisdom and knowledge characterize those that know God (Isaiah 33:6).

The direct relevance of revelation to teaching is shown by such biblical passages as I Corinthians 12:8 where New Testament teaching was described. Here we are told that truth is arrived at by the teacher's powers of observation and reason -- the word of wisdom (logos sophia). The word of knowledge (logos gnoseos) is bestowed as the gift of the Spirit. The first enables the teacher to explain truth; the second qualifies the teacher to interpret it.

6. The Master Teacher. Jesus Christ was the Master Teacher. He taught by His life, His life-style, His relationships with people, His demonstration of love, and His utilization of the best principles of teaching. It is not possible within the scope of this study to deal adequately with this subject, but an analysis of His teaching skills yields valuable educational principles and practices for any program of Christian education.

Some implications of the "Christ-controlled" principle reveal several facets of His manifestation as Lord of Life and Lord of the Church through the power of the Holy Spirit, revealed in the diagram forms below. In keeping with the God-centered philosophy which posits all life and truth in God, Jesus Christ mediates and supervises the transmission of these facets of divine provision in a twofold manner: (1) into the life of the church, and (2) through the ministry of the Church. Thus we see divine life and truth.

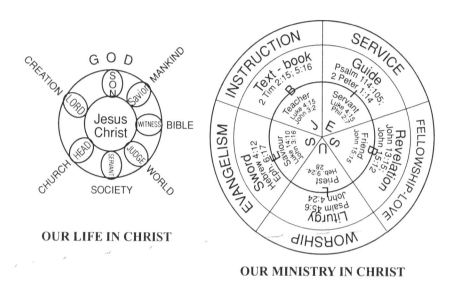

OUR LIFE IN CHRIST

OUR MINISTRY IN CHRIST

7. <u>The Church</u>. Christian education is education that is church-oriented in its context. The doctrine of the church, as recorded in Scripture, shows that the church teaches both by what it is and by what it does. Jesus Christ, the Head of the church, seeks to share both His life and His light to all mankind. This He does through individuals who have experienced His redemption as they live, witness, and serve, and also through the corporate life and ministry of the church which serves as the body of Christ.

In the Lordship of Jesus Christ as Head of the church we see His plan to provide a distinctive quality of life for the world. By being Christlike people, His followers both demonstrate and teach that kind of life. Thus, Christian faith becomes a Godlike life-style.

The body-life of the church also teaches through corporate relationships and nurture. Such teaching is provided internally in the church for its own fellow Christians by mutual support, love, and prayer, making contributions toward individual Christian growth and maturity. By serving one another in Christian love the church members minister to one another both individually and corporately (Rom. 12:9-21; I Cor. 12:14,27-31; Eph. 4:17-32). The church teaches in many ways: (1) by example (Acts 5:42; chap. 17), (2) by manifesting brotherly love (Matt. 18:15-18), (3) by manifesting brotherly concern (Gal. 6:1,2), (4) by good conduct (Gal. 6:1-5), (5) by good relationships (I Cor. 6:1-8; 11:17-34), (6) by concern for one another (I Thess. 4:18; 5:11), (7) by united prayer (James 5:14-16), and (8) by mutual teaching (Col. 3:13,16).

The church teaches by sharing truth. This truth is not only propositional in character in the sense of transmitting the facts of our faith, but it is also living truth. Jesus was the Word made flesh (John 1:14) and His followers will also be "living epistles." Here is seen the importance of teaching by means of modeling the truth and faith. Thus, the life and truth principles are integrated in practice. People who look on are able to learn to be like what they see. Furthermore, if the church is true in the manifestation of Christ-like living, the world, as it looks on, can also learn what it means to be Christian.

The church's ministry in Christ enables it to teach. Following the example of Jesus the church expresses its service through evangelism, worship, instruction, fellowship and service. This teaching ministry is manifested, not only in local church education, but also in other forms and levels of education such as Christian day schools, colleges, seminaries and special schools.

8. The Marks of a Christian Educational System. Simply stated, an institution is Christian when it operates as an expression of Christian faith and ethics. Of course, one does not expect perfect results in this effort but all too often inadequate expressions of the faith are taken as normative.

To identify an institution as Christian one must recognize that the institution is not Christian merely because:

1. It has required courses in religion
2. It has required chapel attendance
3. It uses the word "Christian" in publicity

4. It has a formal connection with some church
5. It has rules and regulations
6. It has extra-class activities and organizations which are religious

Rather, an institution is a Christian one which is committed to give vital expression to the Christian faith in _every_ facet of its life. It is an adventure in learning in which the best educational approaches are interpreted and integrated by a disciplined and constantly-renewed Christian experience. It is only as the institution is true to its distinctive nature that it can fulfill its historic role and its worldwide task.

From the foregoing discussion of a revelational perspective, we can now identify the outline and summarize the marks of a Christian educational system more specifically as follows and or previously discussed:

1. God-centered as to concept of reality
2. Revelation-derived in its concept of knowledge and life
3. Learner-related in its concept of psychology
4. Spiritual quality in its value system
5. Christ-centered in its goals
6. Holy Spirit possessed in its control
7. Bible-based in its curriculum
8. Learner-focused in its methodology
9. Christ-dependent in its responsibility
10. Love-directed in its motive
11. Spirit-controlled in its leadership
12. Bible-revealed in its authority
13. Church-managed in its programs
14. Growth-achieved in its evaluation
15. God-glorifying in its entire process

This kind of education might be defined as a re-interpretation of God's revelation; it is thinking God's thoughts after Him. It is the process of understanding and exemplifying the Christian gospel. The professors section of the former research commission of the National Sunday School Association has defined general Christian education as "the Bible-based, Christ-centered process of leading the student into a transforming experience of Truth, ever maturing into the fullness of Christ, and of equipping him by fundamental knowledge, attitudes, skills to render effective service in the will of God." When this kind of education goes on in a local church the term "church education" is more commonly used to distinguish this kind of education from that which goes on in other fields, such as higher education, or at the lower levels in schools like Christian day schools. The essential philosophy, however, which governs the Christian approach to education will be the same for all types of education sponsored by Christian people.

The evangelical makes a sharp distinction between religious education and Christian education. The former could very well apply to any religion while the latter is used distinctively in connection with orthodox and historic Christian faith. The distinctive element here is its Christocentric quality. Christian education must be centered in Christ and empowered by the Holy Spirit, for without these emphases the character goal cannot be reached. Furthermore, Christian education is in the church, of the church and for the church. The mission of the church is that of Jesus Christ, therefore it has a ministry. Christian teaching is an integral part of this ministry, therefore Christian education is vitally related to and integrated with the mission and ministry of the church.

In contrast to some liberal views, Christian education does not depend on a rational approach to our faith but rather on one which emphasizes faith in and commitment to the God of Revelation, a Person, Who becomes the dynamic of one's life and hope. In the light of this there is an integral relationship between the Christian faith and its education. Evangelism becomes the controlling purpose of Christian education, for without evangelism Christian education degenerates into mere moralism.

Roy B. Zuck has summarized the distinctives of evangelical Christian education when he says:

> *The three indispensable factors that make Christian education dynamic, and at the same time distinctive, are these: (1) the centrality of God's*

Written revelation, (2) the necessity of regeneration, and (3) the ministry of the Holy Spirit. <u>These are the dynamics of Christian education</u>. The presence and functioning of these three together comprises a distinctive education from the evangelical standpoint. To seek to have Christian education without the Word of God is to extricate the basic core of the curriculum. Unregenerate teachers cannot communicate, in the full sense of the word, Christian truths, which they themselves do not know experientially. And the Holy Spirit's work is necessary for spiritual enablement in every phase of teaching and learning.[11]

Thus, Christian education begins in personal experience with and commitment to God and continues in a process of growth and development in the total person toward the character goal of Christlikeness and the ultimate goal of the Kingdom of God to come.

E. Revelation and Local Church Education

1. <u>Focus of Attention</u>. For local church education past efforts to provide an integrating factor by which theory is developed have largely focused on a theological approach. Our purpose here is to sample some of these efforts and compare them with evangelical theories.

2. <u>Traditional Approaches</u>. In his excellent book <u>An Invitation to Religious Education</u>, Harold W. Burgess identified representative Protestant and Catholic theological approaches to religious education. He identified the following common criteria for these approaches as

(1) Authoritative, normative revelation -- the Bible for Protestants; the Bible and church tradition for Catholics

(2) Transmission of God's authoritative message in revelation

(3) Faithful and qualified teachers who transmit the message

(4) Students who live and apply the message

(5) An emphasis on supernaturalism[12]

Both Roman Catholic and Protestant religious educators, he says, drew heavily from such antecedent sources as Augustine and the early church catechumenate systems. Religious teaching, even in the nineteenth century, was largely dominated by a rationalistic approach to education dedicated to the development of reason with its natural counterpart in religious education, the development of memory in early twentieth century church circles. Among Roman Catholics the catechetical method, based on Herbartian teaching theories, was utilized.

Among Protestants, Burgess cites the works of Frank Gabelein, Lois Lebar, and Harold Mason as advocates of the traditional approach. Among Catholics, he names Jungmann, Hofinger and Marcel van Caster as sources.

Among all of these educators, theology exerted the primary influence on the total educational process. The character of this kind of education is manifested as follows:

(1) The aim of education is to be found in divine revelation

(2) The purpose is to transmit a body of divine truth

(3) The element of the supernatural takes the educator beyond mere factual knowledge

(4) Formation of Christian character and Christian living are immediate goals

(5) The content of religious education is an authoritative, biblically, and theologically founded message from Scripture

(6) Jesus Christ is the central and supreme theme of the message

(7) The method is that of impartation and transmission of divine revelation as the Word of God

(8) The teacher must have eminent and personal qualifications for the teaching task and be well trained

(9) The teacher's major method is transmissive in character but the utilization of a wide variety of teaching strategies

is recommended

(10) The student receives the message, but developmental characteristics dictate personal involvement in classroom activities, all with the help of the Holy Spirit[13]

3. <u>Contemporary Theological Approaches</u>. Harold Burgess identifies four major criteria for certain contemporary theological approaches to religious education:

(1) Divine revelation is not limited to the Bible only but also to the continuing revelation activity of God in experience

(2) Religious education aims to establish individuals in right relationships to God within the church and equip them for Christian living

(3) The teacher's task is to enter into a communal relationship with students and serve as a guide to Christian living and development

(4) The student's spiritual life is developed in the fellowship of the church[14]

A survey of the literature of writers advocating a general theological approach to church education reveals that it is not easy to classify writers and their educational approaches. The writer has found it helpful to classify writers into three general categories: (1) those advocating a rather clear-cut theological approach; (2) those who advocate what might be termed a church-centered approach, including both Protestants and Catholics; and (3) neo-orthodox adherents.

Prominent writers in this group include Randolph Miller, Sara Little, Iris Cully, Howard Grimes, Dora Chaplin, Wesner Fallaw, and G. Campbell Wyckoff. The aims and goals of this school of thought might possibly be summarized as follows:

<u>School</u>	-	Neo-orthodox
<u>Aim</u>	-	Conversion; Growth in grace; nurture
<u>Goal</u>	-	Christian discipleship
<u>Philosophical Rootage</u>	-	Christian Theism; Humanism; Realism
<u>Basic Theological Rootage</u>	-	Transcendental; Theocentric

School	-	Church Emphasis
Aim	-	Tranmission of culture and spiritual heritage; growth in grace
Goal	-	Realize the authority of the fellowship of the church
Philosophical Rootage	-	Christian theism; Realism
Basic Theological Rootage	-	Transcendental; Theocentric

School	-	Relationship Theology
Aim	-	Dialogue confrontation
Goal	-	Christian Discipleship
Philosophical Rootage	-	Martin Buber's I-Thou; Realism; Christian theism
Basic Theological Rootage	-	Transcendental; Theocentric

Reflecting on historical developments the theological emphasis in church education theory probably began with H. Shelton Smith's work <u>Faith and Nurture</u> (1941). Reactions against the Social-Gospel approach and other philosophical approaches to church education which proved to be nonproductive, also in response to an effort to revive a social, scientific and liberal approach to church education, Smith opened the door to theological emphasis by attacking the tenets of philosophical humanism and classical liberalism. He pointed up the essential non-Christian position of the views of the social and scientific approaches to religious education. His effort was shortly followed up in 1947 by Paul Vieth's work <u>The Church and Christian Education</u>.

Paul Vieth stressed the importance of theology in religious education which was to be practiced in the context of the church. However, it was Randolph Miller in his <u>The Clue to Christian Education</u> (Scribners, 1950) who advocated an outright theological approach to church education. Theology, he maintained, is the source of theory and practice. He recommended how various theological doctrines should be taught.

Lewis Sherrill in his <u>Gift of Power</u> (1955) stressed the context of the church as a Christian community as the best way to meet man's need for God. Joining him in church emphasis was James Smart and Donald Butler. These men argued that Church education could be understood only in the light of biblical concepts of God and the church. Smart contended that Christian education itself is a theological discipline.

Among Roman Catholics Gabriel Moran asserted that religious education theory flows out of theology and revelation and should go on in the context of the church.

As a partial reaction against the unrealistic approach of classical liberalism, neo-orthodox writers stressed a return to a realistic and biblical view of man and acceptance of divine revelation. They sought to strike a compromise between liberal tenets and some orthodox tenets, stressing the importance of Christian relationships in the context of the church.

An analysis of the writings in the neo-orthodox school of thought reveals an educational system for church education with the following characteristics:

Aim
    (1) Church education aims are derived from the Bible, the life of the church, the culture, and the human situation
    (2) There must be commitment to divine revelation

Purpose
    (1) The purpose of church education is to produce people who are committed to the Christian way of life through the church
    (2) Personal growth and development in the fellowship of the church are important
    (3) Social and moral responsibilities are encumbent upon individual Christians and the church body

Content
    (1) Christian content is to be connected with both the Christian heritage and contemporary culture
    (2) The church is a community of love and concern

Teacher
    (1) The teacher depends on God the Holy Spirit and serves as a model for Christian living
    (2) The teacher is a mediator

<u>Teaching</u>
  (1) Any method can be a vehicle of divine revelation
  (2) There must be full participation in the light of the church on the part of leaders and students
  (3) Guided thinking and the use of Christian responses are necessary
  (4) Group sharing is strategic
<u>Learning</u>
  (1) The student is both a child of God and a sinner, both a person and a learner, the goal of which is to become a knowledgeable and responsible Christian
  (2) Participation on the part of the learner leads to response to God and commitment to the Christian faith

4. <u>Representative Theological Approaches</u>. A search of the literature shows that a few writers have attempted to attack the problem of discovering an integrating factor for local church education. Randolph C. Miller in his work <u>The Clue to Christian Education</u> (Scribners, 1950) advocated theology as the source for integrating church educational theory. Most certainly theology has an important place in Christian education, providing an emphasis on God and content for study. However, in spite of this, critical examination forces one to ask the question: which theology? Obviously, this is not satisfactory. Furthermore, it is not doctrine which is of paramount importance, but rather the Person of God Himself. Who He is and His self-revelation stand far above any theological system.

A second suggestion was made by Lawrence C. Little in his work <u>Foundations for a Philosophy of Christian Education</u> (Abington, 1962). He suggested that a synthesis of theory and the behavioral sciences would yield an integrating factor for theory. While there is much to commend this approach, one must conclude that it is too rational and man-centered in emphasis.

A third suggestion was made by D. Campbell Wyckoff in his work <u>The Gospel and Christian Education</u> (Westminster, 1959). He points out that the Gospel is the heart of the Word which in turn is the heart of the church's ministry. The writer's heart is warmed with these suggestions. This approach has much about it which is both commendable and acceptable. On the other hand, certain objections to this approach must be raised. The Gospel itself is a derivative of something greater than itself -- revelation. Is the Gospel the secret of biblical unity or is it rather revelation and redemption? The Gospel is a channel, not central.

Similar objections can be raised for making the church and the Bible integrating factors. Both of these factors are likewise derivative of something greater -- the Person of God and His revelation. The church is a fellowship of believers for service. The Bible is a channel for the truths of redemption. To place either one of these factors in the center as an integrating factor is to replace the only One worthy to be placed there -- God Himself!

On the periphery of a theological emphasis is that of the humanistic approach which emphasizes a child-centered and life-experience approach as the integrating factor for theory. In this view man replaces God. Little or no direction to curriculum building can be provided because guidance is lacking. Then, too, the question must be asked -- experience in relation to what? What experience? For what purpose? Obviously, this approach is too vague.

Upon examination of the suggestions above the conclusion to be drawn is that these approaches are earthbound, fragmentary, largely unchristian and lacking in the genuine power of integration. One must look elsewhere for help in this matter.

5. Representative Evangelical Approaches. Among evangelical writers who have utilized revelational principles and focused on local church education are Lois Lebar, Lawrence Richards and the writer. Lebar's approach might be termed a Word-Centered approach where the integrating factor is the Word both Living and Written. To Richards the approach becomes one of creating and developing disciples within the context of the church as the Body of Christ and is accomplished by what he calls socialization. The writer holds both of these views in high regard but finds an approach which might be termed theocentric and bibliocentric where stress is laid on the Person of God as He has revealed Himself. This becomes the

integrating factor of church education theory.

6. <u>Implications of Theocentric Revelation for Local Church Education</u>. From what has been said previously about an evangelical proposal for theory for Christian education at all levels can be focused also on the implications of theory for the program of Christian education in the local church. Perhaps it is possible to summarize the discussion on theory in the following diagram which will show the relation of theory to the total program in the local church. Please notice in the diagram the centralized position that Christian epistemology has in the local church theory and which is held in common by all other forms of Christian education.

RELATION OF THEORY
TO TOTAL CHURCH PROGRAM IN THE LOCAL CHURCH

God has revealed Himself in all His redemptive works. With God working dynamically and progressively in His Son Jesus Christ and through the work of the Holy Spirit, the great objectives of redemption are being accomplished. With the church working in close relation to the Holy Spirit and being guided by Him and the Scriptures, the Gospel message and various program agencies of the church become instrumental to this end. The five great methodologies of the early church were evangelism, instruction, worship, fellowship,

99

and service (Acts 2:41,42). With the Holy Spirit empowering these methodologies the church proceeds to serve God and administer His program in the world. The great goals toward which the church moves are individual, social, prophetic and ultimate. The individual goal is to reveal God in Christlike character, the social goal is to extend the individual goal to include every possible individual, the prophetic goal is to wait for the Second Coming of Christ, and the ultimate goal is the Kingdom of God to come. Thus, theory issues in practice.

From the chart one can see that service has two aspects: (1) service by individuals who seek to practice their faith both personally and socially, and (2) service through administration. Administrative aspects of service are to be directed and controlled by the five program elements and expressed through a wide variety of program agencies. Such agencies will meet both on Sunday and through the week. Organization of people and resources become means to this end. Supervision of the program in general and workers in particular will be necessary to assure success with the help of the Holy Spirit. Thus the service elements of the program will be the means by which the servants of God will find outlets for the utilization of their gifts and stewardship. All elements of a revelational approach are to be seen here. Prominent among them are the Life and Light principle and the total life and work of the Master Teacher. We can hopefully claim that the theory proposed above is both consistent and clear. Furthermore, we believe that it is philosophically and theologically valid, and educationally sound. Still further, we believe that the theory is practical and can be clearly and simply communicated to lay workers and members in the church.

F. Revelation and Other Christian Schools

1. <u>Types of Christian Schools</u>. In addition to the local church educational program, called the Church School, there are other schools which are sponsored and operated by Christian people. One of these is the Christian day school, operating at the elementary and secondary school levels. Most of these schools operated by evangelical Christians make a real effort to utilize divine revelation as the

integrating factor for educational theory and practice.

Other schools operate at the higher and graduate levels of education. Christian liberal arts colleges, Bible institutes, and Bible colleges are illustrations of these schools. Theological seminaries are schools for the training of pastors and church workers at the professional level but also serving as post-college schools. One of the problems of post-high school institutions is to find and utilize an integration factor for their administration and curricula. Failure to do this has created a two-track system of education at the college and graduate levels of education. So many of these schools merely emulate secular institutions and even adopt secular patterns for their curricula. Christian emphasis in schools of this kind stress chapel, have Bible and religion departments but fail often to adequately integrate the Christian faith and education in the classroom situation. These schools need an integrating factor which is Christian to give them true distinctiveness.

2. A Common Foundation Needed. As mentioned above, Christian schools at all levels need an integrating factor for theory and practice. This factor is based in the Christian philosophy of life as it is developed from Christian theological, philosophical and biblical sources.

At the undergraduate level, Christian private and day schools have largely adopted the secular elementary and secondary school curriculum patterns but have injected into their curriculum system biblical principles and practices. All teachers in these schools are expected to make an effort to show in all subjects taught that "all truth is God's truth." For theological seminaries Christian education theory becomes an extension of local church theory with practice at the graduate level. For Bible schools and colleges a revelational approach is directly practiced with a biblical emphasis in every class and educational program. Christian service activities further reflect a revelational emphasis on service.

Such schools reflect a revelational approach to curriculum building by drawing from revelational epistemology as it is focused on the redemptive phase in that epistemology, as follows: (Note the top half of the diagram)

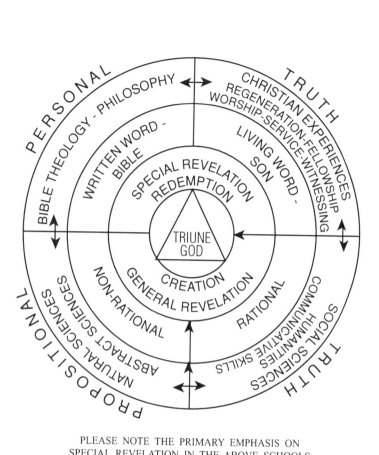

PLEASE NOTE THE PRIMARY EMPHASIS ON
SPECIAL REVELATION IN THE ABOVE SCHOOLS

3. <u>The Christian Liberal Arts College</u>. Perhaps the Christian liberal arts college needs greater help with an integrating factor than any other type school. One reason for this is a tendency to emulate secular institutions, utilizing traditional liberal arts curriculum structures. This has created a two-track system. To overcome this problem the following suggestions are made.

In the chart diagram below one will note that a revelational basis is laid in Biblical epistemology along with all other Christian schools. Where churches, Bible schools and theological seminaries lay emphasis on the redemptive and special revelation side of this epistemology, Christian liberal arts colleges reflect the general revelation side, as follows:

102

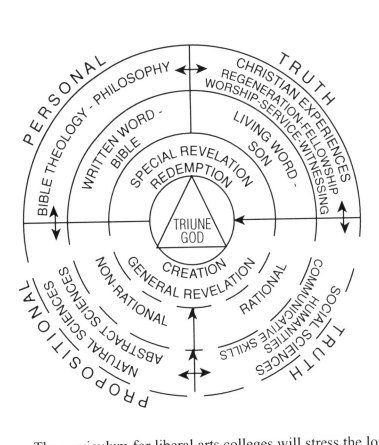

The curriculum for liberal arts colleges will stress the lower half of the above chart. The purpose here is to provide general education for character development and specialties in the sciences and humanities. Spiritual emphasis will be stressed through the curriculum and the unity of God's truth will be reflected in the classroom situation as well. Christian ministry is needed out in society as well as in the church itself.

The curriculum pattern for this type of college will emphasize the following elements:

103

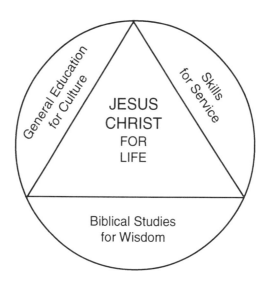

Jesus Christ is the Source of our life, the Bible is the source of wisdom, general education provides the basis for culture, and skills for service prepare one for a life vocation. The first three of these elements will provide a basis for overall general education for character development while skills for service will be reflected throughout the various academic majors offered in the curriculum. All of this will go on in the atmosphere characterized by Christian faith, Christian love and obedience.

Curriculum patterns for Christian schools will be dealt with in the next chapter devoted to practice.

NOTES

1. James MacDonald, "A Transcendental Development Ideology of Education," <u>Heightened Consciousness, Cultural Revolution, and Curriculum Theory</u>, ed. William Pinar, Berkeley, California: McCutchass Publishing Corp., 1974.

2. Little, Lawrence C., <u>Foundations for a Philosophy of Christian Education</u>, Abington, 1962, p.173.

3. Chamberlain, J. Gordon, <u>Freedom and Faith</u>, Westminster, 1965, p.97.

4. Cully, Kendig B., <u>The Search for a Christian Education -- Since 1940</u>, Westminster, 1965, p.162.

5. Wyckoff, G. Campbell, <u>The Gospel and Christian Education</u>, Westminster, 1959, p.69-70.

6. Gabelein, Frank E., <u>The Pattern for God's Truth</u>, Oxford, 1954.

7. Fakkema, Mark, <u>Christian Philosophy: It's Educational Implications</u>, Book III, The Author, 1962, Appendix c-4-2.

8. Jaarsma, Cornelius, ed., <u>Fundamentals in Christian Education</u>, Eerdmans, 1953.

9. Lebar, Lois, <u>Education that is Christian</u>, Revell, 1958, p.205.

10. Richards, Lawrence, <u>A Theology of Christian Education</u>, Zondervan, 1975.

11. Zuck, Roy B., <u>The Holy Spirit in Your Teaching</u>, Scripture Press, 1973, p.5.

12. Religious Education Press, 1975, p.21.

13. Ibid., Chapter 2.

14. Ibid., p.94.

OUTLINE FOR CHAPTER FOUR

REVELATION AND GENERAL CHRISTIAN EDUCATION PRACTICE

A. The Process of Education
   1. The Educational Process
   2. Implications of Revelation for
      Christian Education Practice
   3. The Teaching-Learning Process
   4. Sources
   5. The Place of Epistemology
   6. Integration and Interpretation

B. Objectives
   1. The Importance of Objectives
   2. The Function of Objectives
   3. The Approach to Objectives
   4. A Revelational Approach to Objectives

C. The Role of the Teacher
   1. The Importance of the Teacher
   2. The Function of the Teacher
   3. A Revelational Concept of the Teacher's Role

D. The Role of the Learner
   1. Concepts of Personality
   2. The Place of the Learner
   3. A Revelational Concept of the Learner's Role

E. The Learning Process
   1. Secular Contributions
   2. Liberal Religious Education Views
   3. Views of Integrationists
   4. Traditional Views
   5. Revelational Concepts of Learning
   6. A Suggested Revelational Concept of Learning

F. The Teaching Process
    1. Three Approaches
    2. Secular Contributions
    3. Church Educator Views
    4. An Evangelical and Revelational View
    5. Styles of Teaching
    6. Characteristics of Christian Teaching
    7. A Revelational View
    8. A Revelational Concept of Method

G. Curriculum
    1. Definition
    2. Liberal Religious Educator Views
    3. Traditional Views
    4. Evangelical and Revelational Views
    5. Subject Matter Content
    6. Curriculum Design

H. Authority, Freedom and Discipline
    1. Authority
    2. Freedom
    3. Discipline

I. Evaluation
    1. Secular Contributions
    2. A Revelational Approach
    3. Values

CHAPTER FOUR

REVELATION AND GENERAL
CHRISTIAN EDUCATION PRACTICE

A. The Process of Education

1. <u>The Educational Process</u>. The educational process is that process which involves all the factors and elements essential to the organization and operation of a school situation. It includes all the elements of organization, administration, supervision, teaching and learning. At least seven factors are involved: (1) objectives, (2) sessions, (3) grouping, (4) leadership, (5) environment, (6) curriculum, and (7) planning.

In any school situation at whatever level of operation <u>objectives</u> are paramount. Stated objectives show the reason why the school exists and provide guidelines for the operation of all educational factors involved. In this way they provide a sense of direction for the operation of the school. They guide in the selection and utilization of curriculum materials and methods. They serve to evaluate educational procedures, methodologies and achievement. Objectives are present at every level in the school system. There are general objectives which provide overall motivation and guidance. There are course objectives which guide the use of curriculum materials, and there are objectives which focus on a particular idea or class situation.

The term <u>sessions</u> refers to placing operational factors in a school situation into a schedule or calendar. In a church school situation, depending on the size of the church, this could involve pre-session activities, worship experiences, and classroom activities. Such activities would go in a Sunday school, vacation Bible school, or some other Bible teaching situation.

In other Christian schools, such as a Bible college, Christian college, or seminary, classroom activities would be integrated with chapel services and a wide variety of extra-class activities. The calendar would take the form of a quarter, term or semester, depending on the type of school being operated.

The term <u>grouping</u> refers to the organization of classes of students into teaching-learning situations. This might take the form of formal classes of instruction, or non-formal small groupings of people for learning experiences.

<u>Leaders</u> involve those people who are responsible for the operation of the school. This calls for a wide variety of personnel, such as administrators, supervisors, teachers, and workers of all kinds at various levels in the school system. Ideally, all of these people should be genuinely Christian and well-qualified for the tasks committed to them.

<u>Environment</u> refers to support factors for the teaching-learning activities. Such matters as buildings, equipment, supplies and provision for comfort and security are involved.

<u>Curriculum</u> points up the importance of organizing sources and materials of knowledge and truth into teachable form. All knowledge that has a direct bearing on the production of Christian character and service should be considered. Various courses of study which lead to achievable goals and degrees will be provided.

<u>Planning</u> covers a wide variety of elements which make successful operation of the school situation possible. Included here would be such factors as organizing, executing, administering, supervising, publicizing, and evaluating. All of these educational factors should contribute to the ultimate realization of the purpose and goals of the school.

2. <u>Implications of Revelation for Christian Education Practice</u>. When one considers the doctrinal and theological aspects of the work of Christian education, certain conclusions regarding the implications of revelation for Christian education practice can be drawn. Some of these conclusions can be listed as follows:

1. Theology and revelation have distinctive contributions to make for the whole process of Christian nurture.
2. Theology and revelation provide a frame of reference through which theories of educational practices and learning may be validated.

3. Revelation is basic to the existence of Christian faith.
4. Revelation is not only the communication of Christian knowledge but a definite personal act of God, a gift to sinful man.
5. Man cannot achieve sufficient knowledge about God without revelation because it goes beyond mere cognitive achievement.
6. Revelation supplies special knowledge about God, not to be found through empirical means, observation, research or reason.
7. Revelation leads man to a knowledge of God personally, not merely knowledge about God.
8. To learn, man needs the help of God.
9. Revelation comes to man personally in his relationship to God and also in the fellowship of the church.
10. Truth, therefore, is not a human invention nor discovery. It entered the human sphere in Jesus Christ.
11. Revelation has direct bearing on the interpretation of truth in classroom situations where students find that "all truth is God's truth."

Upon the basis of these revelational evidences it is possible to see that an educational process is an actual derivative of revelation. This gives Christian learning and nurture a divine dimension not to be found in non-Christian systems of education.

By yielding the Christian philosophy of life, divine revelation becomes the foundation for the entire educational program. The Christian view of God and the world furnishes the highest principle of unification, not only for the subject matter disciplines on the philosophical level, but also for uniting the concerns of theory with those of practical living.

The pattern by which the thinking of faculty members and administrators is to be guided regarding achieving integration is shown in the following chart.

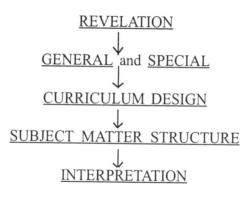

REVELATION
↓
GENERAL and SPECIAL
↓
CURRICULUM DESIGN
↓
SUBJECT MATTER STRUCTURE
↓
INTERPRETATION

Starting with divine revelation, which is reflected in both general and special revelation, curriculum construction and design should show direct relationship to revelation. Each subject matter discipline, which reflects some aspect of revelation, would then be interpreted and taught in the light of the unity of truth as it has come from God. In the chapter to follow suggestions on methods of achieving integration in curriculum design and in the classroom are made.

3. The Teaching-Learning Process. Within the framework of the educational process lies that of the teaching-learning process. It is the process by which the content of the Christian faith is communicated to the learner. More specifically, it is the process in which the intellect, emotions and will of the student are transformed by the teacher-learner relationship under the direction of the Holy Spirit in order that the learner might become the "perfect man in Christ." It is the means by which theory is translated into practice. Various factors in this process must be dealt with in practice. They include:

1. Purposes and objectives provide guidelines for initiating and culminating the educative process.
2. The teacher stands before the student as the oracle of God with the truth of God.
3. The focus of the educative process is the student.
4. The structure of Christian education provides the

112

atmosphere in which the whole process takes place. This structure is provided by Christian love, faith and obedience.

5. The curriculum provides the truth-content by which the revelation of God is organized and presented to the pupil. The pattern by which this is accomplished is fourfold: (1) evangelism, (2) information, (3) worship, and (4) fellowship; (5) All of these issues in service.

6. The methods provide the mediums of communication through which the curriculum content reaches its destination. Such methods must be spiritual, varied, graded, unified, integrated, comprehensive, flexible, personal, social, and biblical. They should be integrated with the principles of teaching and learning.

4. Sources. In approaching the operation of the various facets in the teaching-learning processes, Christian educators need to draw from certain Christian sources to find the guidelines for their work. Such sources, in keeping with the concept that all truth is God's truth, can be divided into two groups: primary sources and secondary sources.

Primary sources of information supply truth from those disciplines in the school system known as Bible, theology and Christian philosophy. These sources yield not only data from which a Christian philosophy of life can be developed but also reveal truths regarding techniques, procedures and methodologies to be utilized in the school system.

Secondary sources of information are derived from divine general revelation. They include such disciplines as psychology, sociology, science and general philosophy. These sources supplement those primary sources indicated above, but they, too, provide information of practical value in dealing with people and in the operation of school systems.

One matter which as generally been neglected in most Christian school systems is that of giving consideration to the ways that God works. Divine revelation clearly reveals how God does things and from this kind of revelation school people can find clear guidance on how to organize, administer and supervise the processes of teaching and learning.

All sources for Christian education should be integrated with the Scriptures. In that sense, the curriculum is biblically based. However, other sources include nature (general revelation), published materials and textbooks, and life situations (experience). Christian education will consider any relevant source which contains truth. It recognizes that all truth comes from God.

5. The Place of Epistemology. It is understood that there is an objective body of content to be considered. Christian education recognizes that there is ultimate truth and that all truth is God's truth. God is the originator of truth. It is also recognized that there is an experimental aspect or level of truth in which knowledge is processed and experienced by the student. It is realized that there is both objective and subjective knowledge. That is, some types of content demand individual creativity and divergent thinking. However, all subjective learning should be kept consistent with God's revealed truth and within scriptural boundaries. This gives one a holistic view of knowledge which sees scientific truth and scriptural truth as complementary and parts of an integrated whole.

6. Integration and Interpretation. Of paramount importance in the teaching-learning process of Christian education is the handling of truth in the classroom. This involves both integration and interpretation. It includes deriving truth from the various subject matter disciplines being taught. It also involves the distinctions to be made between truth and error.

To discover and utilize the principles of truth in the classroom Christian teachers must learn how to use the principles derived from Christian epistemology, mentioned above. Such principles involve not only the interpretation of Christian truth in subject matter but also provide the basic propositions which shape preparation and planning as well as teaching. Administrators must also integrate Christian principles in all organizational, administrative and supervisory activities in the school as a whole. Such practice will call for the exercising of the Christian spirit in both content and practice. This demands that there be the deliberate practice of Christian truth in program and personnel.

In classroom practice and all other aspects of the curriculum all its parts must have their first point of reference in the Word of God, draw their materials from the Bible wherever possible and return to the Bible with their accumulation of facts for interpretation and practical application. Each student should understand, not only content to be studied, but also the process of integration itself. In this way the student will learn how to utilize God's truth in thought and action. In all of this it will be the work of the Holy Spirit to guide both the teachers and students in the processes of integration and interpretation. Thus the student can see the unity of both Natural and Special Revelation.

There are three levels in the teaching-learning process where integration needs to take place. The first level is philosophical and theological. Here emphasis is laid on the principle that all truth is God's truth, reflecting His work and character as Creator and Revealor. The second level may be termed relational where concepts of truth are related and unified with God's revelation. The third level involves application. Here teachers show the relation of truth to personal development, building God's Kingdom, and enriching life in every possible way for His glory.

The process by which this is accomplished is to discover and stress points of common truth between God's revelation and truth in subject matter disciplines. Where truth in God's revelation and truth in subject matter disciplines are harmonized and the unity of truth revealed thereby, it is possible then to apply truth in a Christian way to life. In Chapter Five more will be said about this process.

To practice integration in the classroom and provide true Christian interpretation of the truth in subjects, teachers need to know Bible and theology. Such knowledge will enable the teacher to "test and measure" all truth to determine truth and error. Distinctions should be made also between those truths which are propositional (that is, academic) and those that are personal (those leading to a personal relationship with Jesus Christ as Living Truth).

True integration is seeing the unity of God's truth in all subject matter, not merely quoting Scripture in the classroom or having classroom devotions. Most certainly these things should be included in the program of the school, but they are not substitutes for discovering truth or distinguishing between truth and error. Interpretations of truth must be sought which are as biblical as possible, or some which are more biblical than others. Both Christian teachers and students should be as open-minded as possible on the one hand while avoiding unjustified dogmatism on the other hand.

The objectives to be sought through Christian integration and interpretation are Christian character, a Christian mind, and a Christian philosophy of life. In this way teachers and students can see that all of life and truth is sacred, revealing God and issuing in a Christian life-style, and providing hope of life eternal in God's presence.

B. Objectives

1. <u>The Importance of Objectives</u>. A formative factor in the teaching-learning process is that of objectives. So much of modern education is characterized by lack of purpose. We have much knowledge but without wisdom. We have much information but without knowledge. Most certainly modern secular education is neglecting character development as one of its aims. Christian educators, of whatever school of thought, generally agree on the function and importance of aims and goals in the teaching-learning process. Generally speaking, aims and goals provide direction for the whole educational purpose. More specifically, they provide values for the teacher and learner. Aims and goals give the teacher the inspiration of worthwhile endeavor. He is constantly motivated by a sense of destiny and purposefulness. Furthermore, aims and goals serve as guidelines in the selection of materials and methods by which the pupil is moved toward the objectives set up. Ultimately, aims and goals provide a method of evaluation. They are points of reference in the evaluative process.

Aims and goals motivate learner responses. When learners are clear on why things are being done and where they are going, the chances for cooperation and effective learning are greatly enhanced. When objectives begin to meet learner needs, there is greater interest, concentration, and effort. These factors motivate learning.

Regarding these factors, secular educators are in general agreement with Christian educators regarding their importance. In addition to these advantages Christians see in aims and goals the means whereby integration and correlation of the Christian curriculum is made possible. Representing as they do a summary of the main points of the Christian world view, aims and goals become practical guides in providing unity and integration for a God-centered and bibliocentric philosophy of education and curriculum construction.

2. The Function of Objectives. To the Christian, objectives represent statements of the Christian philosophy of life. They make possible the use of this philosophy in the teaching-learning process and in curriculum construction. The first step, therefore, is to formulate a list of general or ultimate objectives which will serve as guidelines in the whole educative process. Following this, the next step is to formulate a set of integrated specific objectives for subject matter by which the general objectives are integrated and correlated with subject matter. This process is illustrated following.

The Christian Philosophy of Life
|
The Christian Philosophy of Education
|
General or Ultimate Objectives
|
Specific Objectives
|
Subject Matter and Biblical Content

The way this process works out in curriculum construction is discussed more fully in a section ahead devoted to curriculum.

3. The Approach to Objectives. Among religious educators of liberal persuasion there are at least three approaches to goal-setting. Naturalistic liberals, such as Sophia Fahs and Ernest Chave, would emphasize aims such as personal creativity, natural growth, and sensitivity, issuing in a goal of social adjustment for the individual. Social liberals, such as George Coe and Harrison Elliott, would stress spiritual growth as an aim toward the goal of self-realization for the individual and the establishment of a "democracy of God" for society. L. Harold De Wolf as a neo-liberal would emphasize the aim of growth in grace, working toward a faith relationship for the individual and social reconstruction for society.

There are at least three approaches to objectives among traditional adherents: (1) neo-orthodox, (2) church emphasis, both Catholic and Protestant, and (3) Evangelicals. Neo-orthodox religious educators would stress conversion, growth in grace, and nurture as aims. Christian discipleship is the goal to be attained. Among those who stress a church emphasis transmission of a cultural and spiritual heritage and growth in grace would be prominent aims. Christian discipleship, church authority and fellowship in the church would be sought as goals. Among Evangelicals aims would incorporate revelation, conversion and growth in grace. Goals would include Christlike character and conduct, the extension of the church in preparation for the coming Kingdom of God.

Three general approaches to aim can be identified among those who hold to an integral view of revelation. Those with a psychological approach, such as Ruell Howe and Lewis Sherill, would stress Christian nurture and encounter as aims. Goals would include acceptance and changes in the self. Integrists who stress relationship theology would find nurture, engagement and relationships as aims. Goals would include Christian character development through conversion, commitment, and Christian living. Drawing heavily upon a combination of theology and social science, men like James Lee and John Westerhoff would advocate Christian understanding, action and love as aims. Christian service to God and man based on Christian love and Christian living would be hope for goals.

4. A Revelational Approach to Objectives. Evangelicals are

strong in their support of the fact that God is the Source of all life, reality and truth. True education, therefore, is a process of Christian education. The Scriptures stand as the Written Revelation of God and serve as our authority. As one reads the Word of God he is impressed with the fact that there is a steady plan of development for human personality, beginning with the creation of a new heart in man and proceeding through stages of integration of character, conduct, and environment toward eternity. This process includes self-adjustment, social adjustment, growth in grace, a place of service, and a view of eternity.

Christian education, therefore, is education that is Christ-centered in its objectives. Based on the premise that true Christian education is God-centered, the purposes of God become the purposes of education. God's first great purpose is for man to seek God's Kingdom (Matt. 6:33). His great goal for man is to dwell in and enjoy His presence forever (Psalm 27:4). This means that God is concerned with the creation and development of a great family of children (Eph. 1:3-11). To do this He revealed to us His knowledge and wisdom (Eph. 1:8) and that forgiveness and redemption come out of this wisdom (Eph. 1:7,8). For man, therefore, God's general purpose is for His children to know the fullness of Christ (Eph. 1:9; 3:11; 4:13). For His church His will is both completion and edification (Eph. 4:11-16). For mankind in general His purpose is for both salvation and holiness (Eph. 1:3-5). This focuses on the need of the sinner for redemption (Eph. 1:8). These purposes are revealed further in God's plan for salvation and redemption (Acts 2:22,23; 3:18-26).

Focusing on the objectives for Christian education in relation to man, the Scriptures are very specific. Truth is centered in Christ (Col. 2:3; Eph. 1:17) and He made God knowable in Himself (Matt. 11:27; Eph. 1:17). Such knowledge we are told is life eternal (John 17:3). In Christ are found the treasures of wisdom and knowledge (Col. 2:3; I Cor. 1:24). All Christian education, therefore, finds its objectives in the life and truth supplied in Jesus Christ. All Christian educators must draw from Him as the Source of the meaning and content of education. This source provides Christian education with its fundamental objectives.

119

The needs of mankind point up the need for Christ-centered objectives. In general man needs the help of God (John 15:5; Phil. 4:13; Job 11:7,8). In fact it takes divine-human cooperation to succeed (John 7:17; II Cor. 8:12; Phil. 2:13; John 16:13).

Man's basic need is to know God (John 17:3; 9:23,24). But man's unaided knowledge is insufficient (Job 11:7,8). Neither is there any place for pride and self-sufficiency (I Cor. 8:1,2; Rom. 12:16; Prov. 26:12; Jer. 9:23,24).

The effects of sin upon mankind interfere with education (John 1:9,10; 3:19-21). The presence of sin is universal (Rom. 3:9-12,23), has brought universal death (Rom. 5:12-21; I Cor. 15:21,22; Gen. 2:17), and spiritual deterioration is therefore a present reality (Gen. 6:3,5,6). The debilitating effects of sin can be seen on the social order (Gen. 3:12; 4:8), on the material universe (Gen. 3:17-19) and in man's broken relationship with God (Gen. 3:9). The effects of man's sin on personality are quite evident. Man was made a slave to sin (John 8:34), to self (II Cor. 5:15), and to Satan (II Tim 2:26). Sin ruined man's personality. It brought death to the human spirit (Eph. 2:1,5). Man's inner life was marred (Rom. 1:23-32; Gal. 5:17-21; Psalm 14:1-3). Sin brought ruin to the human soul. The mind was blinded (II Cor. 4:3,4; Titus 1:15; Col. 1:21). It became corrupt (Titus 1:15), and characterized by ungodly wisdom (I Cor. 1:20,21), self-love (II Tim 3:1-4), pleasure-seeking (II Tim. 3:1-4) and rebellion (I Cor. 2:14).

The heart was defiled and polluted (Jer. 17:9; Mark 7:21-23; II Tim. 3:1-4). The will was perverted (Judges 17:6; Rom. 8:7). The body became a battlefield (Rom. 3:23; 6:12,13; 7:5; II Cor. 5:4), and the future foreboding (I John 1:5-6; Eph. 5:8; I Cor. 6:9; Rev. 21:27). Original man became the natural man (I Cor. 2:14; Rom. 8:9).

All of this points up the first major Biblical objective of education -- the preeminence of spiritual life and its development (Matt. 6:33). The ideal for this spiritual development is revealed in Jesus Christ (Eph. 3:11). His life and character become the pattern and process to be developed. The great personality goal, therefore, is Christlike character (Matt. 5:48; John 15:4; 17:20-26; Rom. 8:29; Eph. 4:11-16; II Cor. 3:18; Phil. 3:21; Col. 1:27,28; II Tim. 3:17;

Peter 1:4; I John 3:2; 5:11,12). This means to be fully grown or developed (Eph. 4:13 -- the Greek, "TELION"), the fullness of the life of Christ (I John 2:6; I Peter 2:21).

New Testament writers laid emphasis on the high priority given to the inward quality of life and genuineness of spirit in knowing and serving God (Rom. 3:28; 10:3,4). Christianity was pictured as a heart religion (Rom. 10:9,10). Victorious living was stressed (Rom. 6:11-14; II Cor. 2:14). To accomplish this goal, teachings were provided on how to witness (Acts 15:14), how to help men come to know Christ (II Peter 3:18; Phil. 4:7-9), how to walk worthily as Christians (I Thess. 2:12; 4:1; Gal. 6:16; Col. 1:10; Rom. 6:4; Phil. 1:27), and how to prepare for the judgment (Rom. 14:10-12; Matt. 16:27). Stress was laid on the importance of preaching and teaching (Acts 26:16-19), on building up the body of Christ (Eph. 4:12-15), on doing God's will (John 6:38), on glorying in the cross (Gal. 6:14), on deemphasizing possessions (Luke 14:33; Mark 8:34-37) and on spreading the knowledge of Christ everywhere (II Cor. 2:14; Acts 5:28,42; 24:24,25).

Perhaps the personality goals of Christian education can be summarized in the creation and development of the fruit of the Spirit (Gal. 5:22-25). The productive outcomes of such a life can be seen in (1) the new man (II Cor. 5:17; Gal. 6:15; Eph. 2:15; 4:24), (2) the spiritual man (I Cor. 2:15; Gal. 3:14), (3) the mature man (Eph. 4:13; Col. 3:14; Heb. 6:1,2) and (4) the loving man (I Cor. 12 and 13).

Because Christian education is in essence a reinterpretation of God's revelation, its purpose is to show God revealed. This, however, is a means to an end. The immediate objective is to qualify man to reveal God in his total life and environment. At the far end of the spectrum lies the Kingdom of God. We must, however, be more specific than this. To accomplish the purpose there must be a goal, a product. There is, therefore, an individual objective or personality objective, a social objective, and a prophetic objective.

The individual objective is Christlike character (Matt. 5:48; 15:4). The analysis of the character of Jesus is revealed in the Scriptures. "He that hath seen me hath seen the Father" (John 14:9). Jesus was like God. God is revealed in Jesus Christ. His Godliness was expressed in all areas of His life and conduct. "Jesus increased in wisdom and stature, and in favor with God and man" (Luke 2:52). Here we see the intellectual, physical, social and spiritual aspects of His character from the human standpoint. Jesus <u>increased</u> in all these aspects. The pattern, therefore, for man is to become increasingly more Christlike.

The Apostle Paul likewise adopted the goal of Christlikeness as the character-goal for Christians. "Christ in you, the hope of glory: whom we preach... that we may present every man perfect in Christ Jesus" (Col. 1:27,28). "That ye might be filled with all the fullness of God" (Eph. 3:19). Using the fourfold description of Jesus recorded in Luke 2:25, some of Paul's marks of Christlike people are listed on the following chart.

PHYSICAL GOALS

Body was considered the
   Temple of the Holy Spirit
     (I Cor. 3:17)
Purity (I Cor. 6:13,18,20)
Not considered most important
     (I Tim. 4:8)

SPIRITUAL GOALS

Spiritual living is paramount
     (I Cor. 2:14; Gal. 5:22,23)
Emotional control and enjoyment
     Joy (I Thess. 5:17; John 15:11)
     Peace (Phil. 4:6,7)
     Love (I Cor. 13)
Sympathy (Rom. 12:15)
Cheerfulness (Acts 27:22)
Thankfulness (I Thess. 5:18)
Hopefulness (Rom. 15:13)
Confidence (Phil 1:16)
Reverence (Phil. 2:12)
Firmness of will (I Thess. 5:21)
Stability of purpose
     (I Tim. 4:16)
Educated wills (Phil 3:16)
Truthfulness (Eph. 4:25)
Kindness (I Thess. 5:15)
Hospitality (Rom. 12:13)
Spirit-filled (Eph. 5:18)
Patience (I Thess. 5:14)
Obedience (Col. 3:20)
Christlikeness (Rom. 13:14)
Humility (Rom. 12:10)
Temperance (Rom. 12:21)
Holiness (I Peter 1:15-17)

MENTAL GOALS
An informed mind
Awakened understanding
Stirred reason
Quickened judgment
References:
    Acts 28:23
    Acts 20:1
    Acts 9:29
    Acts 19:8,9
    Acts 20:7
    Acts 20:20
    Acts 23:11
    Acts 20:25
    Acts 20:31
    Acts 20:32
    Acts 21:19
    Acts 24:10
Exalted thinking (Phil. 4:7-9)
Faith (Romans 1:17)
Avoid speculation
    (I Tim. 6:20; 4:7)
Exactness of thought (Col. 4:6)
Prayer (Luke 6:12; Eph. 6:18)
Independence of thought
    (Eph. 5:6)
Application in study (II Tim. 2:15)

SOCIAL GOALS
Good citizenship
    (Rom. 13:1-7)
Sound business (Rom. 13:8)
Good ethics (Rom. 13:9)
Respect for the rights of
    others (Rom. 14:13)
Neighborliness (Rom.15:1,2)
Thoughtfulness (Rom.16:19)
No partisanship (I Cor. 1:10)
No class rivalry (I Cor. 4:6)
Good company (I Cor. 5:13)
Lawsuits (I Cor. 6:1,7)
Industry (I Thess. 5:14)
    (II Thess 3:6)
    (II Thess. 3:10)
    (I Thess. 2:9)
    (I Thess. 4:11-13)
Merciful (Rom. 12:17)
Forgiving (Eph. 4:26)
Stewardship (Matt. 6:19-21)
Lights (Matt. 5:14-16)
Salt (Matt. 5:13)
Conduct (Matt. 10:16)
Attitude (I John 2:15-17)

Such a list by no means exhausts the traits which are expected to be revealed by the child of God. He is to be educated to live like this and manifest the truth. The ultimate result of this process is <u>integrated</u> personality, another way of expressing the concept of <u>spiritual maturity</u>. According to God's Word, it is not His will for the new-born Christian to remain in a state of spiritual babyhood (I Cor. 3:1-3). Instead, God expects maturity (I Cor. 14:20). Each Christian is admonished to be filled with the fullness of God (Eph. 3:19; 5:18). The goal is the perfect man in Christ (Eph. 4:13).

    According to Ephesians 4:1 spiritual maturity is achieved by walking worthily as a child of God; this, Paul tells us, is characterized by lowliness, meekness, longsuffering, forbearance, love, unity, peace (vs. 2 and 3), and watchfulness (5:15). Christians are not to act like children (4:14) but are to be stable (vs. 14), truthful (vs. 15, 25), constantly growing (vs. 15), manifesting self-control (vs. 26), overcoming (vs. 26), overcoming temptation (vs. 27), laboring honestly (vs. 28), speaking purely (vs. 29-31), and being kind, tenderhearted, and forgiving (vs. 32). The whole life is to issue in service (Eph. 2:10; 5:16).

The process by which this is achieved is described in Ephesians 6:13-18 where the Christian is to follow after truth, righteousness, the Gospel of peace, faith, salvation, the Word and prayer. Colossians 3 also provides some good advice.

To become integrated a personality must become a unity, an integer, and the educational process should be one by which a person becomes a unit. In the words of Paul, "that the man of God may be perfect, thoroughly furnished unto all good works" (II Tim. 3:17), we see the picture of an integrated personality.

An analysis of the human personality reveals that there are various manifestations of the ego or the self. Man is more than intellect; he is also feelings and will; he is spirit, soul, and body. The purpose of education is to integrate the powers of the personality so that they work as a whole. Knowledge should not be divorced from the feelings or the will. Here, again, it is to be noted that education is education for life and living. At this point is where much modern education has failed. Failure to observe the needs of the moral and spiritual aspects of man's nature, and to provide educational assistance in these realms, has resulted in a fragmentary type of education and a stunted personality. Thus the moral and spiritual development must be integrated with the other aspects of the self. As this integration progresses in the individual, there results to a greater degree in him the powers of self-mastery, self-control, and self-determination. All of this, however, must, to be effective, be guided by the Christian philosophy of life. To be complete the integration of personality includes not only education for life, but also for death. Since attitudes toward death affect life, they also affect education.

The purpose of the integration of personality, therefore, is to help man increasingly to be raised to the higher spiritual levels which are supplied by the Christian philosophy of life and the grace of God.

The self-realization of the Dewey school of thought, therefore, seems to fall short of an adequate goal. From Dewey's viewpoint one is tempted to think more of self-indulgence than self-realization through self-expression. A faulty psychology and philosophy here are revealed. The Christian viewpoint provides a higher level upon which to integrate personality.

It can be safely said, therefore, that the purpose of Christian education is the development of human personality but it is development toward a designed end, guided by obedience to the will of God. In this sense, the personality is freed. Sin causes disintegrated personality but the Christian school must integrate that which sin has disintegrated. This includes, of course, the restoration of the personality to the image of God. From this point on, the life is centered in God and lived in the center of God's will.

Christian education is education that is <u>love-directed in its ethics</u>. The true sources of ethics are in Jesus Christ (John 1:9), in the Moral Law (Ten Commandments) (Matt. 5:17-19), in the teachings of Christ (Matt. 5-7), and in the heart of man (Rom. 2:14,15; Heb. 8:10). The motive for ethics is the law of love (I Cor. 13) and the regulating factor is the conscience (I Tim. 1:5).

The nature of God is the ethical norm. God is love (John 3:16; I John 4:8), is holy (Lev. 11:44-45; Matt. 5:48; I Peter 1:14-16), and is righteous (Psalm 145:7). God is quite concerned about the inward quality of life for man (Deut. 6:5; 10:12; 13:3; Prov. 23:26; Psalm 1:2; 119:34). He is concerned about man's moral life and development (Titus 2:14). The Bible is clear on right and wrong (Isaiah 5:20; II Cor. 6:14,15) and it lifts the highest moral standard (Psalm 1; 24:3-5; Matt. 5:34-37; Mark 2:23-28; Eph. 6:1-3; Matt. 5:21-22; 5:27-32; Eph. 4:28; Col. 3:9; and Col. 3:8).

Duties of all mankind are clearly revealed in Scripture. Such duties include those we owe to God, to self, and to others; duties within the family; and duties to the state. Man's overall duty is to fear God and keep His commandments (Micah 6:8; Eccles. 12:13; Prov. 13:13,14). The supreme social virtues are the cardinal virtue of love (Luke 6:35), the cooperative virtue of service (Gal. 5:13; I Thess. 1:3; I John 3:18) and the consummatory virtue of self-sacrifice

(John 15:13).

There is also a <u>social aim</u> of Christian education. Two primary concepts are at the very heart of the Christian religion: (1) man is built in the image of God and should strive toward the perfection he finds in Him, and (2) man is a social creature; he was made for fellowship with his God and fellow man. The social purpose of Christian education, therefore, includes more than individual development; it includes social development and this, in turn, implies the highest possible development of each individual. In this view life is seen in its wholeness -- the rounded development of the individual who lives in harmony with his fellows. The nature of this harmony requires a philosophy of life, and this rests upon the Christian theistic world view. This view demands the highest possible degree of social serviceability. The curriculum and learning processes must be developed to this end. The child must be trained to take his place in society and to so live and work that social relationships will conform to the ideal. What better place is there to do this than in the church!

The social aim should eventuate in the social goal of Christian education. The social goal of Christian education places stress on what Christians can do together for the common welfare. Two agencies are used by God in bringing to realization His social objective: (1) the Church, and (2) the Kingdom.

The Church is composed of the body of Christ, the corporate body of believers. The goal here, therefore, is to form a great Missionary Society in which the goal is to enlist every disciple of Christ in this body and to develop them into efficient disciples. The methods to be employed are witnessing and evangelism, expressed in the Great Commission. In order to facilitate this objective, the Church, as the Kingdom of Christ, moves out into society as a spiritual leaven with a spiritual program called the Kingdom of Heaven. This Kingdom is to develop the inner man into the image of Christ as the Head of the Church.

Beyond the personality goals were those of the <u>improvement of society</u>. Included here is the development of a good and just society (Lev. 19:2ff), righteousness (Job 27:5,6; Prov. 14:34), good relationships (Rom. 14:7), relief of the poor (Acts 11:29), sensitivity

(Luke 15:1,2), and fellowship (I John 1:3). Not to be overlooked here is the development of good citizenship (Rom. 13:1-7) and practical Christian living virtues, such as good ethics (Rom. 13:9), neighborliness (Rom. 15:1,2), thoughtfulness (Rom. 16:15), sound business (Rom. 13:8), and respect for the rights of others (Rom. 14:13).

The Kingdom of God is the ultimate objective for society. Here is where God has perfect control. The Theocracy is re-established. Perfect love will prevail. "Thou shalt love thy neighbor as thyself." In the meantime, while we await the coming of the Kingdom, the child of God is expected to move out into society and prove that the purposes of God can be increasingly effective in human relations. The ultimate results of this kind of living will be a manifestation of individual Christians of the following social characteristics:

1. Perfect brotherly love
2. Sacrificial service
3. Christian culture
4. Good citizenship

The ultimate goals would include qualification to participate in the resurrection (I Cor. 15:19-20, 51-57), to pass the judgment of God (Rom. 14:10,12; I Cor. 3:12-15), to reach heaven (John 14:1-4; I Cor. 2:9), and to enjoy eternal life with God in His Kingdom (Rev. 21:1-7; Rom. 15:12; I Cor. 15:24-28).

There is finally a prophetic goal for Christian education. Christian education gives the pupil a perspective for eternity. Provision has been made, through the atonement of Jesus Christ on the cross, for the eternal welfare of God's children. Rightly so, this should consume a major share of present concern, but not enough stress thus far has been laid on the Lord's return. A view of eternity will emphasize the return of Jesus and the hope that this offers for the life to come. This will create a sense of balance between time and eternity, but at the same time will provide added incentive and highest motivation for maximum development and preparation now.

Beyond the character and personality goals stated above, lie aims and goals stated also in academic terms. In addition to those goals involving commitment to God and awareness of His presence, character and power, are those goals dealing with student abilities. These abilities will vary according to age and individual differences and will serve to shape the school's objectives for individuals. Within the framework of the student's development, the Christian curriculum should be utilized to develop each student's ability to read, understand, communicate, make judgments and discriminations, and serve God and fellow man in a chosen life's vocation. This is accomplished through the presence and power of the Holy Spirit.

Educational objectives are developed from primary sources found in the Christian world view. From this view, which supplies a Christian philosophy of life, the general objectives for Christian education at all levels are derived. Such objectives will touch upon God, the world, man, truth, and values, all of which supply the norms and direction for Christian education.

The objectives derived from revelational sources, therefore, will demand that each subject be taught through a Christian world view perspective. Furthermore, biblical reasons should be given for teaching all subjects in all Christian schools. Every subject in the curriculum should be justified on the basis of a Christian philosophy of life. It is the conviction of this writer that the objectives for Christian education are so clearly revealed in the primary Christian sources that there is not too much room for modification or change in their application to the school situation.

C. The Role of the Teacher

1. <u>The Importance of the Teacher</u>. The teacher is held in high regard in all types of education and is considered to be one of the most influential factors in the teaching-learning process. The fact that most of the people in the nation contact the teacher in the formative years of their lives places this person in a critical position for both the individual and society. Permanent changes are wrought in a society through the influence of the teacher. In fact the teacher's attitudes and general conduct have greater bearing on pupil development than his knowledge of subject matter.

Among liberal religious educators, the place of the teacher in religious education is based largely on the effects of the personality of the teacher on the learner. Such influence, they feel, is based on genuine personal interest, mutual admiration, and the practice of democratic principles. The role of the teacher in this viewpoint is to create group fellowship in which growth in "Christian" personality is encouraged.

Among evangelical Christian educators the concept of the teacher is a high one. In this view the place of the Christian teacher is determined by the place given to the Master Teacher. The qualifications of the Master Teacher should be the qualifications of the Christian teacher. The functions of the two are the same. In the Bible, Christian teaching is considered to be a ministry. The teacher is a minister of God (Eph. 4:1), an oracle of God (I Peter 4:10,11) and as such has a mandate from God to provide instruction.

Teaching is a God-given responsibility (Isaiah 28:10), should begin early (Isaiah 28:9) and be done a little bit at a time (Isaiah 28:10). It is best accomplished, not by might (human means) but by the Holy Spirit (Zech. 4:6; Acts 17:28).

2. The Function of the Teacher. Among secular educators the function of the teacher is that of a guide, one who motivates, inspires, leads and guides learner activity and growth to win learner cooperation; one who arranges learning activities.

Among liberal religious educationists the teacher functions as a facilitator of learning. Because they feel that all experiences have revelatory value, the teacher is one who functions in the capacity of helping learners participate at the highest level in those experiences. Since God is present in all human experiences to them, the teacher's job is to facilitate observable religious behavior in students.

For the integrationist the function of the teacher is to bring both supernatural and natural experiences into good balance. The teacher functions to help students to recognize and respond to God's revelation in all experiences of life. There is close personal interrelationship between the teacher and student to accomplish this goal. They believe also that the Holy Spirit must be depended on for guidance in both teaching and learning.

Among Evangelicals the teacher functions as an instrument

in the hands of God to bring His message and life in cooperation with the Holy Spirit into the hearts and daily lives of learners.

3. <u>A Revelational Concept of the Teacher's Role</u>. The Christian teacher functions as a Christian educator. As a Christian he so lives as to reveal God through the power of the Holy Spirit. As an educator he functions in accordance with the mandate of God to teach and in accord with the educational principles contained in the whole educative process. Receiving a mandate from God the Christian teacher becomes the oracle or mouthpiece of God (I Peter 4:10,11; John 7:16-18).

The Christian function of the Christian teacher is that of a model in three ways: (1) he models Christlike character, (2) he models Christian truth, and (3) he models Christian teaching at its best. The authority that the teacher has is not in himself but in God through the Bible, a fellow learner with his students. This demands a close relationship with the student characterized by love, mutual respect, trust, honesty and acceptance. In other words the teaching-learning relationship involving teacher and learner should reflect the character of the church as the body of Christ. Such teaching and learning can go on in the home, the classroom, and informal social relations.

As an oracle of God (I Peter 4:10,11) the teacher follows in the train of Jesus Who said, "My teaching is not mine but his that sent me ... he that speaketh from himself seeketh his own glory" (John 7:16-18). Thus, the abilities and talents which the Christian teacher possesses are to be considered God-given and should be used in His service and for His glory. He functions to witness regarding the God-revealing character of creation and providence.

The function of the Christian teacher is also seen in relation to God-given principles of good teaching. The teacher is not only obligated to be a witness, but also must <u>operate</u> properly as a witness. This brings into focus the matter of methodologies which will be dealt with later on.

The teaching process itself bears witness to the function of the teacher. There are many terms which could be used to describe the function of the teacher in this process. Such terms would probably include helping, awakening, imparting knowledge, inspiring students, guiding and correcting, handling subject matter effectively so that the goals kept in mind can be achieved. More details on the teaching process itself will be dealt with in a later section of this chapter.

If administrators are going to develop faculty members with a revelational view of education, obviously those people of genuine Christian character should be selected. Such people will be growing Christians, filled with the Holy Spirit, having a gift for teaching, a genuine love for students and a carefully worked out Christian philosophy of life and education.

School leaders must be intentional in their efforts to develop a Christian philosophy of education based on revelational principles. Such intentionality will demand faculty meetings and studies devoted to developing a Christian philosophy of education.

D. The Role of the Learner

1. <u>Concepts of Personality</u>. Among liberal religious educationists, particularly those who advocate an immanence approach to revelation, the student is viewed from the standpoint of psychology, sociology, and personality development. They reject the theological notion that man is a sinner in need of redemption. Character development is primary in this view, because they see that the human and scientific development of personality is inherently religious and revelatory.

Integrationists see both godly and natural elements in students. God's supernatural power must invade man in his natural state and environment to bring about changes in religious personality.

Among Evangelicals a biblical view of the nature of man prevails. Here man is viewed as a creature of God, but fallen into sin and in rebellion against God. He is thus a sinner and in need of redemption. Man thus lives in two worlds -- the natural and the supernatural. Only through God's redeeming power can man overcome sin and the dominance of the natural over the supernatural.

2. <u>The Place of the Learner</u>. Among secular educators the goal of education for the learner is the good and efficient citizen. This goal is man-centered and the learner becomes, therefore, the

end of the educative process and thus is at its center. This view is based on the belief that man is a functioning organism, capable of perceiving the natural world.

In religious education, the social and educational philosophy of John Dewey and advocates of Progressive Education have led the way. Here too the learner becomes the end of education and the children central in the process. In fact child-centered theories and creative concepts of the teaching process have dominated religious educational circles now for many years. The failure of liberalism, however, is quite apparent today; therefore the advocates of religious education are finding themselves hard put to justify their practices.

3. <u>A Revelational Concept of the Role of the Learner.</u> In Christian education, God, not man, is both end and central. In this view, therefore, the learner becomes the <u>focus</u> of the educative process but not the end. The entire educative process is directed toward the learner but becomes a means to an end in bringing the learner to Christlikeness.

Christian education therefore is education that is pupil-focused in its psychology. All the Life and Light of God are focused on disciples (learners). Jesus said, "I am come that <u>they</u> might have life" (John 10:10). "<u>Ye</u> shall know the truth, and the truth shall make <u>you</u> free" (John 8:32). Christ is the center of Christian education but all His life and truth are focused on the pupil as a learner and disciple of Him.

Learners have personality created by God with attitudes, desires, knowledge and skills (John 2:23-25). Originally created in the image of God (Gen. 1:27) learner personality has been marred by sin (Rom. 3:23) but still owning personality powers which are mental, physical, spiritual and social (Luke 2:52).

Learners, as disciples, have been endowed with minds to discover, understand and perceive truth with which they are confronted (Matt. 5:1-2; Rom. 1:14), hearts to appreciate and desire truth (Phil. 1:8-10), and wills to appropriate and respond to truth (John 7:17).

E. The Learning Process

1. Secular Contributions. Much learning about learning is still needed. What actually happens to the mind when learning takes place is still a matter for further study. Actually, it may be impossible to find out, but still we try. In spite of the difficulties involved, psychologists and students of education have devised several <u>theories of learning</u>. Perhaps the earliest of these was that of <u>faculty psychology</u>. Two schools of thought known as <u>assimilation</u> and <u>discipline</u> became primary. The premise of this position was as follows: mind functions as an entity distinct from the rest of the human organism. The mind can assimilate ideas and be disciplined in the use of them. To this view, mind consists of compartments and faculties, such as memory, judgment, reasoning, imagination, purpose, motivation, etc., as functions. In this view learning becomes a process of taking in ideas and assimilating them and thereby forming and exercising the mind. The teacher, therefore, transmits ideas and compels the learner thus to be exercised. The form of teaching was logical, deductive, and verbal memory.

To <u>association psychology</u> mind consists of the association of ideas, not as an organ which assimilates ideas and exercises itself. Learning results rather from the connection of ideas according to mental laws. Teaching in this view consists of relating new ideas to old ones, the principle of apperception.

<u>Conditioning</u> or <u>connectionism</u>, as advocated by John B. Watson and mechanistic psychologists, stresses the centrality of the nervous system rather than ideas. The mind is composed of neural connections in the brain and is centralized in the cortex with its multitude of connections. Learning becomes a matter of connecting stimuli and responses and establishing them. Establishment takes place through conditioning the responses.

<u>Gestalt</u> and <u>Wholistic</u> schools of psychology advocated a theory of learning based on insight. The core term in this view is <u>wholeness</u>. Man does not react to isolated stimuli but rather to organized wholes. Learning, therefore, becomes a matter of the organization of responses in relationship. It may come in a flash

when the whole is perceived. This is insight. Teaching in this view is the presentation of organized wholes perceptible to the learner. This view is known also as a field theory of learning.

John Dewey advanced the theory that learning is based on experiencing. In this view mind and personality are experience. Human behavior is not individual but social, therefore experience is the interaction of the organism with its environment and this environment is largely social. The heart of experience is to face problems and solve them. The scientific method is the medium through which this is done. Teaching, consequently, becomes a matter of guiding the learner's experience to achieve foreseen ends which are valuable. Pupils learn by doing.

A contemporary theory is known as creative expression. This is an eclectic view which combines the latest findings of both psychology and sociology. Learning is expression which takes place in a social setting. The expression is creative because it originates within. Impressions are not "stamped in" but energize and motivate action. The whole-person-in-action seeks activity. Teaching becomes a matter of guiding the expressions of the whole-person-in-action in security to desirable ends.

In the past psychologists have done much through research to enlighten us on the nature of learning. The following laws and principles of learning have been discovered:

A. The Principle of Pupil-Activity (Self-activity)
    1. Learning comes from the pupils own responses to stimuli
    2. Repetition – the more often something is repeated, the better we remember, the deeper our self-activity.
    3. Teachers control direction.

B. The Principle of Motivation (Interest)
    1. The intensity of the learning response depends upon interest.
    2. Effect – we remember and want to repeat pleasant experiences while trying to forget and avoid unpleasant ones.

3. Use – the use of knowledge and practice of what we know tends to make truth more easily remembered and understood.
4. Recency – the more recently we've studied something, the better we remember it.
5. Make teaching interesting.

C. The Principle of Apperception
   (Preparation and Mental Set)
   1. The nature of the learning response depends upon past experience and present frame of mind.
   2. Readiness – there are special times when a pupil's mind is unusually open to certain kinds of learning; age and maturity also enter in here.
   3. Teaching is related to pupil experience.

D. The Principle of Individualization
   1. Learning responses are determined and limited by individual differences in ability.
   2. Teaching attempts to meet individual differences.

E. The Principle of Socialization
   1. Every response has its social implications.
   2. By-product learnings – all truths are accompanied by many by-product learnings; sometimes these concomitant learnings are more important and valuable than the central facts being considered, for as the pupil learns he is forming vital attitudes.

Recently, some new attempts at learning theory have been made by combining psychological theories with clinical studies of personality development. Cantor records a list of learning propositions which lend support to a teaching-learning process based on such studies:

1. The pupil learns only what he is interested in learning.
2. It is important that the pupil share in the development

and management of the curriculum.
3. Learning is integral.
4. Learning depends upon wanting to learn.
5. An individual learns best when he is free to create his own responses in a situation.
6. Learning depends upon not knowing the answers.
7. Every pupil learns in his own way.
8. Learning is largely an emotional experience.
9. To learn is to change.[1]

Adults bring much more to the learning process than children do, therefore the approach should vary accordingly. Where children are dependent, adults are autonomous. Where children are told what to learn, adults like to choose and evaluate their own achievement. The curriculum for children is largely ready-made, whereas adults like to have a part in self-directed enquiry. Both the quantity and quality of experience differ greatly between children and adults. In time perspective the two differ greatly. Where both children and youth look for immediate satisfaction, adults look to the future. Children study subjects largely for future preparation whereas adults stress problem-solving for the present. Most certainly adults come to educational activities with a great difference in developmental tasks. Adults are facing life-roles which involve responsibilities undreamed of by children and many youth. All of this has meaning not only for methodology but also for curriculum construction.

A rather recent attempt to describe learning is to be found in the theory of <u>concept learning</u>. This view arises out of a background of studies by developmental psychologists who look largely to the cognitive theories of Jean Piaget and the moral development views of Lawrance Kohlberg. The basic premise is that only certain concepts can be processed by children in their early years so we teach in accord with the abilities of children as they develop. On this last point this view also follows in the trend of psychologists who for many years have described the development of personality as people mature.

Piaget maintained that his system of structuralism was a good explanation of learning theory. He took the position, based on his research studies, that learners, particularly children, are limited by their cognitive structure from understanding some things, particularly adult learnings and understandings. He believed that cognitive structures grow and change in sequence the same for all human beings everywhere. Learning for children takes place by active involvement with the physical and social environments but is limited by structural development (maturation). He suggested that children are incapable of doing abstract thinking until about age seven. Kohlberg built his moral development theories on the premises of Piaget and parallels his suggested levels of moral development on the progressive scale suggested by Piaget's cognitive system.

One of the emphases in Piaget that some American psychologists and educators differ with is his denial of the ability of the child to do abstract thinking until he reaches age seven. Because of cultural factors in our society many believe that our children are able to do such thinking long before age seven. Among those advocating this possibility is Jerome Bruner who says that young children are often underestimated in their ability to learn. He advanced the thesis in 1964 that at least half of all human intelligence is developed by age four. This was reflected in the book Stability and Change in Human Characteristics. This thesis was very largely supported by White and Watts at Harvard and revealed in the book Major Influences on the Development of Young Children. This view has gained rather wide acceptance among educators in this country.

Jerome Bruner advanced the premise that "any subject can be taught effectively in some intellectually honest way to any child at any state of development," at least among school age children. Significant work to support this thesis was done at several places in the United States. Oscar Moore at the University of Pittsburgh found that three-year old children can learn to write stories on coded key typewriters with the use of pictures. Experiments at the High/Scope Research Foundation in Ypsilanti, Michigan, show that educators and parents are learning how to give even crib-bound infants an educational head start.

Dr. Kagan at Harvard, in research on the power of infants to think, found that babies react much like adults when confronted with new situations. Burton White, also at Harvard, points out that year two is very critical for the child. At the Harvard Preschool Project, 1965, they discovered that the period between ten and eighteen months is the most significant period in the child's life. They also discovered that three-year olds have relatively the same cluster of abilities as six-year olds. The role of the mother in guiding the child's learning experiences becomes very critical. We thus see in this the significant value of the home. We also see the values of freedom, responsibility, guidance, exploration, and involvement in learning. Both love and learning flow from the conditions of real life.

The Christian looks at these varied learning theories and attempts to evaluate them. To do this, observations are made on the basis of reason. Other observations are made by "filtering" such views through the eyes of revelation and theology. There are elements of truth in most learning theories but they have to be examined in the light of faith.

In responding to the learning views involving connectionism, conditioning and reinforcement, the following observations can be made:

1. Such views have no category for revelation, theology, and spiritual realities. Conditioning is purely materialistic and mechanistic.

2. Not all learning results from reinforcement. In fact, the use of reward in Christian situations must proceed with caution.

3. Reinforcement does not issue in experiencing God. He comes to us first, not by trial and error.

4. All learning is not necessarily rewarding because some learning comes through pain (see the book of Job).

5. From a biological point of view habits can be formed through skills. But because man is a transcendental being he is not formed only on a behavioristic basis.

6. The learner may or may not be ready. Sometimes it takes the Holy Spirit to get one ready to learn.

7. Man is more than reactive, he is a personal and responsible being.

8. There is no purpose in conditioning but man is purposive.
9. Conditioning is valid in the church on the basis of communication but not on the basis of forcing acceptance.
10. Such views do not take into account the effect that sin has on human personality, which hinders thorough learning.
11. The association view destroys spiritual identity.

Gestaltism has some favorable points by emphasizing that learning takes place by <u>intentions</u>. Problems are solved <u>internally</u> through intelligence, not merely by trial and error. The emphasis on the "total field" so necessary to learning looks acceptable, for the Christian insists that the church is part of that total field. Intelligence, however, needs the help of the Holy Spirit. Learning through insight may come also at times by the work of the Holy Spirit in man.

Learning by doing has its place. It does not fully describe, however, all possibilities for learning, for man can also learn vicariously through the experience of others as well as through the use of imagination. Furthermore, for children, learning by doing is often beyond their possibilities because of the lack of maturity or opportunity.

The Christian doctrine of man is a theological description of the learner. As a sinner man does not find it possible to restructure his learning processes without the help of the Holy Spirit. His perceptual processes have been affected by sin and therefore have deteriorated. The Holy Spirit brings about change in the person and thus becomes the power of the Christian in learning. Learning theory might call this motivation, or need states, or readiness, but man needs the help of the Holy Spirit to guide the perceptual process so that he can learn at the deepest level -- in the heart.

Revelation provides the "stuff" for learning. God, through the Holy Spirit, works at the deepest levels of learning by stimulating the learner to respond to His revelation. In this function, the Holy Spirit does not merely validate learning, but is a part of the very process of learning at every point.

The prominence of Piaget's work and its apparent effect on Christian education in some circles demands some response also. A

139

number of questions need to be raised by the Christian as he views Piaget's work.

1. Does the claim that limited cognitive structure really touch the matter of understanding or does it merely indicate limited perception? Why not test understanding <u>after</u> instruction?
2. Is it possible to use the results of research data produced by people who are largely non-Christian to draw conclusions for use among Christian people?
3. Is it possible to structure an experimental situation among children to get adequate results without <u>first</u> preparing them for the experiment?
4. Do cognitive structures grow and change in sequence the same for <u>all</u> people in <u>every</u> culture? What about research evidence by American psychologists and educators which seems to point to the contrary?
5. If children cannot process biblical truth, does this not mean that one has to turn to environmental conditions <u>only</u> to stimulate internal development? What about the category of the supernatural and spiritual?
6. Is it not true that in Christian circles there <u>does exist</u> genuine Christian education of children in Christian concepts?
7. While we admit that there are limitations, is it not also true that God can break through at any level regardless of limitations or lack of maturity?
8. For the Christian, is it not true that there is also revealed truth as well as discovered truth?
9. Is it not true that <u>incomplete knowledge</u> does not preclude the value of <u>partial knowledge</u>?
10. Is it necessary to know Truth perfectly in order to know that Truth?
11. How many adults understand <u>fully</u> what God has done in us?
12. Should we not let children respond <u>on their level</u> to

Christian truth because it is the heart that counts more than the head?

13. Should we not give children the data to work with so they can make adjustments (equilibration) in life? Should we not let children develop what they have now and add to it at later development?

The study of biblical terms in the light of their original meanings might throw some light on the nature of Christian learning:

1. The Hebrew LAMAD stresses application beyond factual knowledge.
2. The Hebrew word for "come to know" (Job 32:7) shows that experience teaches.
3. The Greek work for teaching (Luke 11:1) indicates that one needs to be "shown how" to pray.
4. "Do and teach" are often combined (Matt. 5:19; Acts 1:1).
5. The Greek word for child learning (Acts 7:22; 22:3) means bringing up, not merely information. This implies also discipline and correction (I Cor. 11:32).
6. The word for "know" refers to fruitage (Matt. 12:33); includes also the idea of knowing a person, a relational word, not theory (Matt. 25:12).
7. We learn from following a model (Matt 25:12 – Jesus) – word example.
8. Jesus said, "follow me" – this includes attitudes and values, as well as acts.
9. Deut. 6:4-6 – parents model, teaching in home relationships.
10. Learning is not merely cognitive, but implies a personal knowledge of and relation to God (Matt. 16:16; Rom. 8:19).

2. Liberal Religious Education Views. Among liberals, particularly among those who take an immanence position in the matter of revelation, there has been a tendency to follow the findings

of secular psychology on the matter of learning. To them there is no supernatural aspect to learning.

Among naturalistic liberals Sophia Fahs finds a theory of learning in what she terms "natural beginnings in children's curiosities."[2] This is equated with the "urge to learn the truth." This is based on a continuous search for self. The questioning method becomes prominent in this view.

For social liberals George Coe equates the learning process with the achievement of character. Using the "democracy of God" as the standard for social culture, the task of Christian education is to produce people who are devoted to social ideals and who will "outrun" the conventional social code, and who will effect social reform.[3] The Dewey principle of learning by doing is fully embraced as the proper learning theory, doing based on the social ideal.

3. Views of Integrationists. In contrast to seeking a basis for learning theory in psychology and sociology, Christian educators today are turning to theology and the Bible to find such a theory. Boehlke has pointed out this trend and others as follows:

When faced with the problem of dealing with learning theory and theology, Christian educators have taken their stance chiefly on four main positions: (a) The process of learning in Christian nurture has been considered independently of learning theory; (b) Learning theory has been held to be compatible with theology and consequently valid for Christian nurture; (c) Learning theory has been held to be so lacking in refinement as to make a legitimate choice from among competing theories impossible; (d) Questions have been raised about the theological validity of learning theory for all the concerns of Christian nurture.[4]

Among those stressing a psychological approach, Reuel Howe stresses the importance of acceptance. Man's greatest need is to find "oneness."[5] Man must find a new relationship with God. Learning takes place in personal encounter with God rather than through transmission of words. Here is a theological basis for learning.

142

Among those stressing relationship theology, Randolph C. Miller accepts current learning theory centering in reinforcement and finds this appropriate for Christian nurture.[6] Learning involves the elements of drive, cue, response, and reinforcement. Drive is related to motivation, cue equated with stimulus, response issues in thought or act, and reinforcement depends upon reward or satisfaction. The latter is most important, for without reward there is no learning. It should be pointed out here that something more than a psychological approach is needed to develop a learning theory on theological and biblical grounds.

4. <u>Traditional Views</u>. Traditional views of revelation and learning bring God into the learning process. Among those stressing church education, Wesner Fallaw says that "learning-theory and the grace of God must be considered together, at least when the problem of spiritual instruction is considered."[7] This means that God acts in us. It takes the fruit of the Spirit to effect learning in us. To accomplish this requires the community of the church, for he says further, "to nurture in the faith depends on growth in grace and the church is requisite for this growth."[8] Such learning issues in changes in a person's values and conduct according to the pattern of Christlikeness.

Among neo-orthodox advocates, Iris Cully stresses a learning theory based on life-centered experiences issuing in participation, becoming involved in the historic events of the Bible. Such participation leads to recognition of God's very presence to which man responds in faith and this leads to commitment and communicating the faith.[9]

In looking back over the survey of the status of learning theory among church educators, several generalizations are evident. Some of them merely use one or more theories and throw them into a Christian frame of reference. Others pick one or more theories and seek improvement of them in the light of theological insights. Still others ignore the entire field of learning theory. A few adopt outright the findings of educational psychologists on this matter. For example, Jesse Ziegler seems to equate learning in religion with that of all or any other type of learning. Differences are recognized in content but educational essentials are the same.

It is apparent also that contemporary learning theory neglects to consider fully the fact that man is a religious and spiritual being. Learning, therefore, is not to be understood fully from the standpoint of biology and sociology but also and primarily on man created in the image of God. Because many of the theories of learning are anti-theistic in their concept of man, they are also anti-theistic in their description and explanation of learning.

It does appear, however, that within the vast field of divine revelation and Christian education it would be possible to discover theological implications for learning theory and curriculum construction. Is it not possible to build a theory based on Scripture and the supernatural work of the Holy Spirit? It is encouraging that one finds a contemporary emphasis among neo-orthodox Christian educators to do this.

5. <u>Revelational Concepts of Learning</u>. Among evangelical Christian educators one does not find a great deal of published material on learning theory. Lois Lebar places learning theory in the context of the pupil's large place in the teaching-learning process.[10] There must be self-activity on the part of the pupil in learning. The role of the teacher is to help the pupil do his own learning. She describes learning as an inner process seated in personal needs. Pupils must see in the Word the source of having these needs met. This provides proper motivation. Learning is also an active process, therefore, the pupil must practice what he hears and receives. Observation here indicates that the treatment is more of a description of the characteristics of learning than it is an analysis of the learning process itself. What happens in the actual process of learning is not fully indicated.

The largest treatment of this subject from an evangelical point of view was given by Cornelius Jaarsma. He described his theory as a Christian anthropological view of learning.[11] Learning theory is here based on a concept of human nature. Man is viewed as created in the image of God in contrast to other views which picture man as a biological or social organism. As a mere social being man learns by reasoning and creative experience. In the Christian view man is not to be fully described in his psychophysical structure but rather in his spiritual being. In the light of this, learning is a phase of human development which issues in personality formation. It is a self-active process of the person who explores reality perceptively, sees meaning in it, and assimilates the truth of God into his being in order to reach maturity in the stature of Christ. The person, as a spiritual being, is rational, moral, social, esthetic, free and responsible. He has a "development urge" toward maturity created in him by God. Learning is the means by which this urge comes to fruition at each stage of development.

In the light of the nature of man's being, Jaarsma defines learning as follows:

Learning is the process by which the I comes into conscious control of the self in his interacting with the environment. In and through the psychosomatic the I or person is constantly interacting with the environment. In the dimensions of his personality, changes occur which the I integrates in the whole-person-in-life. These changes become a permanent ingredient of the total personality as the person commits himself to them.[12]

The process of learning on this basis is further indicated by Jaarsma in the following way:

As Christians we remind ourselves of the fact that a child is a religious being and that human learning as we described it is the learning process of a religious being. The Scriptures tell us and we see it evidenced in human life, that the religious being, being made in the image of God, finds his final and deepest security in what he feels to be true. Notice that we say what he feels to be true. This is said advisedly. As a rational-moral-social-esthetic-free-responsible person the learner merges with a situation in understanding. As he forms concepts truth is disclosed to him which he relates to himself. It is a primary need of every learner to commit himself to truth when he can embrace it as relevant to himself. Truth understood in relation to felt needs cultivates a feeling-tone of identity, of being one-with. Truth felt is accepted as that to which one surrenders for control. It is in this surrender that one's personality is formed.[13]

145

The writer finds himself very largely in general agreement with Jaarsma and Lebar. In the material which follows we hope to give further illustrations of learning from an evangelical standpoint and with particular emphasis on describing what actually takes place in learning. To begin with it is recognized that learning is a dynamic and very complex thing. Perhaps it is really not possible to understand fully how it actually takes place.

6. <u>A Suggested Revelational Concept of Learning</u>. Since man is a religious being and a spiritual being, the Christian concept of learning begins at this point. The Christian is not truly and fully educated until he experiences God. Learning to the Christian is not narrowly conceived in intellectual terms, change, or adjustment, but it embraces all of these and much more -- regeneration by the Spirit of God.

The Christian insists on the importance of certain spiritual factors in the learning process. These include the capacities of the regenerated heart-life of pupils, the Person and work of the Holy Spirit, Who is the Spirit of Truth, the power of the Word of God, and the spiritual affinities of the nature of man to respond to the wooings of the Spirit and divine truth. Furthermore, the power of faith provides a way for truth and personality to meet most effectively. The more frequently one dwells upon an object by faith, the more he feels its power.

The Bible does not neglect the subjects of teaching and learning. One illustration of this is found in Psalm 119:11,25-27,33-45. Verse 11 indicates the inward quality of learning. The Word motivates mean from within, beginning at verse 25 the quickening quality and effect of the Word is revealed. This shows that Christian learning begins with the quality of spiritual life imparted by God to the soul. Verse 26 places emphasis on the necessity of information, "Teach me thy statutes." This is followed by understanding (verse 27). Understanding leads to verbalization, "So shall I talk of thy wondrous works." Verses 33-40 seem to imply a process in learning. Verse 33 says, "Teach" -- here is the factual basis of knowledge which begins in storing up information in the memory. Verse 34 shows, however, that understanding is needed to keep the law. The goal is

146

"observe it with my whole heart." The whole person is involved. Verse 35 shows how such learning issues in life application. "Make me to go in the path of thy commandments; for therein do I delight." Emphasis on "delight" shows the place that love for truth plays in the learning process. Such love results in being "inclined unto thy testimonies" (verse 36), motivating desire, and a "quickening" for the life process. It also issues in establishment of character and righteous living (verses 38-40).

Proverbs 2:1-5 reveals the attitudes of the true seeker after knowledge. Learners must be <u>receptive</u> by "receiving my words." They must be <u>retentive</u> by "hiding my commandments with thee." They must be <u>attentive</u> by "inclining their ear." Learners must be <u>applicative</u> by "applying thine heart." They should be <u>supplicative</u> by "crying after knowledge and lifting up the voice for understanding." They must be <u>active</u> in seeking knowledge "as silver and searching for her as for hid treasures." <u>Results</u> are to be evident when the learner "understands the fear (reverence) of the Lord and finds the knowledge of God."

Learning to the Christian is more than obtaining factual knowledge. Learning is living (Matt. 28:19-20; 2 Tim. 3:16,17; Acts 17:6). While factual learning and intellectual skills are important they are secondary to the development of attitudes, interests and purposes. The true mark of a person is to be found in conduct (James 3:13).

True education and learning take place when truth is understood in the mind, not by mere mental assent of repetition (Acts 8:30-35). It must be believed in the heart (the total person) (Acts 8:37; Rom. 10:9,10), and then utilized in life, or adopted by the will (Acts 8:38; Prov. 3:6).

Learning depends on objectives, giving pupils a sense of direction. We see this in Deuteronomy 6 where parents are admonished to instruct their child as they walk and talk.

Learning depends on readiness. We see this in the Corinthian letters where Paul talks about approaching natural, carnal and spiritual people in different ways because they are either ready or not ready.

Learning depends on meeting individual needs and differences

147

in a wide variety of ways. God used a diversity of ways of speaking (Heb. 1:1,2). Jesus used a wide variety of methods and situations in teaching people.

With such observations serving as a biblical and theological basis for a Christian theory of learning, we are able to turn our attention now to the problem of how learning actually takes place. An attempt will be made to look at this from physiological and psychological viewpoints. To facilitate our thinking on these matters reference is made to the chart below.

LEARNING PROCESS
Perception -- Conception -- Application

(1) Physical	(2) Phases	(3) Process
Perception	I. Observation of Phenomena (whole man) Facts - Memory	Mental Attention - Interest
Concepts	II. Organization of observations 1. Comprehension 2. Understanding 3. Conceptualizing 4. Expression 5. Verbalization	Emotional Needs in thinking and living
Reasoning	III. Application of thinking 1. Processes 2. Reasoning 3. Evaluations 4. Convictions	
Living	IV. Restructuring of Relationships 1. Wisdom 2. Applications	Volitional Will Self-activity
	V. Catalytic Agent Work of the Holy Spirit	Heart and Action Wisdom Application

148

Supplying conviction for sin, enlightenment, illumination, power for growth, fruit and maturation in character.

The physiological aspects of learning have been widely studied by educational psychologists. Christian educators can accept many of the findings of scientific psychology on the physiological basis of learning. They will insist, however, that beyond the physical nervous system lies the soul or spirit, the I, which is responsible for conscious responses. These data reveal that learning begins with perception. God has made the mind with the ability to perceive. In this process, pictured in Column (1) in the chart above, mental data are received over the neural system into the brain and subsequently into the mind which is in the brain but separate from the brain. Fastening upon these data the mind has the God-given capacity to see signs, patterns, clues in his perceptual field of experience and to comprehend them, then to turn conscious perceptions into concepts or ideas. This process results in comprehension and understanding which in turn leads to significance. While it is observed that certain chemical results take place in the brain at this point, such chemical results do not make learning possible as concluded by mechanistic psychologists. A higher level of thought process takes place in the mind when concepts are arranged, compared, analyzed and judged through a process of advanced thinking or reasoning. Judgments and discriminations are then made possible and resulting knowledge is used in daily living.

In looking at this process psychologically and making an appraisal of it, one seems to see some phases of learning through which the mind travels in the learning process. Refer to Column (2) in the chart above. This is not to say, however, that there are "steps" so-called to learning. The dynamic quality of learning itself precludes that possibility. There is no such sequential scale to mental processes known. It does appear, however, that learning develops at lower and upper levels of quality.

Psychologically speaking, the first phase is that of the observation of phenomena, involving the perception and appropriation of the facts of knowledge to be stored in the memory. This is the lowest level of learning, important but limited. At a higher level of learning is that of the organization in the mind of the observations and perceptions supplied in the appropriation of factual knowledge, involving comprehension and understanding of the concepts present. The learner here conceptualizes in a perceptual field. When one is able to express such thoughts and ideas verbally, to converse about his understandings, this leads to self-activity, a still higher level of learning. Ideas are developed by conceptualizing. A third phase, still higher than the first two mentioned, involves applications of thinking processes. Here we have reached the level of reasoning, a very dynamic and complex phase of the process of learning. This phase involves the acquisition and classification of data related to observations previously perceived. It involves reflective thinking by which evaluations and discriminations are made. It should result in "creative" thinking which involves the point to which the mind has come in the establishment of personal convictions which are original and the use of insight by which possible applications are envisaged and innovations are conceived. At this point, perhaps, is where love for truth motivates the person to persevere in the acquisition and understanding of truth and knowledge in their relationships. Here is where change takes place, not only in the thinking, feeling, and choosing of the individual, but also in the person himself. The I himself is modified in basic character and condition. As a result of all of this, the mind reaches the point of wisdom by means of which a total restructuring of relationships is achieved. Such applications of knowledge and thought processes are made to the point where rather permanent changes affect thinking, feeling, and conduct. Truth in this way is related to self, surrendered to by the self, and thereby a control factor is instituted into personality. Personality formation thus becomes a reality. When this point is reached, the learner can make fullest applications of the data, which came originally to him in perception, to life situations. In all of this complex process the Holy Spirit is present, working as a "divine catalyst," performing His work of conviction, enlightenment, illumination, anointing, deepening, developing, and molding human personality toward maturity into the image of Jesus Christ.

Column (3) in the learning chart above calls attention to the fact that learning involves the whole man. Because the Christian point of view is the whole-person-in-life, learning is not confined merely to "mental" processes. Instead, other factors are present. These include purpose, maturation, emotions, motivation, understanding, apperception, individual differences, and the pupil's attitudes. Certain external factors also affect learning directly, such as class spirit, class size, building and equipment, and others. These factors are descriptive of an integral phase of learning termed "concomitant learning," for while formally planned activities are in progress in the teaching-learning situation, the pupil is learning other attitudes and ideas related indirectly to the situation.

In reaching the mind with truth, the learning process begins with the achievement of attention and interest on the part of the pupil. Having been motivated, the pupil must discipline thought processes in an effort to grasp the mental data provided. Here is where the critical moment in teaching is revealed. Unless attention and interest can be created and maintained, true learning cannot take place, nor can it be perpetuated. The novelty and drawing power of new experiences and knowledge should be attractive to the learner. Beyond this lie the emotional aspects to be involved. The pupil must come to see the value of what is to be learned. He must develop a "feeling tone." He must recognize that his needs are being met and that satisfaction is being realized as a result. Here is where love for the truth plays such a great part, for it leads to anticipation for further learning and is the first step which leads to surrender to the truths perceived. In fact "love for truth" motivates the mind to discipline itself to perpetuate thought processes involved. The learner must have a sense of expectancy and anticipation as he looks ahead.

Beyond the mental and emotional lies that of the will. There must be a choice; either acceptance or rejection of the truth must be made. The will must surrender to truth recognized and cherished as valuable. This surrender must be self-active, not imposed. When this point is reached and the total person is involved, truth is said to be accepted in the "heart," the total person. Such surrender leads both to allegiance and obedience, to commitment. In turn, this leads to a sense of personal identity to truth. This institutes control into the situation and thereby Christian personality is developed. When applications of truth are made to daily living, the point of wisdom has been reached. This changes one's mode of living. Again, all of this takes place in the context of the presence and work of the Holy Spirit Who brings conviction, enlightenment, illumination, and anointing to the mind and heart. He continues this work in intellectual growth and development and thus has a large part in accomplishing the fruit desired.

While it is recognized that the learning process is essentially the same in any given situation, we also recognize what might be termed "kinds" of learning. Cognitive learning is primarily mental in character and largely restricted to "knowing." There is social learning based largely on a feeling of acceptance and social competence, and a sense of "one-ness" with fellow Christians. Christian fellowship (koinonia) is important here. There is emotional learning in which the value of the truth under consideration is felt. Manual learning involves skills and body functions, mechanical and motor in character.

While there are recognized differences between adult and child learning, perhaps there is not so much a difference in character as it is in degree. Two evidences for this possibility might be cited. L. Harold DeWolf stresses a God-centered approach to Christian education in terms of theology; faith in God is the central focus. This is not confined to a set of beliefs but has direct implications for both purpose and method. He says,

> *If for life that is life indeed and for life eternal all are dependent upon all that God has done for us in Christ, then the whole of God's gracious work is for all and all are in need of it. There are no exceptions. But note that this is very different from saying that all the ideas or words of the message are for all ages . . . . The whole range of the reality of God's dealings with men needs to be brought to all, even little children.*[14]

Thus, DeWolf feels that the whole message must be taught at all levels of personality development and his whole book is based on this premise.

A second trend to be noted is that of the theories of Jerome S. Bruner.

> *We begin with the hypothesis that any subject can be taught effectively in some intellectually honest form to any child at any state of development. It is a bold hypothesis and an essential one in thinking about the nature of a curriculum. No evidence exists to contradict it; considerable evidence is being amassed that supports it...research on the intellectual development of the child highlights the fact that at each stage of development the child has a characteristic way of viewing the world and explaining it to himself. The task of teaching a subject to a child at any particular age is one of representing the structure of that subject in terms of the child's way of viewing things. The task can be thought of as one of translation. The general hypothesis that has just been stated is premised on the considered judgment that any idea can be represented honestly and usefully in the thought forms of children of school age, and that these first representations can later be made more powerful and precise the more easily by virtue of this early learning.[15]*

The implications of this position are tremendous and seem to fit into the Christian frame of reference. Since God's revelation and redemption are for all men, certainly there must be enough flexibility and possibility within the work of the Holy Spirit to accomplish His work of revelation and redemption at any stage of personality development. To accomplish this a great deal of study and work will be needed to produce a learning theory and curriculum materials to achieve this exciting possibility.

The approach to learning involves what psychologists call "the learning set." For children this involves more than rote memory. Their learning set involves concrete reality, things they can see, smell, touch, taste, and hear. Experiences involving these factors are meaningful to them and go beyond rote memory. Teaching of concepts which related to these concrete experiences make for meaningful learning to children because they relate new experiences to things they already know. The more stimulating their perceptual field is based on these concrete experiences, the more meaningful their learning is, so teachers should provide their students with experiences through which they enlarge their scheme of reality. If each subject matter discipline is handled in this way, learning can become meaningful to students. These principles apply at all levels of student life and development.

Christian educators must recognize the presence of certain barriers to learning. A common one is that of language. If the language used in the teaching-learning process is not common to both teacher and learner, verbalism becomes a real barrier. The common men heard Jesus gladly because they could understand Him. Big ideas do not necessarily need big words and long involved sentences for their expression. Time can be a barrier, particularly to children. By means of visuals, particularly that of a time-line, the concept of time can be communicated more clearly. The same is true of spatial relationships. This might call for the use of three-dimensional maps for children. The strange customs in the Bible need to be clearly explained to people in our culture. Tradition, or the way things have always been done in the past, may prove to be a barrier to some people.

The Apostle Paul refers to a particular barrier in making reference to the carnal mind and original sin. To the Corinthian church he pointed out three classes of people to be dealt with in the church. He referred to spiritually minded people. These people find it much easier to accept, believe and live spiritual truths because they are spiritually minded. A second class he referred to as "the natural man," who finds himself incapable of receiving spiritual truths because he is naturally minded, even to the point of completely rejecting spiritually projected truths. The third group of people he referred to as carnally minded people, or "babes in Christ." These are very immature Christian people who, because of being dominated by selfishness and self-will, often find it difficult to accept, understand and live spiritual truth. They are often insensitive to God's truth and are like spiritual babies in that they are too immature to handle spiritual revelation. The use of much prayer, patience and practical application of truth to daily living is necessary for all these people (I Cor. 2).

F. The Teaching Process

1. Three Approaches. A study of the literature on teaching reveals three general approaches to the process of teaching: (1) "pouring in", (2) "drawing out", and (3) "bringing up". The concept of pouring in implies that the mind is conceived as a receptacle into which information is poured by the teacher. Drawing out seems to indicate that the function of teaching is to elicit self-active responses from pupils, to motivate rather than to inform. In Christian education the third concept -- bringing up -- is the most satisfactory one. This seems to be in keeping with Paul's advice to the Ephesian church when he exhorted them to bring up children in the fear and admonition of the Lord (Eph. 6:4). The idea here is to nourish.

Great demands are placed on the teacher today. He is not only to impart knowledge, but he is also expected to inculcate attitudes, develop essential skills, strengthen loyalties, promote allegiance to our way of life, and reinforce moral codes. The Christian teacher is expected to do all of this and cultivate deeper spiritual life as well.

2. Secular Contributions. As one studies the wide variety of approaches to teaching advocated by secular educators he is struck with their conclusion that there is no easy way to teach, no one best way to teach. Scores of research studies have been made which indicate the truth of this. For example, Joyce and Weil in their Models of Teaching (Prentice Hall, 1972) identified at least eighty different schools and theories of thought along this line. This is true because teaching is not static, but a dynamic process, therefore, there are many "good ways" to teach. There seems to be no single teaching strategy which can possibly accomplish all the goals set up.

The evidence from research shows some of the following characteristics of teaching models:

1. There is very little difference in the outcomes of various teaching models.
2. There is very little to support the identification of a single reliable, multipurpose teaching strategy as best.
3. It is hard to measure exactly education outcomes, particularly those of emotion, personality development, creativity, and even intellectual development.
4. There is a rich variety of teaching models.
5. We need to be sensitive to student needs and development.

From such evidence one might also conclude that educational procedures come out of one's view of man. Such a view will determine what to teach and how to teach.

In surveying the many models of teaching Joyce and Weil have classified them into four general families of models.[16] The paradigms of teaching which result from their research appear as follows in outline form:

I. The Social Interaction Model
   A. Philosophy
      1. Priority -- social relationships
      2. Two sub-families
         a. Concepts of society
         b. Concepts of interpersonal relationships
      3. Leaders
         Dewey; Kilpatrick; Counts; Bodie
   B. Educational Theory
      1. Social concept stresses the production of a democratic society
      2. Interpersonal relation stresses skills of group processes in solving social problems and issues
   C. The Role of the Teacher
      Counselor, consultant, critic
   D. Process
      Problems, exploration, options, possible solutions

II. Information - Processing Model
  A. Philosophy
     1. Aim -- skills in data gathering
     2. Goal -- integrated self, good thinker
     3. Concept of attainment and use
  B. Leaders
     1. Bruner; Taba; Suchman; Schwab
     2. Piaget; Sigel; Sullivan
  C. Educational Theory
     1. Purpose -- better thinkers
     2. Inductive processes, group enquiry,
        concept attainment, science enquiry,
        developmentalism (Piaget)
     3. Assimilation accommodation
  D. Role of the Teacher
     Guide, resource person
  E. Process
     1. Confront with problem
     2. Guided enquiry
     3. Present options
     4. Confront with new situations
  F. Kohlberg's Moral Development Strategy
     1. Based on Piaget's work; includes six levels
        of moral development
     2. Leader moves from egocentricity,
        where decisions are based on personal wants
        and avoidance of punishment on the other
     3. Then moves through a stage of rules and
        authority to the highest level of living
        by principle
     4. Teaching strategy is to expose the learner to
        conflicting situations and introducing him to
        new levels of reaction to them; the teacher
        serves here as a guide
III. Personality Development Model
  A. Philosophy
     1. Personality development necessary to

social adjustment
2. Goal -- self-development and productivity
   in the environment
B. Leaders
   1. Carl Rogers -- non-directive teaching
   2. William Glasser -- classroom meetings
   3. J.J. Gordon -- synectics (creativity)
   4. William Schultz -- awareness training
C. Education Theory
   1. Democratic processes
   2. Small groups
   3. Interpersonal relationships
D. Role of the Teacher
   Counselor; group leader; facilitator
E. Processes
   1. Freedom to learn
   2. Small group work
   3. Open discussion
   4. Interpersonal relationship activities
   5. Creativity exercises

IV. Behavior Modification Model
A. Philosophy
   1. Behavior changes by means of manipulative
      reinforcement through operant conditioning
   2. Goal -- to change external behavior in terms
      of visible outcomes resulting in reinforcement
B. Leader -- B.F. Skinner
C. Educational Theory
   1. Stimulus -- response -- reinforcement
   2. Behavior control under the control of
      subject matter stimulus
D. Role of the Teacher
   Initiator; controller
E. Process
   1. Operant conditioning
   2. Programmed instruction

3. <u>Church Educator Views</u>. Parallels to the above secular models of teaching can be seen in the writings of church educators. The information processing model is seen best in the early traditional approaches and in some liberal approaches in Christian education circles. The primary aim of this approach is to improve the teaching-learning process. The paradigm resulting looks like the following:

Information Processing Model

<u>Purpose</u> – the transmission of factual knowledge of Christianity, concept development, the creation of skillful Christians

<u>Teacher</u> – structurer of the learning situation

<u>Teaching</u> – the process is the same as for any other kind of instruction, presentation of factual data

<u>Learner</u> – listener, Christian thinker

<u>Content</u> – the Christian faith

<u>Curriculum</u> – Christian truth is organized in a school setting to meet the developmental, personal needs and interests

Closely related to this model is that of one based on the ability to make <u>skillful interpretation</u> of data. In this model the teacher becomes a guide to the learner as he seeks to interpret Christian faith and experience. Contemporary life and experiences are interpreted in the light of the Christian faith.

Social-Cultural Model

The socialization-cultural model stresses the body-life concept, appealing to the total congregation as the setting for education. The Christian faith is communicated through the life of the church in this model. The paradigm looks like the following:

<u>Purpose</u> – transmission of the Christian life-style

<u>Teacher</u> – minister to all, counselor, consultant, guide

Teaching – stresses the community of the church, using interpersonal relations, small groups, sensitivity methods, problem-solving, seeking solutions to the contemporary social problems

Content – the Christian faith in relation to the life of the church

Learner – active participant in the social process

Curriculum – the Christian community (the church), worship, ritual, Christian answers to social concerns

Personality Development Model

The personality development model is brought into church education circles with the emphasis on spiritual development. Here spiritual maturity is the goal. The paradigm might take the following form:

Purpose – spiritual growth toward Christian maturity

Teacher – a spiritual guide, counselor, facilitator

Teaching – democratic processes, meeting life's crises and issues in the light of the Christian faith

Content – total life process, warm relationships

Learner – needs freedom to learn and grow, participant

Curriculum – encounter groups, life issues, Christian solution to life's problems, self-realization, standards of behavior, creative experiences

In some circles the current "liberation" movement based on "liberation theology" is influential. The position taken here is that spiritual maturity can take place best through a teaching-learning process which focuses on cultural reflection on modern life-styles in the light of the Christian life-style. Deep involvement in the issues of social justice and the transformation of society is required in this model.

The Behavior Modification Model does not find large acceptance in church educational circles because of its humanistic philosophy. The effects, however, can be seen in the use of

160

programmed instruction and the setting of objectives in terms of Christian behavior.

It is necessary at this point to pause and take a look at another late development in secular education which has made impressions on Christian education in some circles. This might be termed a three-component teaching model incorporated into a systems approach. The instructional design involves (1) instructional objectives, (2) instructional activities, and (3) performance assessment. Subject matter and learning activities become the general goal rather than the means to achieve clearly the stated objectives.

The instructional objectives component is based on behavioristic psychology, a concept which declares that learning results from experiencing a change of behavior that can be described in terms of observable performance. Thus, usable objectives must state the intended outcome in terms of terminal behavior, behavior which follows instruction. The writings of Robert F. Mager reflect this performance philosophy. His most popular works include Preparing Instructional Objectives (Fearson, 1962), Analyzing Performance Problems (Fearson, 1970), and Goal Analysis (Fearson, 1972).

Admittedly, there is value in stating objectives in terms of performance, for objectives are clear to the student and measurable for the teacher. Good teaching, however, is not always dependent on behavioristic terms. Certain intangibles and spiritual outcomes to both teaching and learning cannot be captured in this way. Many things are learned spontaneously and in interpersonal relationships in the classroom. It is often difficult for Bible teachers, for example, to list spiritual outcomes in terms of observable behavior. How can feelings, appreciations and even the work of the Holy Spirit be measured in this way? On the other hand, when it comes to the development of certain skills then one is on much firmer ground in measuring what has happened.

The influence of the systems approach to education is resolved in the trend in some circles toward utilizing the total church congregation as a school of Christian faith and living. Here the congregation engages in theological reflection and corporate planning

161

to the end that the body-life of the church is utilized in accomplishing the ends of the Christian faith. The paradigm might take the following form:

A Systems Approach Model

<u>Purpose</u> – to develop the total congregation into a true and faithful Christian community

<u>Teacher</u> – guide, facilitator, counselor

<u>Teaching</u> – the total life and ministry of the church congregation is used to model and communicate the faith

<u>Content</u> – the life and work of the church

<u>Learner</u> – the congregation itself as a whole cooperating to practice vital Christianity

<u>Curriculum</u> – evaluation of total program, define the mission of the church, planning educational strategies to accomplish the goals of the church

Among naturalistic liberals Sophia Fahs advocates an approach to teaching based on the "child's natural schedule and development." The method is basically to answer questions about life which children raise naturally out of wonderment. Among social liberals the approach will be very similar except that the social and cultural heritage in the democratic setting are used to motivate pupils. The position here referred to follows the drawing out method very largely.

Among neo-orthodox advocates Iris Cully thinks of the teacher as an agent who mediates the gospel.[17] The content of this teaching is the basic message, the <u>kerygma</u>, and its resultant teachings, the <u>didache</u>. The teacher is to both lead and guide the pupils into this faith. He will not, however, impose this knowledge on the pupil.

Among those stressing relationship theology, Miller thinks of teaching as "the way in which the learner is led to see the relevance of subject matter to the problems of his own life."[18] The function of teaching in this view is to get the student to think and use Christian resources to solve life's problems. There must be pupil acceptance and love on the part of the teacher. The approach is life-centered and the primary emphasis is on pupil development rather than content mastery.

Among psychologists Sherrill stresses the concept of encounter and at the heart of this is communication, two-way communication.[19] The teaching process is one of interaction. An effort must be made to help pupils "participate" in what the people of the Bible saw, felt and did. Such involvement leads to personal identification with them and the truth.

Among those stressing the centrality of the Church in Christian education, one would expect teaching to take the form of group sharing so that the koinonia idea might be practiced.

4. <u>An Evangelical and Revelational Approach</u>. As an Evangelical, Lois Lebar says:

> *Teaching then is guiding and declaring, guiding pupils and declaring truth. A real teacher does not hesitate to declare truth in a context of guidance. But if he only declares, he becomes a preacher. A teacher must be skilled in guiding, direction, helping pupils in their learning.[20]*

Generally speaking, in Christian education the teaching process must follow the pattern of the learning process. Psychological laws provide assistance to the teacher in his task. Self-activity demands that the teacher control the activity of the learner in the right direction. Motivation and interest demand interesting, attractive lessons. Apperception calls for materials and stimuli to be adapted to the experience and mental set of the learners. Individual difference must be recognized. Finally, the principle of socialization requires that all learning responses be developed in natural social settings and that the environment be conductive to developing good attitudes.

The biblical pattern for teaching and learning is learn, then do. Learn through new life and new knowledge (Eph. 2,3), and then do by walking worthily (Eph. 4:1).

To accomplish these factors, Christian education involves a

teacher-pupil subject relationship. The teacher introduces, interests, explains, and encourages (John 4:7,14). The pupil investigates, appreciates, assimilates, and applies (John 4:15). The subject is the truth around which this interaction revolves (John 4:26).

The pattern which teaching takes involves an <u>introduction</u> to truth which motivates pupil investigation (Mark 4:7), <u>interpretation</u> which utilizes the principle of apperception (known to unknown) in handling spiritual truth (Mark 4:10-14), and <u>integration</u> which assimilates new truth into the heart and life (Mark 4:29).

The process of instruction involves more than listening, telling and showing. It requires <u>participation</u> (Matt. 22:19). A wide variety of techniques in communication are utilized by the Christian worker (Matt. 5:1; 21:28). <u>Application</u> to life is the climax of the whole process (Matt. 22:21,36-40). This kind of teaching demands that the whole process of teaching and learning be directed toward the creation of a Christian life-style as the goal to be achieved. It also requires close personal interrelationships between teachers and pupils in the context of love.

Any study of teaching theory by Christians must not only note the developments in the secular world but also must take seriously the methods of Jesus and the Apostle Paul. Some of the outstanding characteristics of Jesus' teaching methods would include the following principles and practices:

1. He taught with authority.
2. He allowed for individual freedom in exploring and discovery of truth.
3. He understood what was in man and how to deal with what He saw in man.
4. He employed a wide variety of teaching methods.
5. He used informal conversation with individuals and groups.
6. He used questions, answers, dialogue, story-telling, proverbs, discussion, demonstrations, life experiences, assignments, and many learning activities.
7. He used familiar things to teach new things (apperception).

8. He was aware of the needs of those He taught.
9. He involved people in the teaching-learning process.
10. He encouraged people to practice what He taught.
11. He employed visual aids.
12. He assigned projects to be performed.

Bolton and Smith made an extensive study of the four gospels and discovered at least fifty types of learning activities that Jesus used.[21] The reader is urged to secure some of the books devoted to the subject of "Jesus, the Master Teacher" to pursue further the way Jesus taught.

David L. Bartlett made an excellent analysis of Paul's teaching theory and practice in his Paul's Vision for the Teaching Church (Judson, 1977), Chapter 3. He indicated four ways that Paul taught: (1) by tradition, (2) by proclamation, (3) by exhortation, and (4) by imitation. The writer lists some of the suggestions Bartlett made for each one of these categories:

A. Paul's use of Tradition -- remember it
  1. The Gospel comes from God
     (Gal. 1:11-12; I Cor. 11:23-25)
  2. The Content of the Gospel (I Cor. 15:3-7)
  3. The church is to remember (I Cor. 11:23-25)
B. Paul's use of Proclamation -- hear it
  1. Preaching and witnessing (I Cor. 1:21-25)
  2. What to proclaim -- Jesus Christ and Him crucified
  3. How to proclaim (I Cor. 2:1-5) -- good communication
  4. Goal of proclamation (Gal. 3:2) -- faith
C. Paul's use of Exhortation -- obey it
  1. Ethical exhortation (Rom. 12:1-2; 6:17,18,22)
  2. Transformation -- urgency -- relationship
  3. Christian life-style (Rom. 12:3-21; 13:1-14;14:1-23)
  4. Reasons why
    (1) Because Jesus taught us (I Cor. 7:10-11)
    (2) Because of theological principles
      (I Cor. 8:8-9; Rom. 14:5-9)

      (3) Because of common sense (I Cor. 7:25; 6:12)
D. Paul's use of Imitation -- imitate it
    1. Follow my example (model) (I Cor. 10:31-11:1)
    2. Some elements of imitation
        (1) Loving kindness (I Cor. 4:14-16)
        (2) Love for fellowmen (I Cor. 10:31-11:1)
        (3) Learn to suffer (I Thess. 1:6-7)
    3. Personal involvement with people

To this the writer adds that if one wants to see teaching methods used by the Apostle Paul, study the Book of Acts (particularly chapter 17) and his epistles.

     5. <u>Styles of Teaching</u>. In general, styles can be classified as follows: (1) traditional, (2) creative, (3) content-centered, and (4) life-centered. All of these styles are employed at one time or another by Christian educators both liberal and conservative. Perhaps the most common styles in current use are the traditional and creative ones. None, however, is to be considered more <u>Christian</u> or <u>correct</u> than others.

    Traditional or content-centered styles are based on a <u>deductive</u> approach to teaching and learning. Starting with a Bible passage, learners are involved in classroom activities which, it is hoped, will result in the application of biblical truth to life situations. It looks like the following:

Bible Passage (Teacher-presented)
↓
Classroom Activities (Learner-involvement)
↓
Life-application (Utilization of Truth)

    The process of teaching resulting from the deductive approach is a teacher-centered approach. Learners are relatively passive, sitting, listening, and watching and at times asking and answering questions. The teacher is very active, having previously studied, prepared, presented and applied the lesson. Some would view this approach as one of almost complete indoctrination and rigidity. It should be noted, however, that this approach does <u>not have to be</u> devoid of excitement, fruitage and participation. Some learners learn best with this approach because of individual differences among them. Teachers need to study and plan carefully when using this approach to get good results and a good balance between content and life-application.

The creative or life-centered style of teaching is based on a more <u>inductive</u> approach to teaching and learning and may be generally characterized as follows:

Life Situation (challenging life setting)

↓

Classroom Activities (Discovery methods)

↓

Bible Passage (apply it)

Beginning roughly with a life situation to initiate the teaching situation, learners are involved in learning activities which will lead them to a discovery of God's truth and will. This approach is more learner-centered, with the teacher serving as a guide to learning activities. This approach is based on the belief that learners learn best in a teaching situation which includes a wide variety of creative methods and group processes. Learners learn not only by listening but also through exploration, discovery, self-appropriation and assumption of responsibility. Such teaching is far more difficult than the more traditional approach, demanding far more skill, time, and preparation on the part of teachers. The two approaches might be compared as follows:

Traditional or Deductive	Creative or Inductive
1. The teacher is a teller	1. The teacher is a guide
2. The learner listens	2. The learner discovers
3. Content -- stresses facts	3. Content – stresses principles
4. Methods -- story-telling and lecture	4. Methods -- discussion, play, many activities, groupings

| 5. Physical arrangement -- in rows | 5. Physical arrangement -- wide variety, small and large groups; circle arrangements; many activities |

The inductive approach calls for restructuring organizational patterns, developing leadership skills, improving organizational units, and expanding leadership and teacher training programs.

In the deductive approach it is possible that too much emphasis might be placed on Bible memory work to the neglect of good teaching and life application of truth. In the inductive approach it is possible that too much emphasis can be placed on socialization techniques and learning methods to the neglect of Bible content. Neither approach has to work these ways, of course, if the teacher knows what to do. Good education, good Bible content and life application of truth are all possible under both of these teaching styles.

Much research took place during the 1950's and 1960's in an effort to confirm the then believed superiority of learner-centered methods over the teacher-centered methods. Dubin and Taveggia studied the data of such studies in over 140 experiments at the college level as measured by written examinations and concluded that there is no difference that amounts to anything.[22] Many other studies compared the lecture versus discussion methods have confirmed the same thing. The same can be said for small group, and discovery learning techniques. A very significant study was made by Lee S. Schulman and Evan R. Keisler who edited the book Learning by Discovery: A Critical Appraisal (Rand McNally, 1966). They surveyed 179 research studies on the strengths and weaknesses of the inductive method. There were no conclusive results from this study regarding the claimed superiority of this method. They concluded that while there are many strong claims for discovery learning made in the writings of educational psychologists few have been empirically substantiated or clearly tested by experiment.

6. Characteristics of Christian Teaching. While it may be true that there is no one best way to teach, there are certain

characteristics of any style of teaching which might be described as Christian teaching. Most certainly in any Christian teaching situation the life and light principles must be manifested. The content and life-style of Christian faith and Christian living must come together. The means by which this is accomplished is through a process of modeling, reflecting the character of the church as the body of Christ and appealing to the total person in the teaching-learning process. The teacher models in three ways: (1) by character, (2) by conduct, and (3) teaching competence.

A second characteristic of Christian teaching is that of nurturing and discipling. These take place best in the framework of modeling Christian living and learning, a spiritual culture, at its best, also characterized by love, trust and acceptance. Thus the light principle, which specializes in the instruction of divine truth, not mere verbalizations, operates within the context of living truth. Each of the members of the body of Christ supports, strengthens, and sustains one another in daily living. Here is where what the church is and does becomes practically applied in a Christian teaching-learning situation.

Henri J.M. Nouwen describes a third characteristic of Christian teaching in his Creative Ministry (Image, 1979). It is a redemptive process. To avoid the pitfalls of what he calls violent teaching listed as competition, alienation, and unilateralness, he proposes instead a redemptive kind of education. Such education, he says, is a close teacher-learner relationship characterized by evocativeness, that is, mutual motivation, devoid of competition, which issues in fear, evoking rather optimism potential. Bilateralness makes it possible for teachers and learners to learn from each other in freedom. To avoid alienation a process of actualization should take place in the classroom where preparation for the future is linked to realities of the present in daily Christian living.

Whatever style of teaching a Christian teacher employs demands a process characterized by inspiring the student through carefully designed teaching objectives, purposeful activities, and spiritual atmosphere; instructional activities -- eliciting the self-activity of the learner but which are varied, graded, and life-related;

discipling activities which denote a control factor operated in the framework of love and kindness, and, finally, evaluating procedures to determine the effectiveness of both teaching and learning.

7. A Revelational View. From an evangelical standpoint one is faced with wading through the welter of information above to determine an approach to teaching. It is possible to learn something from the wide variety of teaching models presented above; however, it is not satisfactory to take an eclectic position by merely choosing the best from such models. Instead, the evangelical Christian believes that the teaching process which has Christian characteristics can be derived from the nature of the Christian faith, the Christian church and the divine element present in the life and light principles previously discussed. From these sources it is possible to identify a teaching-learning process as a nurturing process. In this process the teacher is God's agent in teaching and learning. As a Christian he functions as a witness, a model, demonstrating the life principle in character and conduct. The light principle points to the function of the teacher as an oracle of God (I Peter 4:10-11; John 7:16-18). To accomplish these functions the teacher functions in a wide variety of ways. He may be a counselor, guide, pastor, facilitator of learning, cooperating with the Holy Spirit in the total process. In doing so he manifests love and concern for his students, giving them individual attention, acceptance, trust and honesty in close interpersonal relationships. Thus conceived, Christian teaching is a ministry. It is not concerned solely with teaching lessons, even Christian ones, but rather should be conceived as a process of teaching lessons to people. The following chart possibly pictures some of these relationships:

In such a relationship all parties in the teaching-learning situation make individual and distinctive contributions while at the same time receiving benefits, help and support from each other. The outcome for the learner will be <u>Christian nurture</u>, not merely the impartation of information or socialization of the individual, resulting in discipleship and spiritual development (Eph. 6:4). All legitimate methods can be utilized, but methods should not dominate the process. However, a good teacher will attempt to use methods best suited to students and the particular subject being taught. The paradigm resulting from this model of teaching will look as follows:

A Nurturing Model of Teaching

<u>Purpose</u> – to show God revealed in revelation
<u>Goal</u> – to reveal God
1. Individual goal -- Christlike character, maturity and Christian living and Christian service
2. Social goal -- building the Christian church and a Christian society toward the Kingdom of God
3. Prophetic goal -- the return of Jesus Christ as Lord and setting up of His Kingdom on earth

<u>Teacher</u> -- a witness, a model, God's mouthpiece, pastor, counselor, friend, leader, facilitator of learning

<u>Teaching</u> -- Combination of inductive and deductive approaches, a cooperative relationship between teacher, learner and the Holy Spirit, a wide variety of methodologies and audiovisuals -- a process of guiding learners and proclaiming the truth; a loving relationship

<u>Content</u> -- the Christian faith, Christian experience, Christian living, and Christian service; all truth is God's truth

<u>Curriculum</u> -- Bible, Christian doctrine, Christian ethics, social concerns, Christian family, worship, church history and outreach, world relations and missions, Christian service and leadership, Christian personality development, spiritual development, vocational preparation, general education, and Christian interpersonal relationships

171

To the Christian, method is the means by which the goal of Christian education is achieved. The goal, as stated above, is Christlike character. In approaching this goal, the Christian educator is concerned with two facets of approach. On the ethical side of method, moral discipline is required in accomplishing the character-goal set up. On the intellectual side of method, instruction in the truth of the Gospel is required to accomplish the goal. The term method is being used in this latter sense. The purpose of Christian methodology, therefore, is to help the learner accomplish the goals set up. Methods are the means by which this is done.

8. A Revelational Concept of Method. The revelational view of method is based on supernatural interpretation. Since God is central, all method must also center in Him. All truth is revelatory of God. He is therefore directly connected with subject matter because through subject matter God is revealed. The learner is also expected to reflect divine revelation. Educational methodology, therefore, is the manner in which the objective revelation of God in school content and the subjective revelation of God in the learner are stepped up from the non-rational level to the rational level of the person who studies. The Holy Spirit is very active also in this process. This process might be described as one of "bringing up" the learner in the things of God. Such a view does not preclude the possibility of using a wide variety of instructional procedures to accomplish this process.

Certain bodies of knowledge will be taught best by lecturing or some other method. Others can be taught inductively through discovery. Methods in themselves are wrong only if they are used improperly to teach a false philosophy. Methods of discovery learning and teaching, however, need to be directly related also to the objective body of knowledge given by God.

The selection of methods is determined by whatever aims are set up, the needs of learners, time at hand, and they should be selected carefully in the light of the teacher's best judgment as to how best to deal with the learner, subject matter and objectives.

More specifically, the process of teaching involves four phases in getting ready to teach: (1) selection of objectives, (2) preparation for teaching, including study and planning, (3) presentation of the lesson, and (4) evaluation of results. In the preparation phase emphasis is placed on individual study and planning. Study is what the teacher does primarily for himself whereas planning focuses on the teaching-learning process. The written lesson plan has many advantages because it provides a blueprint for designing the processes of teaching and learning. Such a plan will guide the teacher in the selection of lesson aims, teaching and learning procedures, focusing too on how lessons are introduced to the learner, developed and concluded. The reader is referred to many good books on the market today to show how to study and plan lessons. Age-group books also are helpful in the selection of teaching methods for children, youth and adults. There are over one hundred different methods of teaching the Bible to be found in such sources.

Not too much is available to church teachers in the field of evaluation. Certain publishing houses suggest testing and evaluation procedures in connection with their recommended teaching-learning materials. For further help in this matter the reader is referred to the writer's publication Improving Church Education (Religious Education Press, 1979).

Teaching theories and procedures should be applied according to the demands of the people being taught. While general principles of teaching and learning might apply to all age groups, it is also true that certain strategies are designed to work best with the learner as the teacher meets him in the learning situation.

The needs of learners provide clues for the planning of teaching processes for them. They need love and affection, freedom of choice and activities, trust, approval, self-esteem, and others. To meet these needs individual differences must be recognized and a wide variety of activities provided for them. To avoid the pitfalls of verbalism, learners should be taught as much as possible through "concrete experiences," and lifelike situations, and the utilization of many audiovisuals.

As a facilitator of learning the teacher should provide learners with a large number of options in learning activities, be open to questions and problems posed by them, and provide specific opportunities for them to cooperate with fellow-learners, all done in

173

a well-ordered atmosphere. Teachers, and parents too, should make every effort to make Bible truths appear to learners, particularly children, as <u>real life realities</u>, not merely ideas and words memorized. In all of this work there should be close cooperation with and relation to the home, providing parents, as teachers and learners, with all possible assistance in modeling Christianity and good teaching procedures.

G. Curriculum

1. <u>Definition</u>. A wide variety of definitions has been given to the word "curriculum". The word itself is derived from the Latin word meaning "a place of running", "a race course". In other words, curriculum is a course of study, a line of progress through a series of subjects.

In its broadest meaning, the curriculum is life-inclusive, but this is not too practical for study purposes. It can be thought of instead as that which includes all activities and experiences which are initiated or utilized by the church and school for the accomplishment of the aims of education and Christian education.

A more narrow meaning, yet commonly held, conceives of the curriculum as areas or fields of subject matter organized into learning areas. For a long time it was a real issue among educators as to whether one curriculum was inclusive of <u>all</u> that goes on under the organized activities of the school, or that it was confined merely to lesson materials. The first view is the one most acceptable today. For the Sunday school, it would include classes, worship, hymns, prayers, lesson materials both biblical and extra-biblical, the ritual, all activities, etc.

What is a Christian curriculum? The meaning of the term "Christian" will determine the answer. Education is distinctively Christian when the authority of Christ and the realization of His authority in our lives is the justification for all educational activity. All subject matter will be recognized as a revelation of His truth. All activities will be motivated by His life, will and Spirit. Whether

174

conceived in broad or narrow terms, a Christian curriculum centers in Christ. It is the medium employed by the school and home to achieve the ends of Christian education.

The curriculum is given design by the course of study. The basic facts and principles of psychological development set the stage for this design. This is all guided by the principles of the Word of God. The whole-person-in-life doing the will of God is the object of the Christian curriculum. Therefore, the curriculum may be thought of as guided experience. Properly, the Christian curriculum includes the elements of evangelism, instruction, worship, fellowship, and service.

2. <u>Liberal Religious Educator Views</u>. Among the naturalistic liberals Sophia Fahs says the curriculum materials should be based on "significant experiences in a child's natural religious growth."[23] Rather than using Bible stories for very small children, stories in harmony with the child's own significant experience are advocated. Bible stories can be instituted later as the child grows older. For Bible content she rejects the old "Story of Salvation" as held by orthodox believers and advocates a "newly interpreted" Bible, the Bible of modern critical scholarship which shows the Bible, not to be a special divine revelation, but a collection of records of human experience and what men believe about God. This demands comparative rather than authoritative study.

Social liberals take largely the same attitude toward the Bible as pictured above but would advocate structuring the curriculum toward active sociality and centered in life situations. Thus, curriculum content is to be found in present relations and interactions between persons.[24] Biblical content will be supplemented with extra-biblical materials.

3. <u>Traditional Views</u>. Neo-Orthodox advocates stress biblical content and the Bible as special divine revelation. In its interpretation, however, many of them seek to incorporate the theories of biblical criticism.

Wyckoff points out that in addition to biblical content the great themes of the Christian faith and life should be included as elements in the curriculum.[25] The person's needs and experiences serve as the organizing principle of the curriculum.

Among relationship theologians Sherrill's theory of curriculum is closely related to the way the Bible is used. He takes the psychological and existential approach that the purpose of the Bible, viewed in neo-orthodox terms, is to prepare men "to perceive God and respond to him in the present." God as Self meets man as a self.[26]

Church educators define curriculum within the context of the community of the church. Butler says that curriculum "is all the media communication and of the influences by which the Church brings itself to bear upon the individual in nurture."[27] More narrowly conceived the curriculum refers to curriculum materials, to Christian literature and the Bible.

4. <u>Evangelical and Revelational Views</u>. Turning to the evangelical viewpoint Lois Lebar defines the curriculum as

those activities in relation to authoritative content that are guided or employed by Christian leadership in order to bring pupils one step nearer to maturity in Christ. These activities imply interaction of both teachers and pupils with the Word of God.[28]

Miss Lebar has developed what is termed a Word-centered approach. The curriculum is centered in divine life Himself. The Word both Living and Written must be a part of the experience of the learner. The Living Word has the primary place and experience a secondary place.

The Bible has an essential place in education. It is both an instrument and a model. Whatever the Bible has to say about education is of significance and some use to anyone who takes seriously both education and the Bible. One of the needs in Christian education at all levels today is to examine the Bible specifically to seek models narrated and concepts expounded as a basis for today's theory and practice.

Regarding the content, it is recognized that the Bible has no formal list of educational principles and methods. In spite of this it is found possible through application of inductive principles to discover such matters within the framework of Scripture. This is particularly true when one studies the work of Jesus Christ and the Apostle Paul. In fact, some would say that the Bible is a veritable history of education.

So often the Bible has been used to illustrate educational ideologies and practices of the day. What is needed is a thorough exegetical study to discover what is the total Bible concept of education.

Because the educational theories and practices of men are constantly changing, a source of timeless quality that does not change is needed. This source is to be found in the Eternal Word of God. Christians cannot afford to accept uncritically secular sources of education. They should not have to seek man-made systems of education. The God of all knowledge is available and He is the Source of all wisdom and knowledge. He reveals to us in His Word the very nature of teaching and learning. Furthermore, the Christian has in his Bible the very best revelation of educational truth which is of the finest quality and of inestimable value. While the Bible makes no attempt to deal formally with the problems of a philosophy of education, it is possible to discover biblical truths about education, teaching and learning in Scripture, and by reasoning to organize these truths into a system of thought about education. The procedure to be followed is to draw from the biblical assumptions about life and develop therefrom a philosophy of education. In doing this, data supplied by Scripture, theology and philosophy are utilized.

As far as its essential place in education is concerned, the Bible functions in three ways. It provides, first, a philosophical function. In doing this it provides the standard of life which supports and gives direction to the total life of the school. Biblical perspectives should guide all school activities and programs. The convictions of both administrators and faculty members should be based on Scripture. Biblical guidelines thus mold the character of the school, making it Christian. Educational theory and practice should be based on the Word of God.

Secondly, the Bible serves as a guide to spiritual and devotional activities on campus as expressed in chapel services, prayer meetings, and personal devotions. Corporate worship experiences draw people together and strengthen common commitments to serve God. They motivate people to renewed dedication and provide the means by which the reason for continued study is realized.

Thirdly, the Bible provides an educational function for the school. It is uniquely the Word of God and therefore deserves study of itself as a field of enquiry. But it also provides a basis for academic integration and the means by which all truth can be evaluated. The biblical point of view should be sought in the teaching of all academic disciplines.

The Christian curriculum, therefore, begins with the Word of God. This is true when conceiving of the curriculum broadly as comprehending all that goes on in the school situation, or more narrowly in terms of factual materials for subject matter. The Word of God as a divine revelation provides both content and principles by which all subject matter content is evaluated and used. In the church, or course, the Scriptures comprise the primary content.

God has not limited His provision, however, to subject matter content. He moves in still closer to human personality by His very presence in the teaching-learning process. This we call the <u>divine element</u> in Christian education. The divine element includes the presence and power of the Holy Spirit, the inherent power of the written Word of God which is "the Sword of the Spirit," the capacities of the regenerated self to learn, and the impact of the Christian personality of the teacher. These factors in themselves provide tremendous teaching atmosphere and power for the Christian teacher and learner. Still another factor, however, is what we call atmosphere or the structure of Christian education. Structure has been defined as that which holds a matter together, much as steel is the framework of a building. The history of education shows that education in every age has had an inner structure to provide coherent power. For the Greeks, it was loyalty and eloquence; for the Hebrews it was knowledge of the law and obedience; in the Middle Ages, it was knowledge and discipline. The structure of education, therefore, is that which gives coherence. For the Christian, the structure of education is found in the threefold provision of love, faith and obedience. It may be charted as follows:

The biblical message and Christian theology along with all the activities involved in the program of Christian education need to be presented within the framework of the structure of Christian education depicted in the chart form above. In this view love is the foundation of it all. The love of God is imparted by the Holy Spirit to the transformed hearts of saved men that they may love God and men. To love is to love from the heart but with the whole man. Sin prohibits love, but a transformed heart can love. Love forms a coherent motivation which directs redeemed man's life. Love is, therefore, basic to Christian education and to the curriculum. Loving interpersonal relationships may be the most significant factor in a Christian curriculum.

Faith is also necessary. Since love fastens the whole man in God, the capacity of faith is turned toward God. The whole man with a new heart of love lays hold by faith upon God and His Word. Faith opens the way to true knowledge and understanding. Unsaved men believe but their faith is in self and social adjustment. Consequently, any integration that takes place is temporary and misdirected hellward. Obedience is also part of the structure. There is surrender in love. No longer does self rule; instead the ego is turned Godward.

At this point perhaps it is possible to summarize the total philosophy of the curriculum as follows:

179

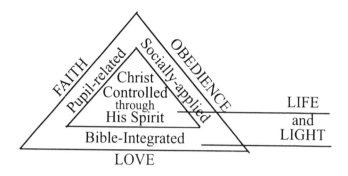

FAITH
Pupil-related
Socially-applied
OBEDIENCE
Christ
Controlled
through
His Spirit
Bible-Integrated
LOVE

LIFE
and
LIGHT

In keeping with the God-centered philosophy of Christian education Jesus Christ is at the center of our curriculum as the Authoritative Head of the Church. He controls the teaching-learning process in person through the work of the Holy Spirit. In this way the life principle is maintained as the motivating and maintaining power of the educational program. In contrast to pupil-centered and experience-centered view, this view keeps God in His proper place in all the work of the church. The Bible provides the light principle through which God's revelation in written form reaches the classroom. In addition the Bible becomes the integrating factor in the subject-matter curriculum, for it is here that we find the great principles by which we operate as well as factual content to master. The life and will of God are focused on the pupil and related to his personal needs and daily living. At this point also is where the developmental aspects of teaching and learning assists teachers and workers to adapt materials and methods to capacities and life situations of pupils. All of this issues in the application of life and truth to society around us. This whole process, as previously indicated, is conducted within the structure and frame of reference of Christian love, Christian faith and obedience, the exemplary features of Christian leadership and expressed attitudes. In this viewpoint, therefore, we see a combination of theological, psychological, and sociological factors which have a bearing on curriculum construction and operation.

The authority for curriculum construction is not found in science, society, or human knowledge, as in the case of secular curricula, but primarily in the will and Word of God which express the purpose of the Person of Christ, the Head.

Like any other kind of curriculum, a Christian curriculum is affected not only by one's philosophy and theology but also by such factors as expressed aims and goals, the nature and needs of pupils, tradition, professional influences, public demand, and even developments in other types of education.

In the field of religious education the problem of the organization of curriculum materials has been deeply affected by various approaches in secular education. In Christian education one must not be unaware of such developments but obviously there are certain spiritual factors which directly affect the concept of organization. First and foremost is the strategic position of the Bible as the written Word of God. Other factors include the person of Jesus Christ, the nature and needs of the pupil, and the needs of society. The Christian concept will also recognize the New Testament pattern provided for and by the Church as embracing four major factors which should be inherent in the pattern of organization: (1) evangelism, which includes Christian experience, (2) instruction, which embraces knowledge and training, (3) worship, and (4) fellowship, including social life and recreation. All of this issues in service on the part of individual Christians and groups in the corporate body of the Church.

5. <u>Subject Matter Content</u>. In secular education subject matter content is very largely equated with the production of culture, the products of the hearts and minds of men. Outside the church, Christian education curriculum materials are comprehensive enough to embrace both the cultural and spiritual elements of society. Inside the church the curriculum specializes in those spiritual products which come to man through creation and redemption by God. They are composed of His Word, the life and ministry of Jesus Christ, the Bible and the work of the Holy Spirit. The purpose of such materials outside the church in Christian education is to help the individual Christian fill his place in the cultural world and in his spiritual activity in fellowship with God. Inside the church the emphasis is placed on the latter. The great overall objective, as we have seen, is "that the man of God may be perfect, thoroughly furnished unto all good works" (I Tim. 3:17). The primary criterion of selection of such subject matter is that of heavenly citizenship as recorded in the Bible. This is the citizenship-

destiny of the Christian.

More specifically, curriculum content is selected according to the categories of Christian life and thought deemed necessary to the creation and development of Christian personality. For a church curriculum, categories of Christian truth thought most important would include faithfulness, trust, total commitment, beliefs, attitudes, motives and skills, touching the total person.

Naturally one philosophy will determine the kind of curriculum to be developed. However, there seems to be rather general agreement among conservatives and liberals, Catholics and Protestants, as to the subject matter areas to be covered by curriculum materials. Such areas would include Bible, Christian doctrine, Christian ethics, church history, life and thought. Some would broaden these areas to include culture and society.

Outside the church those holding certain philosophical positions choose subject matter according to the dictates of the philosophy they hold. Among the advocates of naturalism and realism the social and natural sciences are considered of highest value because they deal with nature. Humanities and languages are secondary. Traditionalists would emphasize liberal arts, natural sciences, and social sciences as subjects of greatest interest. For the pragmatist subjects which he considers more important in the development of the mind, such as history, biography, literature, philosophy and math. The revelationist would select subjects reflecting the nature and character of God first, then subjects reflecting God's general revelation, such as the sciences and liberal arts.

From a revelational standpoint, the general content of the curriculum is concerned with two great subjects (I Peter 1:11): (1) the sufferings of Christ, and (2) the glory of Christ. The great message contained in God's curriculum is that God is Life and Light (John 1:1-3,5,12; I John 1:5). The source of both of these is in Jesus Christ (I John 1:1,5) and they are available through Him (I John 1:2,7; John 14:6). The central message is the cross (Matt. 27; Gal. 3:10-14). The two great commandments to be considered are (1) love to God and (2) to others (Mark 12:29-31). All of these matters are embraced in the Gospel (Acts 13:38-39,47; I Cor. 15:3-4). The substance of the content of the Gospel was expressed in Paul's teachings as repentance toward God and faith toward the Lord Jesus Christ (Acts 20:20,21).

The purpose of the curriculum was to afford Christians with an opportunity for growth (I Thess. 4:10). The very grace of God teaches Christians (1) to live, (2) to look, and (3) to labor (Titus 2:11-16).

The supreme end of the curriculum is to produce the perfect man in Christ (Col. 1:28), one who does the will of God and serves Him in some life vocation. To accomplish this requires crowning Jesus Christ not only as Savior but as Lord (Acts 10:36; Rom. 10:12; I Cor. 15:47). Thus, by showing such truths, freedom would be gained (John 8:32). The purpose of grace and truth is conformity (James 1:22ff; II Cor. 3:18). This is reflected in the spiritual characteristic of perfect love (Matt. 22:36-40; I Cor. 13; Gal. 5:14; 6:2), faith and love (Gal. 3:1-6,23-26; 5:6; Rom. 13:8-10; I Thess. 1:4-9; Phil. 1:9-11; John 20:29,31).

Very specific curriculum content is provided in the record of the early church activities. Through the Kerygma, they proclaimed the Gospel (John 1:9,10; 3:16; Rom. 5:8). This was followed by the Didache (teaching) where the Kerygma was explained (I Thess. 2:13; Eph. 4:20,21; I Cor. 11:23; 15:3; II Tim 2:2; II Thess. 2:15; II Tim. 3:16). The Great Commission was a teaching commission (Matt. 28:19,20). They emphasized fellowship (Gal. 2:9; I John 1:3,6,7) which involved being partners with God (Luke 5:7), sharing (Heb. 2:14), communication (Heb. 13:16), the communion of the saints (Rom. 1:7; I Cor. 1:2; Heb. 2:11; Acts 10:44-47; Eph. 4:12-16), brotherhood (Acts 9:17; Gal. 6:10; Eph. 2:19; Mark 3:31-35) and participation (Phil. 3:10; 1:1-5). They stressed the importance of diakoina (service) which as an expression of gifts (Eph. 4:11f; I Peter 4:10,11) and love (Mark 10:42-45). All Christians were expected to serve (John 12:2; Luke 22:27; Acts 6:1f).

Among other matters included in the curriculum were the oral teaching (II Thess. 2:15; 3:6; I Cor. 11:2,23; I Tim. 6:20), the apostles' writings (Gal. 1:8; II John 9,10; Acts 20:27), the heritage (Ps. 44:1; 61:5; 78:3-6), preparation for the future (I Thess. 1:9,10), some pagan learning used with discretion (Acts 17:28; I Cor. 15:33; Titus 1:12; I Cor. 3:19) and the ordinances (Gal. 3:26,27; Rom. 6:3,4; I Cor. 11:24,26,28,29; Acts 4:29,30; 6:2-4).

Special warnings were taught regarding the difference between false and true education -- James 3:15-17:

False Education	True Education
Earthly	Heavenly (from above)
Sensual	Pure
Devilish	Peaceable
Bitter Envying	Gentle
Strife	Easy to be entreated
Every evil work	Full of mercy and good fruits
	Without partiality and hypocrisy

False education is the wrong kind of wisdom (I Cor. 1:21), in fact it is foolishness with God (I Cor. 3:19), and leads men to many ungodly practices (Rom. 1:21-28). But the reward of faithful education is successful childhood (Prov. 22:6).

General education was not overlooked. The works of creation are to be studied by man -- plant life (Matt. 6:28), animal life (Luke 12:24; Matt. 6:26; Prov. 6:6; Job 12:7-10), the earth (Job 12:8) and the starry heavens (Isaiah 40:26). The works of God are regarded as an exhibition of the love, wisdom and power of God (Prov. 3:19,20). The operations of nature are direct manifestations of the wisdom, power and love of God -- the snow (Ps. 147:16), the rain (Matt. 5:45), the beasts (Ps. 147:9), vegetation and wine (Ps. 104:14,15). A study of the Scripture reveals an almost unlimited number of subject matter areas for study, covering language arts, the arts, communications skills, sociology, economics, music, etc.

The prominence of education in the home is an outstanding characteristic of biblical education. Parental instruction was required (Deut. 6:1-9) and a great many of the subjects mentioned above were covered. Children were taught to share (Heb. 13:16), to love (I John 4:7), to be kind (Eph. 4:32) and helpful (II Cor. 1:24), to be thankful (II Tim. 1:3; Eph. 5:20) and remember God's creation (Acts 17:24;

184

John 1:3; I Tim. 6:17).

Curriculum outcomes were fourfold in nature: (1) to develop spiritual life, (2) to gain knowledge, (3) to appropriate truth, and (4) to utilize wisdom. The ultimate spiritual development for the Christian is "the perfect man of God thoroughly furnished unto all good works" (II Tim. 3:17).

Christian education, therefore, is education that is Bible-based in its curriculum. God wants all men to know the truth (I Tim. 2:4) and it is the responsibility of Christians to perpetuate His teachings (II Thess. 2:15). In doing this, major truths should be taught, not fables (I Tim. 1:3,4). Supreme faith should be placed in spiritual things above all else (Mark 10:21,24; John 3:18,30). This involves emphasis on such matters as repentance (Matt. 3:2,8; Luke 13:3,5), prayer (Mark 11:17,24), sound doctrine (Titus 2:1,2), and citizenship (Mark 12:17).

The appropriation of God's truth is a curriculum objective. Truth is Living Truth in Jesus Christ (John 14:6) and written truth is the Word (Eph. 6:17). Truth is something to be done, not merely known and is found by doing the will of God (John 1:12-14; 8:32; 17:16-26). Christians are to walk in His truth (Eph. 4:24; III John 4). The function of Christian education, therefore, is centered in a workman with truth (II Tim. 3:15).

While truth can be expressed in terms of scientific formulas, mathematical equations, and grammatical structures, these are only expressions of a much more comprehensive source of truth. This source will serve as a unifying principle for all knowledge and life - - the answer is Christ (John 14:6; John 1:3; Col. 1:16,17).

The Greek -- "SOPHIA" -- speaks of the wisdom of God (Luke 11:49; Matt. 23:34). The Scriptures speak of two kinds of wisdom: (1) of God (I Cor. 2:7) and (2) of the world (I Cor. 1:20,21; 2:6,7). Worldly wisdom is found in man (Gen. 3:6), does not reveal God (I Cor. 1:21), is foolishness (I Cor. 3:19,20) and should be avoided (I Cor. 2:1ff). Godly wisdom is from God (Prov. 15:33). It is a gift from Him (Prov. 2:6) and equated with life itself (Prov. 8:35). It is revealed in revelation, redemption and forgiveness (Eph. 1:7,8). Such wisdom should be sought by man (Prov. 15:14), accepted (Prov. 21:11) and stored by man (Prov. 10:14) because it is the principle thing (Prov. 4:5-9). Such wisdom is imparted by Jesus Christ (Col. 2:3; I Cor. 1:24,30) and is supplied by the Holy Spirit (I Cor. 2:13). It comes to man by means of prayer (James 1:5-6), by hearing, believing and trusting (Eph. 1:17-19; Prov. 2:2), obedience (Eccles. 12:13; 5:1-7) and faith (I Cor. 3:18f; I Tim. 3:15; I Cor. 1:24,30). The final outcome is the glory of God (Col. 1:18).

6. <u>Curriculum Design</u>. All of this information is formed into a curriculum plan and design to cover all age groups and their needs. Then various administrative procedures, such as organization, management, and supervision, are set up to implement the plan.

Most church groups select curriculum materials which are either designed or approved by denominational boards and publishing houses. Among evangelical groups certain independent publishers provide these materials. A wide variety of these materials is available to include uniform lessons, group graded lessons, closely graded lessons, broadly graded lessons and specialized lesson systems, designed for such agencies as vacation Bible school and weekday groups. There are specialized materials prepared for special people, such as blind, deaf, and handicapped people.

The large mainline denominations have often cooperated in the production and distribution of curriculum materials. Perhaps the finest illustration of this is the Cooperative Curriculum Project which was issued as <u>The Church's Educational Ministry: A Curriculum Plan</u>, (Bethany, 1965).

Regarding the sequence of instruction of curriculum content there is not common agreement. DeWolf has indicated some principles by which an approach to the problem of sequence can be handled. He describes this as an approach to sequence that requires "a different perspective" and one which flows "from the message of the Christian faith." Some of his views can be summarized as follows:
    A. The whole faith should be presented at every age level
       1. Because <u>all</u> need the benefits of God's saving acts
       2. The whole range of God's dealings with men needs to be brought to all, even to little children
    B. The methods and depth of the faith will be communicated according to capacity

1. Because there is one message but changing language
2. Realities of the faith can be communicated, not only by words, but also through relationships
C. Theology provides some guidelines for sequence
   1. Adults are mediators and models of the faith to infants
   2. We can teach beginners through attitudes and loving Christian relationships
   3. God does speak to children and children can know God as presence and love
   4. By modeling forgiveness children can see what this means as they observe adults
   5. Children can learn by experience when ideas and concepts fall short
   6. As children mature, more advanced learning activities can be utilized
   7. In Junior and Senior High departments evangelism is very central
   8. In High School the message should be relevant to adolescent needs and life-style
   9. After High School comes a challenge to face new life issues and situations in the light of the Lordship of Jesus Christ
   10. Adults need to have the message applied in the home and work situations.[29]

Instruction of children in their early years would probably focus on developing in them an awareness of God and their need for Him and on matters concerning the created environment and interpersonal relationships. As children mature the scope of studies would broaden to include the suggestions made above under curriculum design. To accomplish this, more than information will be required. The right Christian information should lead to Christian discipleship which in turn will help students become successful in Christian living and service. Thus, Christian students are prepared for life in God's service.

Among older students in Christian day schools and higher education any curriculum system which purports to be Christian should be based on a Christian view of reality. The general pattern by which this is accomplished in any Christian school is to provide this point of view in required courses which reflect this philosophy and then reflected, as far as possible, in all other subjects taught. The main purpose is to help students formulate a Christian view of life and the world. Among educators stressing an immanence kind of revelation stress would be laid on all experience as the Christian view. Among those who attempt the position of the integrationist there would be emphasis on both natural and supernatural experiences.

For any curriculum design, particularly among those engaged at the higher levels of education, all faculties need a skeleton outline on curriculum design and development. There are at least five factors from a revelational standpoint which need to be considered in this work as follows:

1. The philosophical and theological factor -- what is believed about God, man, truth, values, life and education
2. The psychological factor -- what is to be known about Christian personality development
3. The cultural factor -- what is believed about the role of the school in society
4. The knowledge factor -- what is believed about the priorities of truth to be taught in the subject matter disciplines
5. The personality factor -- what is seen as the goal for the development of Christian character and work

To achieve integration in the total curriculum faculties must have common understandings and commitments about all of the above factors. Principles involved in factor one above will directly impact all the other factors involved. In addition to these factors attention should be given also to the so-called extra-class activities, for these too are part of the curriculum as a whole. This is important because interpersonal relationships are important in Christian education. Here again, Christian concepts and values are determinative factors in bringing about such relationships on campus.

In factor number five above Bloom's Educational Taxonomy

should prove to be helpful in focusing on what aspects of personality we have to develop. This would involve determination of what is to be taught regarding (1) factual knowledge, (2) conceptual knowledge, (3) values, and (4) skills, including psychomotor skills, such as reading, writing, etc. as well as mental skills of understanding and reasoning. It is important, however, for a faculty to be selective at this point because obviously not everything about everything can be taught.

At the college level a revelational approach to this matter would stress a fourfold outline to curriculum building. First, through Bible and theological studies fundamental themes would be provided which set the stage for all Christian thinking. Second, an overview of the History of Western Civilization is tied in with biblical/ theological themes to show how our civilization has been affected by Judeo-Christian developments. Third, an exposure to contemporary philosophical thinking reveals the basic humanism and self-centeredness of modern man and how God has been excluded. Fourth, a study of modern science and technology is given so that Christian students can assess its possible role in building the Kingdom of God.

Some of the biblical/theological themes to be emphasized would include the following matters:

1. Redemption
2. Creation as affected by sin and renewal
3. The history of God's Covenant people
4. The New Testament concept of the Kingdom of God
5. The strategic importance of the incarnation and its relation to history, culminating in the return of Christ
6. A Christian world view

Illustrations of how this is done are given in the following chapter.

H. Authority, Freedom and Discipline

1. <u>Authority</u>. Christian education is education that is Bible-revealed in its authority. This word is a derivative of the Greek, EXOUSIA, which means power granted from a higher source. God-centered education, therefore, finds its authority in the highest of all sources. It involves a God-given right over something, to do something. It is permission and freedom to act. In the Hebrew it refers to the absolute, sovereign power of God.

Paul reveals that our source of authority is in God (Rom. 13:1). Jesus Christ has been clothed with supreme authority (Matt. 1:23; 28:18). He taught with authority (Mark 1:22; Matt. 7:29). Jesus manifested His authority over nature (Mark 4:39), over death (Luke 7:14,15), over demons (Luke 4:33-37) and by forgiving sins (Mark 2:10).

The disciples of Jesus served with authority (Luke 6:12ff; Acts 22:6-10; 2:12-47) and they preached and taught with authority (II John 10; II Cor 11:4; I Thess. 2:13; Titus 1:3; Gal. 1:6-12).

Our authority is based on the authority of Jesus Christ (Matt. 5:17,18; John 10:34-38). It should be exercised only in the power of the Holy Spirit for teaching (John 14:26) and for ministry (John 16:7-14). The teacher's authority is to be reflective of God's authority. The teacher is to be authoritative. This means that the teacher will not be permissive nor authoritarian. The teacher is to be in a leadership role and is to be respected for a healthy and redemptive teaching-learning relationship to exist.

2. <u>Freedom</u>. The teacher in Christian education should recognize individuality and respect the personhood of each student. Students must have the freedom to be themselves and to develop in a healthy manner. However, students (as is the case with all persons) will find true freedom only within proper boundaries. Rules and discipline are necessary to freedom. In the spiritual realm, it should be noted that true freedom is found only by coming under the Lordship of Jesus Christ (John 8:32-36).

In Scripture freedom is linked with responsibility and our calling in Christ; it is to be used to serve others, not as an opportunity for the flesh (Gal. 5:13). Since yielding to the flesh and to wayward living are dangers for students in Christian schools, discipline is called for. In a true Christian community, however the discipline will <u>start</u> with the students themselves. Christian students should maintain Christian expectations for proper behavior and not be exposed to situations in which "anything goes." However, officials in Christian schools should not hesitate to step in when such situations do arise. No Christian school should tolerate open, persistent immorality on the part of students or faculty.

3. <u>Discipline</u>. Positive discipline will arise from the program of studies and the work to be done. Where students are thus involved they will make good use of their time, set a good example and uphold Christian standards. Discipline arises out of love for God and a purpose to please Him.

The origin of discipline was in the Garden of Eden (Gen. 3). The purpose of discipline is to make us true children of God (Heb. 12:5-11). Without discipline there is lawlessness (Judges 21:25). Disloyalty and disobedience (Gen. 3) results in sin (Rom. 3:23; 5:12; Ps. 51:5; 58:3; Gen. 8:21) and calls for correction (Prov. 3:11-12; 15:10; 22:15).

The spirit of discipline is love. Jesus reproved others but He also encouraged them (John 8:11; 5:14). The Holy Spirit reproves, but He is also the Comforter (John 16:7-11; 14:26). Discipline is the evidence of God's love (Prov. 3:11,12). The best method, therefore, is love (Prov. 13:24; 23:13,14).

Discipline has an important place in God's plan (Job 5:17), and in education (Job 12:5-12). Chastening comes out of love (Heb. 12:6; Rev. 3:19), and true love requires the discipline of obedience (I John 5:2-4). Children need discipline at times (Prov. 23:13,14), but its application should be graded (I Cor. 5:6,7,13).

True discipline results in good fruit (Prov. 23:13,14; John 15:2), produces wisdom (Prov. 29:15), rest and delight (Prov. 29:17), holiness (Heb. 12:10) and righteousness (Heb. 12:11). It makes God's blessings possible (Gen. 18:19), and leads to our greatest freedom (Ps. 119:44-45).

Discipline, therefore, is necessary. It is necessary for students to experience true freedom. It is needed for personal development, spiritual development, class procedures, and a healthy teaching-learning process. However, various types of disciplinary procedures are used depending on teacher personalities, teaching styles, and teacher expectations. But the teacher must be in control.

Appropriate discipline sets the stage for discipleship. Christian discipleship implies that a person will come under the discipline of Jesus Christ. An observation can be made at this point that persons who received good discipline as children usually found it easier to take the step into real Christian discipleship. Appropriate discipline is redemptive in nature and helps set the stage for spiritual formation.

As to punishment, it is social in nature -- if we are to learn from God. This is so because the Kingdom of God is social. This means that a Christian academic community is also a social community. Christian administrators, therefore, need to view both the individual and the community in the approach to discipline and punishment. While it is important to remember that what is best for the community must be done. If we are to learn from God's way of doing things, it seems certain that all discipline should be unsentimentally social in nature and application, but by a community that is concerned also with the good of each individual in it.

Punishment should have the whole academic community in mind. The forgiveness of the individual is an expression of personal love, not of community discipline. God forgives one who repents, and administrators should also be concerned for individuals who need discipline. But the fruits of repentance should be allowed to ripen and be tested before any individual is restored to the academic community; membership is a holy privilege, to be held in high respect. As far as possible, therefore, equal concern must be manifested by school administrators for both the individual and the community.

There are three styles of discipline: (1) the extreme authoritarian, where student wills are crushed; (2) permissive, where students are conceived as naturally good and thus left to do as they please; and (3) firmness qualified by love. The third one is the most acceptable for Christians. Here the student is given respect as the image of God but viewed also as sinful, thus, in need of definite control. There are also three levels of disciplinary control: (1) corporate discipline and/or expulsion, used only as a last resort; (2) corrective discipline, using corrective measures, such as withdrawal of privileges, verbal rebuke, suspension, isolation, parental consultation and other similar methods; and (3) preventive discipline brought about through the use of positive techniques of good rules, good communication, good teaching, etc. The latter is preferable for Christians.

I. Evaluation

1. Secular Contributions. Secular education for many years has been able to develop systems of evaluation to be used in educational situations of all kinds. Norms and standards of criteria have been utilized to test and measure almost any kind of experience and personality development one can think of. On the other hand, Christian educators have been slow to develop such standards because of the erroneously perceived notion that subjective matters and spiritual matters cannot be adequately assessed and evaluated.

2. A Revelational Approach. Dealing as we do with souls of immortal value it does appear that some effort should be made to determine the place and value of measurement. Scripture might be of possible help here.

We have seen previously in the consideration of objectives that for the Christian spiritual maturity is the character goal. Any evaluation, therefore, should be at this point. How Christlike are my students now? Based on the aspects of the life of Jesus we should ask: Are our students increasing in wisdom, in stature, and in the favor of God and man? This includes the personality factors of the spiritual, the physical, the intellectual and social. Do we see evidences of spiritual growth, greater interest in serving God, and increased service activity? Do we see evidences of loving one's fellow man, traits characterized by cooperation, friendliness, purity, good health, and the ability to use intellectual skills? These might indicate growth and development.

Early uses of the principle of evaluation by God can be seen at creation when God saw that all things were created "good" (Gen. 1:4,10,13,18,21,25,31). From the very beginning Adam and Eve were made subject to a probationary test (Gen. 2 and 3).

Other early uses of evaluation is the trial of Bible characters, such as Abraham (Gen. 22) and Joseph (Gen. 39). God Himself evaluates. The Holy Spirit evaluates (Rom. 8:27; I Cor. 2:10). All men will give an account to Him (I Pet. 4:5,6; I Cor. 3:13; Rev. 20:11-15; 22:12). In fact, judgment begins at the house of God (I Pet. 4:17). There will be a great judgment day as a day of evaluation and testing (Heb. 9:27; 10:30; Rom. 2:15-16; I Cor. 2:10). All Christians will appear before the Judgment Seat of Christ (Rom. 14:10-12; II Cor 5:10; II Tim. 4:8). The final evaluation will take place at the Second Coming of Christ (I Cor. 4:5). God will evaluate the churches (Rev. 1-3).

We see the use of testing in the Levitical laws. God tested Israel for sin (Ex. 20:20) and allowed pagan nations to prove them (Judges 2:22; 3:4). God will test the works and actions of men (Eccl. 12:14; I Sam. 2:3). His method is inward testing (Ps. 17:3).

God tests believers in a variety of ways: (1) by demanding great sacrifices (Gen. 22:1,2), (2) by leading men in a difficult way (Deut. 8:2), (3) by giving opportunities for choice (I Kings 3:5), (4) by proposing hard tasks (John 6:5,6), (5) by permitting men to suffer (Acts 16:23,24), (6) by permitting temptation (James 1:2,3), (7) by divine delays (Ps. 13:1; 119:52; John 16:6,21; James 1:12; 2:17; II Peter 3:9), (8) by testing faith (Matt. 9:28; Heb. 11:8,17) and faithfulness (I Tim. 3:10), (9) by testing alertness (I Thess. 5:6) and the use of judgment and discernment (Luke 12:54-59), (10) by approving things excellent (Phil. 1:10), (11) by trying our spirits (I John 4:1-3) and (12) by putting our entire lives to the highest and best test (I Cor. 11:28; II Cor. 13:5).

Various types of tests can be seen in Scripture: (1) the service test (Matt. 25:35; Luke 10:37), (2) the leadership test (I Tim. 3:10), (3) the test of repentance (II Cor. 7:9-11,16), and (4) the test of hearing (Luke 8:4-15, four kinds of hearers).

The source of our standards is to be found in God (II Cor.

10:13; Rev. 1:8) but not in others or ourselves (II Cor. 10:12,13). The methods of evaluation are many: books (Rev. 20:2-15), God's holiness (I Cor. 3:11-13), proving of works (Gal. 6:4), and admonitions. The rewards of evaluation are also many (I Cor. 3:14) and will be seen in the various crowns issued to God's children: for self control (I Cor. 9:25), for service (I Thess 2:19,20), for faithful testimony (II Tim. 4:7,8), for faithful shepherding (I Pet. 5:2-4) and for faithfulness in trial (Rev. 2:10). One might conclude in the light of these matters that Christian education is education that is growth-determined in its evaluation.

3. Values. Christian education is education that is eternally-oriented in values. Values for Christian education are present as a result of God's creation which was deemed "good" (Gen.1:4,10,12,18,21,25). Values from God are also universal (Ps. 139:8,9; Eccles. 3:11) and eternal ones (II Cor. 4:18). To love and obey God is considered of highest value for man (Deut. 30:15-20).

Of all the gifts of God to man Christ is the most precious one (II Cor. 9:15; Phil. 3:8). Life in Christ is both good and rich (Mark 5:34; Luke 5:31; John 10:10; Luke 19:9,10; Rom. 1:16; John 14:27). He offers many blessings (Matt. 11:3-5; John 14:8; Acts 9:5).

Among the highest values for Christians are (1) wisdom (Job 28:18), (2) obedience to God (Deut. 6:4-9), (3) instruction and reproof (Prov. 15:32), and (4) victory over sin and death (I Cor. 15:51,54-57). Human personality itself is of supreme value (Luke 12:7,15).

For the Christian true happiness is not found in pleasure or mirth (Prov. 21:17, Eccles. 2:1), nor in great possessions (Prov. 23:5; 27:24; Eccles. 2:11) but in love for God and others (I John. 4:7-8; Luke 10:27).

The writer of Ecclesiastes sums up the whole matter when he says, "Let us hear the conclusion of the whole matter: Fear God, and keep His commandments: for this is the whole duty of man" (Eccles. 12:13).

Notes

1. Nathaniel Cantor, <u>The Teaching-Learning Process</u>, Holt, Rinehard and Winston, 1953, chapter 13.

2. Sophia Fahs, <u>Today's Children and Yesterday's Heritage</u>, Beacon, 1952, chapter 4.

3. George A. Coe, <u>A Social Theory of Religious Education</u>, Scribners, 1924, chapter 14.

4. Robert R. Boehlke, <u>Theories of Learning in Christian Education</u>, Westminster, 1962, p. 19.

5. Reuel Howe, <u>Man's Need and God's Action</u>, Seabury, 1953, p. 9.

6. Randolph C. Miller, <u>The Clue to Christian Education</u>, Scribners, 1950, p. 42.

7. Wesner Fallaw, <u>Christian Education for Tomorrow</u>, Westminster, 1960, p. 33.

8. <u>Ibid.</u>, p. 35.

9. Iris Cully, <u>The Dynamics of Christian Education</u>, Westminster, 1958, pp. 119-120.

10. Lois Lebar, <u>Education that is Christian</u>, Revell, 1958, p. 135.

11. Cornelius Jaarsma, ed., <u>Fundamentals in Christian Education</u>, Eerdmans, 1953, chapter 17.

12. <u>Ibid.</u>, p. 330.

13. <u>Ibid.</u>, p. 273.

14. L. Harold DeWolf, <u>Teaching Our Faith in God</u>, Abingdon, 1963, pp. 44-45.

15. Jerome S. Bruner, <u>The Process of Education</u>, Harvard University Press, 1960, p. 33.

16. Bruce Joyce and Marsha Weil, <u>Models of Teaching</u>, Prentice Hall, 1972.

17. Cully, <u>op. cit.</u>, p. 111.

18. Miller, <u>op. cit.</u>, p. 159.

19. Lewis J. Sherrill, <u>Gift of Power</u>, Macmillan, 1955, p. 184.

20. Lebar, <u>op. cit.</u>, p. 136.

21. Barbara J. Bolton and Charles T. Smith, <u>Bible Learning Activities</u>, Gospel Light, 1973, chapter 1.

22. Dubin and Taveggia, <u>The Teaching-Learning Paradox</u>, Center for Advanced Study of Educational Administration, University of Oregon, 1968.

23. Fahs, <u>op. cit.</u>, p. 56.

24. Coe, <u>op. cit.</u>, p. 100.

25. D. Campbell Wyckoff, <u>The Gospel and Christian Education</u>, Westminster, 1959, p. 136.

26. Sherrill, <u>op. cit.</u>, p. 95.

27. J. Donald Butler, <u>Four Philosophies and Their Practice in Education and Religion</u>, Harper, 1951, p. 236.

28. Lebar, <u>op. cit.</u>, p. 203.

29. DeWolf, <u>op. cit.</u>

CHAPTER FIVE

REVELATION AND INSTITUTIONAL CHRISTIAN EDUCATION PRACTICE

A. Local Church Practice
   1. The Total Church Concept
   2. Principles
   3. Pattern
   4. Philosophy
   5. Practice
   6. Curriculum Possibilities
   7. Leadership
   8. The Home
   9. Organization, Administration and Supervision
   10. Resources

B. Christian Day School Practice
   1. Philosophy of Education
   2. Implementation of the Philosophy
   3. Integration Practices
   4. Organization, Administration and Supervision

C. Christian Liberal Arts College Practice
   1. Background
   2. The Need
   3. Distinctives
   4. Liberal Arts Education
   5. Integration
   6. Interpretation
   7. Administrative and Supervisory Means to Achieve Integration
   8. Functional Principles of Curriculum Practice
   9. Suggested Curriculum Themes to Achieve Integration
   10. Academic Freedom
   11. The Challenge

D. The Theological Seminary and Educational Practice
   1. The Purpose and Needs
   2. The Program

CHAPTER FIVE

REVELATION AND INSTITUTIONAL
CHRISTIAN EDUCATION PRACTICE

A. Local Church Practice

1. <u>The Total Church Concept</u>. Revelation has implications for local church education. A comprehensive program of church education is based on the <u>total church</u> concept of Christian education. This means that the program must embrace elements not only within the traditional Sunday school but also outside it. While it is true that the Sunday school is the primary instructional agency of the church program, the needs for all ages in the church demand the use of a great many agencies in the development of a total church program.

A total church program of church education will include all the activities, materials, resources, physical facilities, and personnel necessary to operate a full-orbed program of teaching and learning to reach the total constituency of the church. All the activities which produce the kind of experiences needed to transform the life into that which God intended for the individual must be planned in such a program.

2. <u>Principles</u>. The development of a total church program is dependent on the recognition and practice of solid principles which yield good Christian education. First, Christian education is the church at work in education. It is the church studying, teaching and learning. Second, the objectives for Christian education and the church are the same. They come to us from the Living and Written Word. Third, the tasks of Christian education and the church are identical, that of bringing the light and life of God to a lost world and building His kingdom in the hearts and lives of the people. Fourth, church control is required. If the total church is involved in a program of education then the governing body of the church will recognize this and through planning and cooperation help to educate it. Fifth, for the church to accomplish its educational mission some centralized agency is needed, such as a Board of Education, to organize,

administer, and supervise the program. Other principles can be listed as follows:

Scriptural -- providing authority and guidelines
Practical -- useful and used
Comprehensive -- adequate coverage for all ages
Integration -- providing unity and good balance
Graded -- psychologically oriented to age levels
Simple -- easily followed
Clear -- easily understood
Flexible -- allowing for change and adjustments
Democratic -- allowing the voice of the people to be heard
Functional -- making responsibilities and duties clear

3. Pattern. The local church has the advantage of following a successful model -- the New Testament church. They followed the revealed Word to discover purposes and objectives. We should follow this church to establish our patterns for action, then follow the pattern in building the program. All activities, materials, methods, and content should be bent to the revealed objectives.

As previously mentioned, the church will look also to its Head, Jesus Christ, Who has modeled in His life and service the way His body would function. The reader is referred to the reference previously made to "Our Life in Christ" and "Our Ministry for Christ".

4. Philosophy. The content of a total church program is based solidly on Christian theory and practice. Therefore, it will be Christ-controlled through His Spirit, Bible-integrated and based, learner related, and socially applied. For more information on this matter the reader is referred to the author's work A Christian Approach to Education (Mott Media, 1977).

5. Practice. Practice will be governed by the five Scriptural program elements: (1) evangelism, (2) instruction, (3) worship, (4) fellowship, and (5) service (Acts 2:41,42). Wide latitude will be allowed for the exercising of various ministries for the edifying of the church and the work of the ministry (Eph. 4:11-13). The program elements are related, interrelated and woven into the total pro-

gram to achieve a balanced program, so that the pattern of these elements can be conceived as follows to produce a <u>church school</u>:

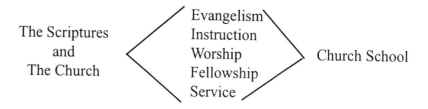

The Scriptures
and
The Church

Evangelism
Instruction
Worship
Fellowship
Service

Church School

Each of the five program elements will in turn provide program suggestions to be utilized in the church.

Evangelism includes
Soul winning
Enrollment and attendance
Follow-up of absentees
Religious census
Outpost and mission schools
Instruction in evangelistic techniques
Missions
Church membership and Christian life classes
Special days
Visitation

Worship includes
Act of worship
Worship training
Atmosphere and setting
Prayer
Devotional arts, such as pictures, stories, etc.
Offering
Liturgy
Leadership
Training period
Service includes
Individual acts of service

Group activities in service
Ministries of total church such as mission projects
Ministries in time of crisis

Instruction includes
Bible study
Christian doctrine
Christian ethics
Church history, policy, organization
Missions
Teacher training
Leadership education and development
Stewardship
Social action
Techniques of evangelism
Worship
Fellowship and recreation
Prayer
Christian home-making
Christian citizenship
Christian culture
Service training

Fellowship includes
Burden bearing
Recreation
Use of leisure time
Christian ethics and culture
Christian athletics
Social etiquette
Leadership development
Personality development; morale building
Correlation, integration of other instructional items
Cultivation of a Christian spirit

6. Curriculum Possibilities. A total church program, as previously indicated, will provide adequate coverage for the needs

of all age groups in the church body. Following is a listing of such possibilities for children, youth and adults. Each local congregation should find helpful suggestions from these listings for program building. One word of caution, however, is in order. A study of such possibilities may also indicate that a church might be trying to do too much.

CURRICULUM POSSIBILITIES FOR CHILDREN'S WORK
Sunday School Classes
Expanded or Extended Sessions
Children's Church (May be Beginner, Primary, Junior)
Sunday Evening Sessions
School of Missions
Weekday Religious Education
Weekday Clubs
Weekday Nursery School
Vacation Bible School
Day Camping
Child Evangelism
Supervised Recreation
Christian Life, Church Membership class
Children's Choirs
Ushers
Acolytes
Story Hours
Summer Program (camping, special activities)
Drama Groups
Hobby Clubs
Extended VBS
Scouting
Denominational Program
Christian Day School
Kindergarten Program

Variations of Above Programs

Extended session of Sunday School on weekdays
Weekday Free Kindergarten for Poor
Six Week Study Group on Sunday Evening
4 Week Study Group on Missions with Bus Tours Included
After school story, activity time -- weekly
After school supervised play
Sunday School extended to Wednesdays for children
   3:30 - 5:30 – paid teacher – small tuition fee
Thursday or Saturday Church school
Winter day camping
Saturday afternoon stamp group
Musical enrichment sessions – listen, sing, study
Choir and Study Sessions
Choir and Church membership session (weekdays)
Choir and activities (arts and crafts)
Junior Fellowship (Grades 4,5,6) – Meets twice a
   month – 1 1/2 hours each
Once a month movie and Recreation Day
Saturday morning adventures – activities, trips
Neighborhood playmate program – club idea
VBS in a Basket
Junior Club Program
   Fall – school of missions
   Winter – hobby and craft groups
   Spring – study groups; pastor's class

Special Groups

Good News Club	Bible Memory Club
Arts and Crafts Club	Scouting
Pioneer Girls	Christian Service Brigade
Sky Pilots	Child Evangelism Fellowship
Children's Bible Mission	Rural Bible Mission
Youth Gospel Crusade	Children for Christ
Challenger Group	Youth for Christ
Christian Endeavor	Special Schools for the
	retarded, blind, deaf, etc.

CURRICULUM POSSIBILITIES FOR YOUTH

Christian Endeavor, MYF, etc.
Sunday School
Youth Choir
Interdenominational programs
Youth Week
Ushers
Membership Training
Service groups -jails, rest homes, etc.
Help with Worship Services
Librarians
Visitation
Recreation and athletics
Visual aid helpers
Musicians
Song Leaders
VBS Students or workers
Church officers
Church offices
Special interest groups
    music, art, etc.

Resident Camping
Special Music -uke bands, etc.
Denominational program
Missions Club
Youth revival
Youth prayer groups
Youth for Christ
Drama
Bible Memorization
YMCA, YWCA
Retreats
College Campus ministry
Conventions
Weekday religious education
Weekday education groups
Debate teams
Pastor's classes
Counseling and guidance
    Projects

CURRICULUM POSSIBILITIES FOR ADULTS

Sunday
Morning worship
Sunday School
Evening study sessions
Evening worship
Choir
Ushers
Host and hostesses
Sermon seminar
Visitation
Drama

Weekday
Midweek prayer and praise
Membership training
Bible-study
Organizational meetings
Christian Family instruction
Board Meetings
Pastor's hour -
    parsonage discussion groups
Retreats
Bible Conferences

Musical groups	Family Camps
Special services	Literature league
Buzz sessions	Social events
Forum, lectures, discussion groups	Evangelistic meetings
School in Christian training	Surveys - census
Home Department	Athletics & recreation
Extension Department	Child-parent activities - PTO
	Mission School
	Workshops
	Special Clubs
	Men's Brotherhood
	Women's Society
	Mother's Club
	Special groups -
	hobby, crafts, etc.

7. <u>Leadership</u>. Leadership in the church program consists of parents, pastors, other professional workers, and laymen. All of these people are considered to be <u>ministers of God</u>. In keeping with their gifts they are to play specific roles as co-laborers with Christ through the power of the Holy Spirit to build the church program in the home and in the school of the church. Each of them must think of himself as the servant of God and man (Matt. 20:25-28). Arbitrary authority exercised by any leader is to be avoided and replaced by serving one another and encouraging one another (I Pet. 5:1-5). Pastors are leaders of leaders, ministers among other ministers, motivating and guiding laymen to carry out God's will and program.

Laymen are to offer themselves in sacrificial service in keeping with the gifts God has imparted to them. They are to form a team to carry out the will of God and responsibilities as the body of Christ. All of their activities are to be considered as ministries, not merely jobs to perform or duties to assume. All should think of themselves as Christian teachers and learners.

8. <u>The Home</u>. Christian education begins in the home as the basic unit of society. The Bible points to the home as the basic

educational institution (Deut. 11:18,19; Eph. 6:4). Parents have been obligated by God to see that their children are properly cared for and educated. The early years of child life are the most impressionable ones. The influence of the parents provides an unmatched teaching situation. Learning is both natural and easy in the home. The security and love of the parents make learning assured.

Parents must be genuinely Christian to carry out their responsibilities. The Bible and prayer must be central in home teachings on religion, so also is evangelism. There must be Christian service training for all family members. The manifestation of Christian attitudes, the sharing of duties in Christian living, Christian conversation, family worship as expressed in grace at the table, bedside prayers, general prayer periods and Bible reading are some of the duties to be performed. Attendance at public worship services and Sunday School meetings are also additional avenues of training and service.

To assist the home with its Christian responsibilities some churches organize a Committee on Christian Family Education. Its general duties would be to find out what is already being done in the church and community to promote Christian family life and then to plan a total program for Christian Family Education. Program suggestions would cover a wide variety of activities to include: informal study groups, organized study groups, led by the pastor or others, leadership classes on home life, correspondence courses, books and library materials, magazines, audio visuals, couples' clubs, a Parent Teacher Organization and special activities, such as sex education, special days, and specialized Sunday School departments such as the Cradle Roll and Home Department. Popular activities utilized by some churches include home Bible classes, family retreats, family finance retreats, open house, nursery school, child care center, family camping and many fellowship activities.

9. <u>Organization, Administration and Supervision</u>. Organization may be defined as "the breaking down of the responsibility of the group as a whole into parts which can be assigned to individuals and committees." It is the framework within which the church program operates. Principles of organization are believed

to be useful in the church because they are in harmony with God Himself, Who is a God of organization as clearly revealed in the work of Jesus and the New Testament church.

Each church congregation through its ruling body will delegate the responsibility of the church educational program to a Board of Christian Education or its equivalent. There will also be designated committees and officers of administration to execute the policies and plans of this board. Each denomination will have its own philosophy and plans by which such organization will be done in the local church.

Adequate administration is both needed and necessary if a program of church education is to work effectively. Each person and committee should be informed clearly what duties and responsibilities are necessary for them to carry out their ministries.

Supervisory functions will seek improvement and effectiveness in all phases of the educational program, seeking to help individual workers carry out their tasks more effectively. The following series of functions will be performed by good administrators and supervisors:

<u>Administration</u>
Concerned with scope and breadth
1. Operation
2. Management
3. Placement
4. Program
5. Finances
6. Resources

<u>Supervision</u>
Concerned with depth and improvement
1. Quality
2. Improvement
3. Objectives
4. Teaching-learning
5. Leadership

6. Leadership training and development
7. Results -- effectiveness
8. Problem-solving
9. Efficiency
10. Standards

10. <u>Resources</u>. No program of church education will operate effectively without thorough support. Such support will be provided in terms of buildings, equipment, curriculum materials, audiovisual supplies, and money. For more information on these matters the reader is referred to the author's work <u>Christian Education for the Local Church</u> (revised edition, Zondervan, 1973).

B. Christian Day School Practice

1. <u>Philosophy of Education</u>. Any well run Christian day school should have a written statement of philosophy of education. Such a statement should be both comprehensive and thorough. This statement will be based clearly on the presuppositions of Christian theism and will show how all truth is integrated with that of God's truth.

A statement of philosophy will probably include two parts; one part will be devoted to a statement of theology, what one believes about God. The second part will reveal what the school believes about life and the totality of the educational process. The whole statement will be definitive in character and will provide the guidelines for the total operation of the school.

2. <u>Implementation of the Philosophy</u>. Ones' philosophy of life must be translated over into practice and communicated in the classroom. This would involve a clear statement of aims and objectives for the school. On the one hand such a statement of objectives will reflect, not only a biblical and theological point of view, but also what some term a "protest" to secular forms of education.

Of prime importance in implementing the Christian philosophy in the school is the matter of providing teachers with guidelines on how to integrate the Christian faith and practice with classroom learning. Here teachers are to show how all truth is God's truth. The unity of all truth reveals God in all aspects of academic life and thought. Thus, God is revealed in every subject and every subject becomes a vessel by which God's life, will and truth are seen. This eliminates the arbitrary distinction between the sacred and the secular. Such integration will affect also those administrative procedures and practices by which the school is operated both in spirit and practice.

In Christian day schools, curriculum design should reflect a Christian philosophy of life and education. For both elementary and secondary levels the curriculum pattern should reflect the following hierarchical pattern:

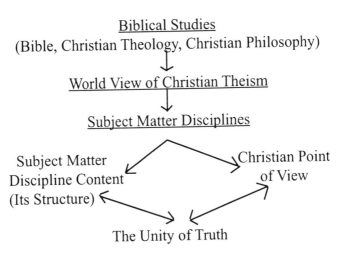

Biblical Studies
(Bible, Christian Theology, Christian Philosophy)

World View of Christian Theism

Subject Matter Disciplines

Subject Matter Discipline Content (Its Structure)   Christian Point of View

The Unity of Truth

Although scholars do not generally agree on the subjects which are most important, some do recommend the use of some kind of core organization. For elementary schools the core would possibly consist of Bible, Social Studies, Natural Sciences, and Aesthetic studies, such as Art, Music and selected Literature. Following this would be emphasis on the skills.

For secondary schools the foundation studies would be largely the same as above. With increasing levels of intellectual ability, however, more specialization would be needed. Biblical Studies would provide the perspectives of Christian philosophy, theology and world view and thus become the integrating center for the curriculum. Following this would be curriculum emphases on communication, health, physical environment, government and citizenship, and skills. Each school will have to decide which courses beyond the core are required and how many elective courses would be provided. It may be that some kind of provision should be made for college preparatory work as well as general courses and vocational courses.

3. Integration Practices. An examination of the research and writings on the Christian Day School Movement reveals that not enough attention has been given formally to the matter of providing teachers with guidelines on how to integrate the Christian faith with the teaching of secular subjects. Some assistance has been provided in curriculum materials supplied to the schools by Christian publishers. Otherwise most of the attention has been given to administering the schools. Teachers are left largely to themselves in this matter.

Christine M. Templar found this to be true in a recent survey of integration practices among teachers in Christian day schools (unpublished dissertation, Southern Baptist Seminary, 1979). That study revealed a definite desire among day school people to integrate Bible and other curriculum areas but also that very little help was available to teachers on how to do this. Three weaknesses were found. One, most of the integrative efforts were left to classroom teachers who were generally too busy with teaching activities to do the necessary work to bring about integration. Second, very little integrative material is available to help teachers and little curriculum philosophy to guide such efforts. Third, quality curriculum materials to bring about integration are not available. The study went on to make suggestions for developing an integrated curriculum for use in Kentucky Christian Church day schools.

In an unpublished doctoral dissertation John A. Burgess wrote on the subject "The Integration of Religious Content in Secular Subjects in Certain Church-Related Schools" (Ed.D., Harvard University, 1967). In his research Burgess studied about seventy Christian day schools recommended to him by the National Association of Christian Schools. He examined teaching practices and content as utilized by teachers in their efforts to achieve integration. Subject areas covered included mathematics, reading, science, social studies and language arts.

In general, Burgess found on examining lesson plans that teachers were not well trained in integration practices but they did make special efforts to bring about integration. There were some general practices in integration used by the teachers in his study. Sometimes religious content was not directly concerned with the objectives of lessons but was used to develop a religious attitude. Other times the secular topics helped develop a religious theme, such as God as Creator. Sometimes religious content was scattered throughout the lessons wherever the teachers deemed it most appropriate. The use of religious vocabulary, however, was found to be quite common. Burgess also found that efforts at integration were initiated very largely by the teachers rather than students. Most student contributions were made in answer to questions.

In his studies Burgess discovered more specific methods utilized by teachers to bring about integration. There were at least three points in the lessons where integration could take place: (1) in the lesson introduction, (2) during the lesson itself, and (3) in the lesson conclusion.

At least four methods of integration were used by teachers in the study: (1) to present religious information, (2) to express a religious thought, (3) to express a religious position, and (4) the prescription of religious behavior.

Burgess was able to classify two aspects of integrating secular subject matter as practiced by Christian day school teachers: (1) categories of intent, showing purpose, and (2) categories of content, showing topics. In the categories of intent integration efforts revealed the following aspects:

Moralistic -- showing acceptable conduct
Factual -- showing facts about biblical information,
     people and events
Similarity of Concept -- showing the similarity of secular
     and religious concepts

Hortative -- urging students to acceptable ideas and actions
Theistic -- presenting secular subjects from a theistic
        perspective
Application -- showing the application of church standards
        in problem situations
Doctrinal -- showing acceptable doctrinal positions

In the categories of content, practices reveal the following efforts:

Religious Content -- referring to events, locales,
        personalities, and objects of religious significance
God-Works -- showing God's acts past, present, and future
God-Attributes -- showing God's nature and characteristics
Holy Spirit -- showing His person and work
Christology -- showing the work and character of
        Jesus Christ
Soteriology -- focusing on the doctrine of salvation
Evangelism -- acts of proclaiming the faith with conversion
Religious Behavior -- showing acceptable conduct,
        attitudes, and personality characteristics
Other Religions -- referring to religions other than that
        of Christianity

In all of these teaching practices it will be noted that special efforts were made to indicate the Christian point of view. However, in some of these efforts the unity of truth is not clearly seen. Other illustrations of integration practices will be given in the discussion ahead devoted to Christian higher education.

4. Organization, Administration and Supervision. Christian day schools are organized and structured along two general lines: (1) those that are sponsored, supported and controlled by some kind of institution, such as a church, and (2) those sponsored, supported and controlled by individuals. If the individuals maintain the school for others, it is known as a "private school." Where parents and others cooperate in the establishment and maintenance of a school, it

is usually called a "parent-society school." Other similar schools are operated by denominational groups and are known as parochial schools. There are some differences in philosophy of these schools. Where parochial schools are generally run for the purpose of promoting the individual concerns of a particular denomination and are rather church-centered in emphasis, private schools place greater stress on the importance of Bible, Christian philosophy of life and education.

Administratively, most of these schools have a sponsoring Board of Education which sets up the policies, rules and regulations by which the school is run. Oversight of the total operation of the school would include giving attention to such matters as public relations, finances, maintenance, transportation, maintenance concerns, as well as the selection of a principal, faculty members and supporting staff. In this kind of work Christian schools find much in common with secular schools. High on the list of responsibilities would be the determination of curriculum plans and programs. In most elementary schools the following study areas are commonly found: Bible Study, Mathematics, Language Arts, Social Science, Science, Physical Education and the Fine Arts. The high school courses are very largely extensions and outgrowths of the same kind of organization.

Supervision refers to the oversight of the quality and improvement of the program of the schools. This becomes the responsibility of the principal and teachers. Every effort should be made to achieve quality in program and practice.

C. Christian Liberal Arts College Practice

1. <u>Background</u>. In general, liberal arts colleges are products of the liberal arts heritage and the early university systems. In fact the university system stems directly from the nature and work of the Christian church. Universities emerged from the cathedral and monastic schools of the medieval period. Thus from the very beginning of higher education the church sponsored education because it was committed to education.

Among the influences which helped to shape liberal arts education were religious, cultural, philosophical and educational factors. The Renaissance and Reformation of the sixteenth century provided formative influences which were Christian, secular, and humanistic. The Renaissance directed attention away from God to man. Man's relation to nature became paramount. Human reason sought to dethrone theology in the thinking of man. A spirit of self-sufficiency was substituted for divine-dependence. Out of this emphasis came philosophical emphases which stressed rationalism, evolution, humanistic psychology and scientific criticism of life and thought.

On the other hand out of the Reformation developments came an emphasis on the primacy of God and revelation. Man's hope did not lie in himself or in humanism but God. A God-centered life patterned after Scripture led to an emphasis on the sacredness of all life -- a Christian life view.

In the West the humanistic view became dominant in circles outside the church. Within the church it spawned religious liberalism on the one hand and led to secularism on the other hand. It promoted a conservative viewpoint which led to the development of fundamentalism and evangelicalism. The great need today is for a return to biblical Christianity as it is expressed through the education programs sponsored by Christian people.

From its inception the Christian liberal arts college was committed to a liberal arts education in a Christian atmosphere and its program was directed from a Christian perspective. The history of the first colleges, such as Harvard and Yale, show clearly the eagerness of their founders to make the colleges true to the Bible and to the Christian faith. Their curricula gave a large place to the "wisdom of Christ." Unfortunately today, so many Christian liberal arts colleges have followed more in the Renaissance tradition than that of the Reformation tradition. This has resulted in a two-track system of education in many liberal arts colleges. Religion, Bible and theology, including chapel services and devotional life emphases, run on one track while that of the academic proceeds largely according to the secular university pattern included from the Renaissance.

2. <u>The Need</u>. In the face of the increasing secularization of American schools the desperate need in Christian higher education is for a Christian philosophy of education. As presently run many Christian liberal arts colleges are beset with the problem of "departmentalitis." Here knowledge is compressed into watertight compartments, with each department separate and distinct from the others. Religion is "added on" rather than integrated into the curriculum as a whole. This practice overlooks the unity of all truth based on a Christian world view. Christianity is the basic foundation and unifying philosophy of the whole educational program. Every course should issue from a Christian conception. All truth is one because God is its source. All departments in the curriculum are interrelated and stem from the idea that God is the source of all knowledge. Where this principle is practiced the program will achieve a unity, an integration, and a comprehensiveness which is truly Christian.

The challenge which comes to today's Christian liberal arts college is to develop a curriculum which is thoroughly Christian throughout and a Christian world view which encompasses re-capturing the world for Christ. It will strive to develop an educational program which reflects the best in educational philosophy and practice and at the same time show itself based on the presuppositions of Christian theism.

3. <u>Distinctives</u>. The distinctiveness of a Christian college lies in its Christian world view which is based on Scripture. It is to be expected, therefore, that the administration, faculty, curriculum, student body, and constituency should reflect this point of view. Based on this general premise, an evangelical Christian college should mani-fest the following characteristics:

1. A Christian world view based on Scripture
2. Christian aims, purposes and objectives based on this view and taken from it
3. A Christian administration and faculty fully committed to these objectives in life and teaching
4. A Christian spirit and atmosphere in school life

5. A Christian curriculum and program which is both theocentric and bibliocentric
6. A Christian motivation and product

Besides being characterized by Christian evidences, the Christian college is expected to be Christian in all of its functions. At the Board level the master policies which yield the guidelines for the total operation of the school must be Christian in character and direction. In the administration of the day-by-day school activities all management functions should also manifest Christian characteristics; all decisions made should be distinctively Christian. All faculty members must be thoroughly Christian in their daily walk as well as in the professional activities of the classroom. They should know how to correlate and integrate subject matter specialties with the Christian faith but at the highest possible level of competence.

4. <u>Liberal Arts Education</u>. Today liberal arts have developed far beyond those which were developed by the Greeks and the Romans because much has been accomplished in these fields of learning since then. But the basic values still remain.

Several views of the liberal arts are evident. The concept of producing the cultured person remains. A taste for and sense of values is developed. The means by which discriminatory thinking is done is emphasized. Most certainly the foundations of all knowledge is stressed. In Christian colleges the feeling is present that liberal arts education produces the scholar and that kind of thinking which becomes the foundation for theological study.

In some circles liberal arts education is equated with the concept of general education. In curriculum building general education is related to other curriculum facets by organizing it according to the following pattern:

1. Jesus Christ for spiritual life
2. Biblical studies for wisdom
3. General education for culture
4. Skills for service

The term "general education" is somewhat vague but there seems to be common agreement that it refers to a common, necessary kind of education. It involves mastery of certain areas of knowledge and shows the interrelationships which exist there. It involves personality development. It includes skills in language use, a knowledge of the social structure, the development of skills of correct thinking, an appreciation for the accomplishments of men in the arts and science, and an understanding of life's highest values. Content is drawn largely from God's general revelation.

General education is non-vocational in character. Content areas are commonly divided into humanities, the social sciences, and natural sciences although not strictly limited to these. These are subjects which, to the Christian, comprehend one's relation to God, to one's self, to others, and to nature.

This kind of education aims at developing the student's capacity for responsible living under God in a human society and a natural environment. It cultivates the feelings, enlarges and infuses the imagination, disciplines the mind, trains the judgment, provides historical perspective, and sheds light on the nature of every reality. It is particularly necessary for contemporary living in an age of science and technology which is perhaps the most pervasive and radically transforming experience in our lives today. In the midst of this kind of culture one function of the Christian college is to foster and nurture Christian ideas, experiences and practices which keep God in our midst and provides hope for the future.

To achieve these exalted goals, the Christian college should sponsor the "sacramental view of life" which means that the physical aspects of the world are the instruments of spiritual purpose. A curriculum, therefore, will reflect this approach to truth and will be characterized by certain priorities which emphasize that character is more important than conduct and being is more important than doing. The curriculum will also reflect the fact that values take precedence over functional efficiency. Christian educators should have the conviction that the development of practical skills will take place better if posited in a foundation of Christian character.

To realize these great objectives requires the development of

219

a curriculum which truly reflects a sacramental and Christian view of life. This further requires careful practice of the principles involved in integration and interpretation.

5. Integration. Integration means to make whole, to unify, to bring parts together. The opposite of this concept is separateness, or splintering. So much of education today lacks a unifying purpose and idea. There seems to be no ordering principle for the whole. As previously noted, a study of the history of this problem in education fails to show that there is any general agreement on what this principle should be. The suggestion was made that we can find it in the source of divine revelation.

The basis of integration for the evangelical Christian lies in the concept that all truth is God's truth. God's truth is universal in scope, therefore every part of education must be brought into relation to it. This includes the way subject matter is handled in the classroom and also all experiences involved in the organization, administration and supervision of the total educational program and setting. There must be a living union of subject matter, personnel and administration with God's truth.

Integration is not necessarily achieved by teachers who open classes with prayer or who might quote Scripture. It is achieved best when teachers see their task as one of teaching all subjects as a part of the total truth of God and pointing out to students the direct relevance of revelation to all of life and truth. All teachers in Christian schools, therefore, should see their subjects, whether scientific, historical, or otherwise, as included within the pattern of God's truth.

There are four general ways to bring about integration in the Christian school. One is through the permeation of the Christian spirit and practice in the total environment of the school where manifestations of the fruit of the Spirit are clearly revealed in lives and activities on campus. Christian education involves more than classroom activities. There are the general policies and practices of the administration as well as the corporate lives of the student body, involving such activities as clubs, athletics, etc. They, too, have their place within the framework of God's truth. Every effort should be made, therefore, to practice the principle laid down by the Apostle

Paul, "Whatsoever you do in word or deed, do all in the name of the Lord Jesus, giving thanks to God and the Father by Him" (Col. 3:17). All matters which cannot pass this test are ruled out for campus life. This principle involves not only <u>what</u> is done but also <u>how</u> things are done. Whatever is done by Christians should be done well and with the motive to please God in all our ways. This brings integration to total campus life.

A second way to bring about integration is through human relationships on campus. It has been observed on campuses that great influence for confronting the student with the Christian challenge is the personality and character of persons in the life of the college -- professors, administrators, and fellow students. The college should become a corporate Christian fellowship which permeates the student's everyday life.

The lives of Christian teachers should manifest the presence of God and the work of the Holy Spirit so that students see God in them and the way they work. Christian teachers should utilize a world view that is Christian. Such a view, as manifested in life and subject matter, will directly affect the thoughts and attitudes of students who observe. On the one hand teachers should manifest a real concern for the development of devotional life, Bible study, and Christian piety so that they will have a background from which to draw a Christian philosophy of life. In this way the teacher can approach a subject of study and show the natural relationships that exist between truth in the subject and the Christian philosophy of life. In doing this the teacher will draw heavily from both Special and General Revelation, showing also the place that consecrated reason has in the teaching-learning process.

A third way to achieve integration is through specific religious and Christian activities on campus. Some of these activities might include the following, as well as others:

1. Private and group worship in church and chapel
2. Active participation in the church life of the community, or in the church of the campus
3. A Christian-oriented counseling program

221

4. The encouragement of a sense of Christian vocation in one's life work
5. Christian student organizations among whose aims should be the development of a feeling of responsibility on the part of the individual college member for the welfare of the whole college community as well as for the success of his own private work
6. Religious emphasis periods which should be integrated with the total religious program of the college

A fourth way to bring about integration is through academic activities. Most important, and most neglected, is the impingement of the Christian presuppositions upon the student through his distinctively academic experiences. There is a disturbing failure on the part of many of the teachers to view their activities in the Christian perspective of revelation. Because they have never given the matter much thought and because of the limitations imposed by the current teaching materials available, many teachers unwittingly present their courses in a manner which is inconsistent with the tenets of the Christian faith. What is needed is a sincere and searching examination by all teachers of the relation of their fields to the Christian perspective given to us through divine revelation. To do this calls for continuing study and discussion of the presuppositions of the Christian faith on the part of all school personnel.

As used in secular education, educators use the concept of integration in various ways. Psychologically, integration is the blanket term employed to denote the educator's concern for the total personality of the learner. Pedagogically, integration is used to describe a teaching procedure which relates varieties of subject matter to units of study or to problem-solving situations. Sociologically, integration is utilized in three different ways, namely: (1) to designate the desired relationship between an individual and other individuals as interacting personalities; (2) to designate the desired relationship between an individual and the organized institutions of society; and (3) to designate the desired relationship between one organized institution of society (the school, for example) and other institutions involved in the complex of culture.

Emphasis here is on helping learners become integrated personalities who function creatively in society. The goal is a well-adjusted person. Obviously, here the emphasis is placed on behavior rather than on subject matter content. The purpose of any curriculum for secular education, therefore, is to aid individuals with improving their life and living. Attempts are made to provide positive aids to learners in improving the process of intelligent interacting and adjusting.

In handling subject matter secular educators have sought to bring about integration between subject matter disciplines, showing relationships of truth within them and how to utilize the information. This is correlation. An illustration of this procedure was given in Integrative Principles of Modern Thought edited by Henry Margenau (Gordon and Breach, Science Publishers, New York, 1972). This work grew out of the activities and experience of the Center for Integrative Education, whose aim was to provide methods and materials to overcome the divisiveness of modern education. Through research and publication this group sought to build bridges between separate disciplines of learning. Concern was expressed over the results of overspecialization and its harmful effects on society, particularly in the arts, philosophy and sciences. This group decried the use of dogmas, facts and language as the basis for integration and advocated instead the use of concepts. They sought to identify the major concepts of truth which unify knowledge and recommended their relevance to modern living. Thus, they sought to provide a synopsis of useful concepts and theories for integrating modern knowledge. Thus, emphasis was placed on the structure of subject matter.

Another way to bring about integration is to unify concepts within each discipline to correlate ideas. This approach was advocated by James R. Miller and Barbara Hayes-Roth in Text Annotation: A Technique for Facilitating Knowledge Integration, a paper published by the Rand Corporation, Santa Monica, California, 1977. They sought to identify facts and facts-and-inference situations in the same text. Here an attempt was made to integrate facts and ideas <u>within</u> each course. They felt that greater understanding of a particular discipline can be realized by integrating the major ideas presented than the facts covered. Here again, we see emphasis placed on the structure of a discipline.

Several types of curricula have been produced by secular educators in efforts to bring about integrative behavior. Where the subject curriculum places emphasis on individual subjects, the <u>correlated curriculum</u> attempts to achieve integration by showing how subjects are related and correlated. The <u>broad fields</u> curriculum lays emphasis on a few fields of greater areas of learning rather than on small subjects. This type of curriculum has been widely used in colleges and secondary schools. Closely related to this type of curriculum is the <u>core curriculum</u> where a fixed, prescribed body of subject matter and learning activities in subjects are required of everyone but with variability of content and activities within the subjects to meet the varying needs of individuals. The <u>experience curriculum</u> provides a series of purposeful experiences growing out of pupil interests and moving toward an ever more adequate understanding of and participation in the surrounding culture and group life.

While these various views of curriculum have some contribution to make, it is apparent that little or no attempt is made to build into them a definite set of values based on an acceptable philosophy of life. It is this need that Christian educators feel can best be met by integrating a Christian philosophy of life based on divine revelation with subject matter and activities.

More specifically, perhaps the best way to bring about integration is in the teaching of the subjects themselves. This does not involve a point-by-point reconciliation of the Bible with all subjects necessarily, although Scripture is important, but primarily an emphasis on the unity of truth; all truth is God's truth.

If the Christian college is committed to the world view of Christian theism, it implies that revelation illumines every sphere of life and learning. A teacher may teach from the presuppositions involved in the Christian faith or from the presuppositions of some rival world view or creed, but he does have a "faith." This faith expresses itself in allegiance to principles that determine the answer to questions such as: "What is reality?" and "How does man know what is real?" and in such practical pursuits as the selection of material to be used in courses.

A first step would demand an examination and explication by every faculty member of presuppositions held by himself in regards to man, nature, and the universe and how these views influence his selection and evaluation of subject matter, methodology, and attitude toward students.

A second step is to bring to bear upon the various disciples in a structural way the implications and interpretations of the Christian world-view. Subject matter should never be taught factually. It does not exist independently from God's creation. Teachers should show how the subject deals with some aspect of God's creation and how it relates to other disciplines to show the unity of God's truth. Each subject should be taught to show how its knowledge contributes to the student's knowledge of how to live and work for God.

In planning for classroom teaching and learning the Christian teacher will intentionally throw his subject matter discipline within the framework of revelation. The following pattern is suggested as a guide for achieving this:

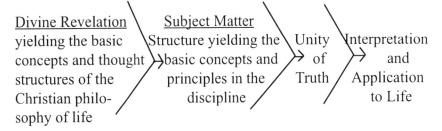

Divine Revelation yielding the basic concepts and thought structures of the Christian philosophy of life → Subject Matter Structure yielding the basic concepts and principles in the discipline → Unity of Truth → Interpretation and Application to Life

To bring about integration in the classroom each Christian teacher needs to combine the basic concepts and thought structures about reality, provided in the Christian philosophy of life recorded in biblical studies, with the structure of each subject matter discipline. This goes beyond merely showing relationships (correlation) and comparisons to merging these concepts into one Christian concept.

225

Thereby the unity of truth can be seen.

Jerome S. Bruner in his classic work <u>The Process of Education</u> (Random House, 1960) refers to the importance of <u>structure</u> in each subject matter discipline. He pointed out that to learn structure is to learn how things are related. Furthermore, the disciplines reveal distinctively pervading and powerful ideas and attitudes in them and can be taught at any age level. These basic ideas should be clearly isolated and revealed to students in each discipline so that they see the rationale for each subject including the purpose and place of each discipline in the total curriculum and the distinctive contribution it makes to total knowledge.

The structure of biblical studies focuses primarily on the teachings about God and a Christian philosophy of life, thus providing Special Revelation. All other subjects provide truth about additional realities derived from General Revelation. By putting together all of these basic ideas into one frame of reference the unity of truth is achieved and integration made possible. From that point both interpretation and application to all thought and life can be made. In this way students are taught to think in a Christian mode as well as to see how truth is related to other truth and to life.

Obviously, not all subject matter is equally revelational. Some subjects have more to say about God and Christian living and service than do others, but in spite of this the full spectrum of truth is provided by revelations of the various disciplines.

Christian teachers must also deal with the presence and effects of sin on both learner and subject matter disciplines. In the learner's case the carnal mind presents communication barriers to learning, particularly to spiritual truths. Furthermore, sin's effect on life and truth in general has distorted truth to such an extent that special efforts need to be made to sort out truth from error. This is done through the utilization of the values and concepts of biblical studies which provide the guidelines for doing this. More will be said about this matter when we discuss interpretation.

It must be recognized also that God's General Revelation has created truth objectively to be discovered. This means that non-Christians can discover truth simply because it is discoverable. Non-

226

Christian teachers, however, do not recognize the source and frame of reference for the truths they discover because in their thinking they have discovered them outside the context of God's revelation. Truth may be revealed through scientific analysis and experimentation but, for the Christian, even these techniques must be recognized as coming from God.

One way to bring about integration and correlation when handling subject matter is to discover instances in which the Bible and the subject matter are talking about the same thing. Parallels with biblical history and secular history is an illustration of this approach. The utilization of Scripture principles in the evaluation of teaching materials is another way. Principles of righteousness, integrity and honesty should be emphasized in the handling of truth at any level of school life. It is also possible to point out the ethical or moral inferences of truths being taught. Questions may be raised as to how Christian people should act or could act in situations prevalent in the subject matter being taught. Still another method consists of the use of biblical illustrations in the areas of instruction. Yet another approach is to spot the corresponding biblical custom and relate it to the question at hand.

There are some teaching procedures which might be utilized by teachers in the classroom to help bring about integration. At the beginning of a course the teacher could identify any secular points of view that might come up and then compare these with the Christian philosophy of life. During the conduct of the course teachers can point out where subject matter proves to be in harmony with the Word of God, or where it might deviate from it. At the end of the course questions might be included in the final examinations to test whether or not the students have been sensitive about the relationship of subject matter to Christian views. Of course, general discussions during the progress of the school terms can often bring out integrative concerns. Assigned readings in supplementary sources and the Bible can also bring to bear Christian views on issues.

Perhaps there are other ways that a Christian teacher can utilize in achieve integration. Suffice to say, unless the truth of God in the Scriptures is related to truth as discovered by man, our educational program is a secular one taught by a Christian. If we really believe that all truth is God's truth, we must show this to our students. They will not guess it.

6. Interpretation. The interpretation of truth among secular educators takes place largely through the use of what might be called "natural" interpretation. Here natural reasoning abilities are used to discover truth, and trial and error are utilized to determine truth from error.

If a professor is a Christian theist, he has a perspective from which he can interpret the facts and deal with the issues in his field more adequately. If Christian theism is a valid position, it asserts the ultimate truth about reality as a whole. Therefore, it provides the key for the interpretation of all truths in special fields of knowledge which deal with particular aspects of reality. God is not only absolute light, He is the source of the light which illuminates every field of reality we explore. A God-centered Christian must have God-centered thinking and reveal this in the teaching process. One conclusion, however, that we draw from all of this is that the Christian professor must never allow his religious perspective to become a substitute for the careful establishment of facts and development of theories appropriate to his field. The role of his Christian perspective is to enable him to see the facts in a deeper dimension and to relate the descriptions of them by the methods used in his field to a more inclusive and in fact to an ultimate interpretation of truth. Furthermore, the Christian teacher should never be afraid of research, discovery, or experimentation because if they lead to the truth, there will God be found.

Christian educators are called upon to think God's thoughts after Him. Thinking, therefore, needs to be both God-centered and biblical. Great reliance on the presence and the work of the Holy Spirit is also necessary. The process might be termed one of "theological filtering." The role of the teacher here is to help identify, by means of Scripture and theology, what is good and bad. How does the subject matter under consideration fit into a Christian world-view? When alternatives are presented to both teacher and student, then the process of thinking will be one of ascertaining which alternative may be better than other ones because they are more biblical and Christian. Since sin is an ever present reality, it will become necessary also to point out its distortions in relation to the subject being considered.

The basic pattern, therefore, by which interpretation can be achieved by Christian teachers might take the following form:

Source of Truth	Integration	Application
Special Revelation	Unity of	Personal
General Revelation	truth	Social
Subject matter structure		Home, church
		School
		Society
		Vocation, etc.

Since all truth is God's truth, the source and beginning point of interpretation is to be found in revelation, both Special and General, and merged with the structure (basic principles) of the subject matter discipline. From these sources a synthesis of truth can be realized thus achieving unity and integration. From this point interpretation and application of truth can be made to all aspects of life.

The clues provided to the Christian teacher from revelational sources, as indicated above, are to be found first in those subjects which reflect most closely and personally the character, nature and work of God. These subjects provide primary sources of truth, both Living and Written, and yield great concepts and thought structures which in turn serve as guidelines to integration and interpretation. Such concepts would include thoughts about:

God	Salvation	The future	Social
Creation	Values	Purpose	Institutions,
Man	Being	Truth	etc.
Sin	Society	Education	

One will notice that all of these concepts and more are included in a carefully worked out Christian philosophy of life.

229

Thought structures provide basic ideas and principles for the interpretation of subject matter disciplines. Such thought structures would include concepts about creation, purpose, process, providence, God's presence in history, His redemptive acts in dealing with sin and man, and the perspective of the future provided in prophecy. This all means that the great concepts and thought structures provided in God's revelation yield a Christian philosophy of life; which in turn provides the frame of reference within which all subject matter is handled and interpreted.

Added to the great concepts and thought structures of the Christian philosophy of life are those basic ideas and principles of the various subject disciplines, which, blended with Christian concepts, help to make interpretation and application possible to all areas of life.

Another approach to interpretation and application of truth is to view the whole matter as a process which involves the following facets:

1. Information -- gathering truth as fact
2. Discrimination -- seeing truth in relation to error
3. Correlation -- seeing truth in relation to other truth
4. Integration -- seeing truth as one whole from God
5. Application -- seeing truth in relation to life

Information focuses on the importance of gathering the facts and identifying clearly the structure of a subject matter discipline. In the ascertaining of such facts, Christian teachers need to be as thorough and professional as any other teacher. This step involves seeing truth as fact.

The discrimination facet involves the evaluation of truth and shows its possible relation to error. Here is where all perceived factual knowledge is run through one's biblical and theological "filter system" to determine its validity and usefulness.

The correlation facet emphasizes the relationships to be seen between truths discovered. This shows truth in relation to other truth. Because there are no such things as "brute facts" to the

Christian, all facts of truth must be seen in relation to God as Creator and Author. This is where the facet of integration becomes important and where the unity of truth is revealed. This is where the truth that all truth is God's truth becomes evident. Here is where it can be determined in what ways, if any, God might be revealed. It is also the place where more than one option of truth might be discovered. At this point it will be the responsibility of teachers and students to determine which option, if any, might possibly be more true than others. The total process becomes one of moving from facts to principles to a Christian point of view.

The whole process is culminated in application to determine the relation of truth to life with all that it might involve. The following questions might possibly be used to determine implications and applications of truth from a Christian perspective:

1. What cultural and factual knowledge is present which can be used in practical situations in the whole of life?
2. What direct parallels can naturally be drawn between biblical content and practical content?
3. What attributes of God are made evident?
4. What kind of person will this help me to be?
5. How will these truths help society? The home? Vocation?
6. How will these truths help build the Kingdom of God?

7. Administrative and Supervisory Means to Secure Integration. While education is a process not limited in the sphere of action to the classroom or even to the school, nevertheless the classroom is the central setting for instruction. The kind of educational product a school turns out will be principally determined by what goes on in its classrooms. It follows, therefore, that if a Christian school is to fulfill its function as such it must acknowledge Christian presuppositions as fundamental to its instruction, not in one but in all its classrooms. This end requires that the school formulate a Christian philosophy of education and effectively translate it by consistent administration and supervision into the concrete realities of classroom teaching. Thus, if a school proposes to call itself Christian and to

offer a distinctively Christian education it must see to it that all its teaching is projected on the basis of Christian presuppositions. This demands deliberate intentional effort on the part of administrators and supervisors to help achieve integration.

The effectiveness of any typical Christian teacher is dependent to a considerable degree on administration and supervision because such teachers have not had adequate training in the techniques and knowledge required. Most teacher training institutions have not provided such training for teachers. Also by its very nature integration in any particular school demands coordinated effort on the part of the whole teaching staff. Only a strong top leadership can hope to produce such coordination. A staff unified by ultimate goals, not individuals working separately, however earnestly, will gain the desired results. For this, school leaders are responsible through good administration and supervision whether at higher, elementary, or secondary levels.

A whole-school program requires whole-school cooperation, which is possible only through effective administrative and supervisory leadership. This view implies a conception of religion based on a clear theological position, and it requires a unified, positive program. In that situation the school head is the key figure.

For this reason, many Christian schools prefer clergymen to head their schools, but this does not necessarily hold in every case, particularly if the school head is knowledgeable about theology and Christian educational philosophy.

High on the list of the duties of a school head is the matter of teacher selection. If integration is to be achieved it becomes necessary to secure teachers and other workers who are Christian and who will seek to present a Christian world view in classroom experience.

Administrators can schedule faculty conferences to discuss the importance of integrating the Christian faith with subjects taught. Such matters as the importance of a point of view, the implications of the Christian faith for each subject, and just exactly what the Christian faith is can be discussed. Perhaps this could be done in on-going conferences devoted to each subject matter discipline.

Following is a list of supervisory methods which might be

232

employed to help Christian teachers do a better job of integration:

1. Holding effective group meetings of teachers
2. Conferring constructively with teachers, individually or in small groups with common interests and needs
3. Being easily accessible to teachers who need help, encouragement, stimulus and direction
4. Encouraging and directing the use of promising strengths
5. Diagnosing troubles and helping teachers overcome them
6. Providing teachers with pertinent information regarding the pupils
7. Assisting teachers to study the pupils -- their abilities, their attitudes, and their ambitions -- and to adapt the work according to the revealed individual differences
8. Sharing in cooperative work -- e.g. improving courses of study, lesson planning, and the like
9. Cooperating in the examination, interpretation, criticism, and evaluation of textbooks and syllabi
10. Advising and assisting in the collection of enriched teaching materials
11. Helping teachers to understand the results of research and to apply them in their own work
12. Directing simple research and experimentation
13. Giving or providing demonstrations of good teaching
14. Directing visits to superior teachers and helping to interpret the reports of observation and to get them used
15. Using stenographic reports or recorded recitation summaries for illustration of good procedures
16. Directing and using the results of professional readings
17. Improving study habits of both teachers and pupils
18. Using effective supervisory bulletins
19. Encouraging self-rating by teachers
20. Keeping supervision above the level of inspection
21. Using intensive "drives" for specific objectives
22. Encouraging cultural enrichment
23. Setting an example of professional efficiency

Almost all of these methods are applicable to a program of integrated Christian education and no doubt many administrators using these suggestions as a checklist could show a considerable amount of supervisory activity by way of in-service training and guidance.

Other administrative and supervisory means employed in the service of Christian education include pre-opening orientation and devotional meetings, the altar or chapel as a focal center, daily morning and evening chapel services, a daily two-minute period of silence each morning, student conferences and assembly program on the subject of Christian aims and goals, evangelistic services and prayer meetings, religious extracurricular activities, and weekly faculty devotional services. To the extent that these are used to help unify the life of a school around a Christian center, they may be said to contribute to integrated Christian instruction.

Problems of integration and illustrations drawn from classroom experience might well be made topics of discussion in group meetings held monthly. These should be supplemented by individual conferences scheduled by the head of the school or his deputy supervisory with teachers to make specific applications to their own situations, and by other supervisory aid given both inside and outside the classroom. Further help can be rendered through keeping teachers informed about appropriate radio programs and books and magazine articles that might prove useful; making it possible for teachers to attend conferences, conventions, institutes, and the like, where helpful discussions are apt to occur; calling in specialists from schools of education and religion to serve as lecturers and consultants; organizing workshops or cooperating in planning and attending them along with teachers, at one's own or another school; preparing supervisory bulletins; assisting in the selection of textbooks and other teaching materials and helping teachers to adapt these materials in effective ways to the purposes of integrated Christian instruction; undertaking cooperatively with teachers, and encouraging them to attempt on their own part, research and experimentation; working with teachers to formulate objectives, both ultimate and immediate, in relation to the Christian purposes of the school. While it is true that the character, convictions, and abilities of the teacher (who should be chosen as much on the basis of the first two considerations as the third) primarily determine the quality of classroom instruction, it is also true that to gain the greatest degree of instructional effectiveness, especially where integrated Christian education is sought, the teacher must become part of a growing cooperative enterprise; and to produce this result, supervision rightly conceived and employed is the essential factor.

The major questions, therefore, regarding the relation of faculty members to the matter of achieving integration in subject matter teaching are <u>where</u> and <u>how</u> this is done. It may be desirable to train each professor as a lay theologian so that factual knowledge and interpretation may be implemented through the same person. Or it may be necessary to augment course work taught from any explicitly announced assumptions with the extra class offerings in a theistic interpretation of all subject matter. It may be desirable to have somewhere in the curriculum courses which give a systematic theological interpretation of the various disciplines. This is done in some Roman Catholic schools where a Thomistic synthesis is used.

In the final analysis, and to summarize this matter, integration by teachers can be brought about by the professor in the manner of teaching and in his attitude as well as in the content of the course itself. Every department in the Christian school has the obligation to leave a Christian impression because the sum of the attitudes of all members of the faculty will make an impression upon the philosophy of the student. It will be expected, therefore, that each professor will observe the following rules in teaching:

1. A revelational perspective requires the teacher to give due weight to the religious facts which are relevant to his field.
2. A revelational perspective enables the teacher to recognize the limitations of the method used in his field.
3. A revelational perspective affects profoundly the interpretations of facts in a field of study.
4. A revelational perspective may often be expressed more effectively through the personal qualities and attitudes of the teacher than through anything else he says.

8. <u>Functional Principles of Curriculum Practice</u>. The approach to curriculum construction and practice in Christian colleges should be as thorough and professional as in any other type of school. This demands certain commitments on the part of Christian school administrators and teachers, such as:

1. A commitment to quality
2. A commitment to curriculum integrity
3. A commitment to professional competence
4. A commitment to liberal education
5. A commitment to Christian theism
6. A commitment to the Christian theistic world view
7. A commitment to particular efforts to integrate the Christian faith with academic matters
8. A commitment to the production of Christian character and life-style
9. A commitment to the objectives of the Word of God
10. A commitment to the hope of the life to come through Jesus Christ as Savior and Lord of Life

In a recent study by the faculty at Calvin College (1970) three Christian views of an approach to the use of the liberal arts at the college level were presented. They were (1) the pragmatist, (2) the classicist, and (3) disciplinary views. All three views were considered to be Christian, but they opted for the disciplinary view in their case.

The pragmatist view utilizes the principle that the acquisition of knowledge is justified on the basis of its use in solving concrete problems in contemporary life. Such use in this view avoids the pitfalls of mere Greek intellectualism. Instead, Christian colleges should utilize the liberal arts also to help graduates prepare for a life's vocation.

In the classicist view the principle of developing the whole man -- morally, intellectually, aesthetically, etc. -- is utilized. The goal is the development of the wise and cultured person rather than the specialist. Rather, general education is used and has priority over specialization.

In the disciplinary view the primary focus is on scholarly disciplines by both teachers and students who are directed by the Word of God. In the study of the liberal arts disciplined efforts are made not only to discover and study the institutions, creations and activities of man but also to determine the religious perspectives and mind behind all of these cultural products. The Christian scholar will utilize the disciplines as an exercise of his Christian faith and will strive to see reality in that perspective. This does not preclude the possibility of specialization however.

9. <u>Suggested Curriculum Themes to Achieve Integration</u>. Due to the character and distinctiveness of the subject matter disciplines, possibilities for integration are almost endless. The writer made some suggestions along this line in a previous work entitled <u>A Christian Approach to Education</u>, rev. ed., Mott Media, 1977.

To accomplish curriculum objectives from a Christian perspective requires constant attention being given to the pattern of integration and interpretation demanded. This pattern requires the following approach to truth in each of the subject matter disciplines.

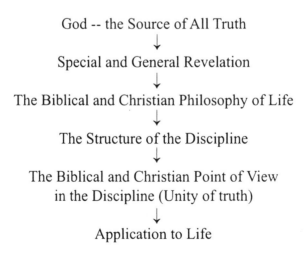

God -- the Source of All Truth
↓
Special and General Revelation
↓
The Biblical and Christian Philosophy of Life
↓
The Structure of the Discipline
↓
The Biblical and Christian Point of View
in the Discipline (Unity of truth)
↓
Application to Life

Some Generalizations

Since all truth is God's truth Christian teachers can confidently approach the classroom and design their work in accord with this principle. An overview of truth from this perspective enables Christian teachers to see their respective subject matter disciplines as "ideas" from God, thus:

> History gives students clear appreciation of the Christian movement through the centuries; it is the unrolling of God's scroll in the dimension of time; it is a record of God's revelation in the affairs of the human race.

> Philosophy shows the contributions of Jesus to the development of modern thought and attitude.

> Sociology indicates the influences of Jesus in creating an attitude of sympathy which makes applied sociology possible.

> Psychology shows an appreciation of religious experience.

> Science shows the working out of God's purposes in the Space dimension; it reveals natural law which shows God's control over His creation.

> Mathematics shows that God's creation involves ideas of number, form, symmetry and system and laws governing the existence and harmonious working of all things; it is essential to ethical dealings between men.

> The gifts of speech, reading and writing are gifts to be used for God's glory.

Citizenship is a result of God's creation of man as a social being and is based on God's laws for society and government.

Geography shows the whole earth related to God.

Physical education is founded on the principle that man's body is a gift of God and a temple of the Holy Spirit.

Art and Music are intended to glorify God since all beauty originates with Him and is a reflection of Him.

Integration can be brought about through assigned readings of the biographies of great figures of American History and correlated with Scripture. John Amos Comenius, a seventeenth century Moravian Bishop, suggested many methods for blending religion and education into an effective whole in his Great Didactic. He advocated the use of the Bible in teaching children to read and write.

The Humanities

Traditionally, subjects classified as the Humanities have included literature, art, history, philosophy, and religion. In liberal education one seeks to develop the personality intellectually, aesthetically, morally and spiritually. In these subjects the subjective life of man comes to its greatest expression. The strict objectivity of the natural and social sciences exclude value judgments and, therefore, they cannot reveal man's personal and inner life, nor give meaning to life. The Humanities tend to develop sensitivity, intellectual enthusiasm, moral idealism, an understanding of man and a life of humility and gratitude before God.

The pattern of integration and interpretation for the Humanities will appear as follows:

239

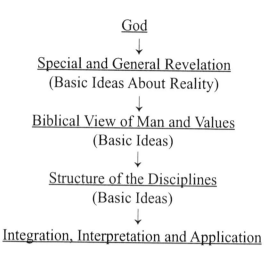

God

↓

Special and General Revelation
(Basic Ideas About Reality)

↓

Biblical View of Man and Values
(Basic Ideas)

↓

Structure of the Disciplines
(Basic Ideas)

↓

Integration, Interpretation and Application

Integration themes and basic ideas (structures) to be stressed might possibly include:

1. Showing the relevance of a world view as expressed in contemporary music, art, poetry and literature
2. Stressing God as Creator, Who is the Supreme Artist and that we can learn from Him as He makes room in our lives for creative expression
3. Emphasizing that literature exemplifies the indirect and vicarious means of teaching that are characteristic of God's pedagogy
4. Showing that poetry, prose and drama are art forms to fill needs for human expression and reveal also methods that God uses to teach
5. Pointing out that the Bible is the example of literature at its best
6. Showing the influence of Greco-Roman culture on th arts and sciences of the Western world
7. Revealing the presence of Christian symbolism in many, if not most, works of art, architecture and philosophical thought and that the vast majority of poetic and musical expressions were religious
8. Showing that the humanities reveal truths which add to

the glory of God
9. Showing that they can lead to greater sensitivity in worship
10. Pointing out that in some cases Christians can see the work of the Holy Spirit in the characteristics of the arts
11. Revealing that the arts can be used in making the Gospel message more vivid
12. Stressing that beauty and music are gifts from God
13. Revealing the effects of sin on the arts
14. Giving students an appreciation of God-honoring music and art
15. Challenging gifted students to consider humanities as a possible vocation under God
16. Emphasize all talents are gifts from God
17. Showing all students the results of a life lived independently of God and how empty such a life can be
18. Use of art to highlight great Christian seasons and themes

History

The sacramental view of life shows that the physical aspects of the world are instruments of God's purpose. History, therefore, is not a blind push of evolutionary mechanism but rather is a sacramental economy in which the hand of God never ceases to cause all things to work together for the accomplishment of divine ends and goals.

Themes and basic ideas to be given attention could include the following:

1. The appearance of God in history is not only true to facts but inevitable from the very nature of God.
2. The natural is a part of the supernatural work of God and is supplementary to Special Revelation.
3. God is an inner directing Presence in history and an Authoritative will above it, directing life toward the goal He has in mind, the Kingdom of God.
4. Show how the Renaissance provided the transition from

Medieval to modern man and what effect it had on philosophy, religion, politics, and art.

5. Show how the Renaissance shifted the emphasis from God to man.
6. Indicate the significance of the Renaissance in the development of humanism.
7. Emphasize the effect of the Reformation on life, religion and education and that it was an effort to restore the biblical and Christian concepts of men, with particular stress on the priesthood of all believers and the sacredness of all life and work.
8. Trace the rise of the secular outlook on life, showing how Humanism pushed God into the background of individuals and society and supplanted Him with an emphasis on man as the measure of all things.
9. Show the importance of our Judeo-Christian heritage as a balance to Greco-Roman influences.
10. Provide a Christian philosophy of history.
11. Show the influences of religion in speeches like those of Abraham Lincoln.
12. Show the place of religion in the reform movements of the 1830's and the progressive movement of 20th century America.
13. Show how Quakerism and Methodism arose to revive depressed conditions in the 17th and 18th centuries.
14. Show place and influence of religion from the colonial period to modern times.
15. Correlate biblical history with secular history.
16. Stress the sovereignty of God.
17. Show God's plan as history.
18. Show God's activities in the rise and fall of nations.

Philosophy

Someone has defined philosophy as "an intellectual discipline concerned with the nature of reality and the investigation of the general principles of knowledge and existence." It involves the study of truth and, therefore, it cannot ignore religious issues and Christianity. Some of the themes and basic ideas to be highlighted might include the following:

1. Show how the current emphasis on Humanism arose during the Renaissance.
2. Define Humanism as the attempt to interpret the world in terms of man's self-sufficiency.
3. Show the attempts of the Reformers and Reformation period to renew the Christian world view.
4. Show that Christian Theism is one of the options to be entertained concerning the nature of the universe.
5. Indicate that evidence from science, art, history and religious experience more fully vindicate the truths of Christian Theism than any other hypotheses.
6. Stress the kind of thinking that is characterized by open enquiry, rational analysis, a fair consideration of opposing views, and the drawing of conclusions based on evidence.
7. Point out that all truth is God's truth wherever found.
8. Study how to think and reason.
9. Show that Christianity is grounded solidly in reality.
10. Highlight some of the emphases of non-Christian philosophies, such as:
    (1) de-emphasis on subjective values and beliefs which depreciate the importance of religion and morality;
    (2) show how this has led to a de-emphasis on the place of God in our lives.
11. Teach the values and use of reflective thinking and the skills of inductive processes.
12. Help students develop a set of Christian values based on the life and teachings of Jesus Christ.

Social Sciences and Social Studies

The Social Sciences are those disciplines which are primarily concerned with social institutions and with individual and group interaction. They are concerned to a large extent with man's efforts to understand himself and influence his human environment. Traditionally, the scope of studies in this area has included the fields of anthropology, history (although some would include history with the humanities), sociology, psychology, political science, geography, economics, law and education. These studies are used largely among adults. Research, investigation, and experimentation are their methods. They are the primary sources of social science knowledge.

Social studies have primarily a pedagogical end, making known to students the human relationships discovered and confirmed by scientific study. Character education is at the heart of these studies which are used primarily in public education. History, geography, and civics are found at the elementary education level and economics and sociology for high schools.

The pattern of integration and interpretation for the Social Sciences and Social Studies disciplines will appear as follows:

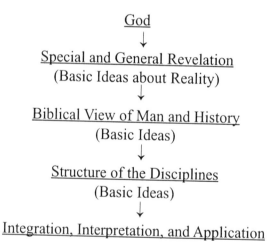

God
↓
Special and General Revelation
(Basic Ideas about Reality)
↓
Biblical View of Man and History
(Basic Ideas)
↓
Structure of the Disciplines
(Basic Ideas)
↓
Integration, Interpretation, and Application

Christian concepts and basic ideas to be emphasized in these studies might include the following matters:
1. The providence of God in the affairs of men
2. The individual dignity of the human person
3. The material and spiritual interdependence of all men;

244

their rights and obligations, as founded upon justice and charity

4. The sacredness and integration of the family and the church
5. The rights and duties of our common protector, the State
6. Creation by God and the consequent dependence of man and the earth on Him
7. Man is a steward over creation
8. In work man can cooperate with God
9. The evils of materialism
10. Geography can be a study of God's providential care and His suggestions on man's stewardship
11. Respect for and appreciation of the contributions of the various races of men, their languages and ideals
12. Consideration of the problem of man, who he is, and what he is in a technological world
13. Point up the importance of the problems of how we deal with men
14. To show the significance of human life and culture
15. Because Christianity on the human side is social, it can utilize the social sciences to assist it in its work in the world
16. Point out that because man is not an automation he is free to choose the conditions under which he lives
17. While society can be objectively studied, this does not mean that humanity must be reduced completely to a natural phenomenon
18. Christian education will gear naturally into the social sciences by the fact that by its very nature it involves concern for satisfactory community
19. Point up the need for both personal and social regeneration of the individual and society by means of the spiritual regeneration of both
20. Indicate the importance of the home and the church as basic institutions of society
21. The cultivation of an objective attitude toward social is-

sues and problems
22. Develop a Christian view of man and society
23. Stress an understanding of the social basis of reality and man's social relationships
24. A study of how sin has distorted man's social relations
25. A study of the task of reconstructing our knowledge and conception of society from a Christian standpoint
26. A study of how Christians should interact with the secular world so that they can be adequately equipped to render service within it
27. Be aware of the dangers of living in a sinful and secular world (John 15:19-20) and prepare a defense for it
28. Equip Christian students with the philosophy of the Great Commission and the skills to carry it out
29. Stress the responsibility of Christians as God's stewards on earth
30. To stress concepts of conflict, secularization, culture, government, justice and freedom, economics, people and land relationships, a sense of history, pluralism, commitment and purpose
31. Develop Christian attitudes about world conditions and problems
32. General topics to be covered might include the comparative study of religions, philosophies of life, interfaith education, school cooperation with community religious groups
33. Develop Christian attitudes toward money and possessions
34. In economics point out the importance to God of finances, property ownership, work attitudes and ethical business principles, and stewardship
35. God's teachings about government and man's responsibility
36. Responsibilities of good and sound administration
37. Christian bases for the principles and practices of good leadership

Natural Science and Mathematics

In a broad sense, science means knowledge; in a narrow sense it means a method for investigating the physical world. The natural sciences are "those systematically organized bodies of accumulated knowledge concerning the physical and biological universe which have been derived exclusively through techniques of direct, objective observation." Subjects commonly embraced in this area are anatomy, astronomy, botany, chemistry, geology, physics, physiology and zoology. Mathematics is an essential tool of science.

The pattern for the integration and interpretation of the Natural Sciences and Mathematics will appear as follows:

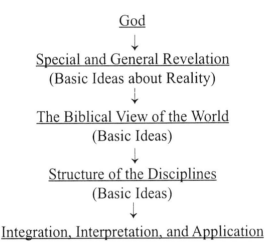

God
↓
Special and General Revelation
(Basic Ideas about Reality)
↓
The Biblical View of the World
(Basic Ideas)
↓
Structure of the Disciplines
(Basic Ideas)
↓
Integration, Interpretation, and Application

Some of the generalizations by which integration and interpretation can take place could be achieved by including the following observations:

1. Stress God as Creator and nature as God's handiwork
2. Study of science may be an act of worship because we focus on God's handiwork
3. Study of science can reveal the validity of our faith in the God of creation
4. Christian theism provides the basic axioms of science –

the unity of the world, the uniformity of the world, and the rationality of the world

5. Thus, Christianity nurtured the post-Renaissance science movement

6. Applied science can help the church accomplish its mission of communication and healing to the world

7. An understanding of science and technological developments with their effect on human life should be provided

8. Deal with the fear that technology now has the power to destroy man

9. Where is man's identity in a "computer age?"

10. What is the place of technology? How can Christian people utilize it?

11. A study of nature as God's handiwork and the results of man's management of natural resources

12. Show the relevance of biblical, theological and Christian philosophical knowledge to such matters as the existence of God, His relation to the world as Creator and the providence of God

13. Show the dangers of restricting knowledge to the physical realm to the neglect of moral, spiritual and social matters

14. Show the relation of science to the meaning of life

15. Work out a synthesis of science, philosophy and religion

16. Point out that when science prevents and disrupts intellectual, moral and spiritual knowledge it can become an enemy of human welfare and of truth

17. The material world reveals the wisdom and power of a Creator

18. Show God's future plans for the universe

19. Teach the merits and limitations of the scientific method

20. Show that the "laws of nature" are methods by which God controls the universe

21. Sex education

22. The purpose and growth of living things are part of God's design

23. Deal with the issue of the conflict between science and Scripture
24. In astronomy show the origin of heavenly bodies and the character and description of the universe, also man's relation to it
25. In earth science show the history and description of the earth, God's control over it, its future, and man's relation to it
26. In physics and chemistry show the origin and character of matter and energy as created by God
27. Chemical and physical laws often illustrate spiritual truth
28. In life sciences show God's relations, the beginnings of life on earth, the principles of life science in Scripture and man's relations to plants and animals
29. In zoology show the history of animal life with its characteristics and how God and man are related to animal life
30. In botany show how plant growth and development follows God-given laws
31. In mathematics show God's concern for numbers and the value of mathematics

Language Arts

The subjects normally included in the area of language arts include Literature, Foreign Languages, Reading, Writing, and Speech. The Bible has given much attention to the matter of communication. God has communicated Himself to man in many ways, and man has also communicated with other men. It is crucial, therefore, that a Christian view of communication be given in the classroom.

The pattern by which integration and interpretation may well take place for the language arts will appear as follows:

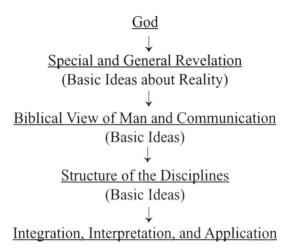

God
↓
Special and General Revelation
(Basic Ideas about Reality)
↓
Biblical View of Man and Communication
(Basic Ideas)
↓
Structure of the Disciplines
(Basic Ideas)
↓
Integration, Interpretation, and Application

Following is a list of suggested themes for presenting the basic ideas of the language arts:

1. To help students use God-given language abilities to full creative expression, thus praising God and helping others

2. To show the importance of communication on God's level and human affairs

3. To stress the four aspects of language communication – reading, writing, listening and talking

4. To stress the importance of Christians being responsible to God and fellow beings for using language in the right way

5. To help students function to highest personal capacity in speaking and understanding language

6. To apply Christian standards in communication

7. Show the values of the Written Word (Scripture) and the spoken Word (preaching) for our faith

8. Show Christian interpretations of great pieces of literature

9. Show the emphasis on religious values in non-Christian literature

10. Correlate Bible with literary selections to show the Bible as great literature

Subjects commonly classified in this area of knowledge are often referred to as Biblical Studies and include those branches of learning and departments of knowledge which draw their content primarily from the Holy Scriptures. The field includes the disciplines of Bible, Christian theology and Christian philosophy.

The pattern by which integration and interpretation may well take place for Biblical Studies will appear as follows:

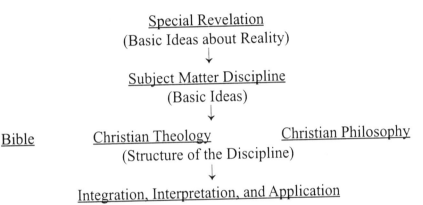

Special Revelation
(Basic Ideas about Reality)

Subject Matter Discipline
(Basic Ideas)

Bible   Christian Theology   Christian Philosophy
(Structure of the Discipline)

Integration, Interpretation, and Application

Following is a list of suggested themes to be stressed in integrating Bible and Theology with other subjects. Philosophy was dealt with under the classification of the Humanities.

1. Show the direct relevance of Bible, theology and Christian philosophy for the creation and extension of a Christian world view
2. Show the relevance of Bible, theology and Christian philosophy to the arts and sciences
3. Show the direct relevance of biblical truth to the realities of every day living
4. Reveal the primacy of divine revelation in the thought and life of true Christian people
5. Provide a thorough knowledge of the Bible as the inspired Word of God
6. Provide students with the ability to make the Bible rel-

evant for current problems and needs, both individually and socially

7. Stress Jesus Christ as Son of God, Logos, Savior, and the key to knowledge
8. Provide through theology a thorough study of the great doctrines of the Christian faith
9. Point up the integrating power of theology and Bible in relation to all truth
10. Show the God-centered pattern of reality
11. Show the destructive power of sin and in the light of this the need for special revelation and spiritual rebirth
12. Show how God restores the image of God in man
13. Development of proficiency in study habits, and effective thinking
14. Foundation ideas about God, man, sin, redemption, values, Christian institutions, prophecy, etc.
15. Thought structures, such as creation, purpose, process, providence and destiny, etc.

It must be recognized, of course, that the above suggestions are by no means exhaustive. Each Christian educator will add many more suggestions. To accomplish all these goals and more, it has been suggested that a complete reconstruction of knowledge becomes a necessity for the Christian. But it is also an unending process. It demands constant study and evaluation of truth on the part of Christian educators.

The curriculum of a Christian school is not restricted to the study and teaching of subject matter disciplines. There is the larger curriculum context of the atmosphere and activities of campus life. The Christian faith and life-style where Christian love is manifested provides the basis for fellowship and motivation as well as the elimination of the problems of lack of purpose present on so many secular campuses.

Research does not yield, however, many efforts by Christian colleges and schools to bring about integration in teaching and curriculum practices. In 1961, Spring Arbor College, in moving from a junior college status to a four-year college, developed a curriculum based on the following principles as stated by its then president, David McKenna. Their purpose was:

> To develop a general education curriculum for a four-year college which is: (a) *philosophically,* liberal arts in content, Christian in perspective, and relevant to the contemporary world in application; (b) *educationally,* descriptive of issues, analytical for alternatives and discriminating in choice, and (c) *organizationally,* economical in structure, enriched in method, and experimental in motive.

The result of this effort was to develop the Spring Arbor Concept known as "The Christian Perspective in the Liberal Arts." Student involvement, Christian commitment, and participation in world affairs were student outcomes to be sought. Using four liberal arts divisions -- Humanities, Natural Sciences, Social Sciences, Philosophy and Religion -- the faculty developed new courses focused upon Christian and other issues which arose naturally out of the study-in-depth of the facts and principles of a given field. Complementary to course offerings pre-college, midyear, and post-college programs were organized to emphasize the integration of academic involvement and spiritual commitment with the responsibility for participation in the affairs of the contemporary world. The learning theory used in this setup was threefold in character: (1) the identification of issues, (2) analysis of the issues, and (3) integration with the Christian perspective. Thus, description, discrimination, and decision were the three elements emphasized.

In 1970 the Calvin College Curriculum Study Committee published a report on Christian Liberal Arts Education (Eerdmans, 1970). In this report a series of essays revealed the nature of Calvinistic-Christian education. They took the position that the "core" of the liberal arts curriculum should on the one hand reflect the best in the liberal arts tradition and on the other an integrated Christian view of reality.

In 1984, the faculty at Central Methodist College, Fayette,

Missouri, instituted a series of faculty workshops to consider the relation of Christian values and the academic disciplines. The result of these studies was published by University Press of America, and edited by Floyd D. Crenshaw and John A. Flanders, and entitled <u>Christian Values and the Academic Disciplines</u>. This study was commendable in lifting up the importance of Christian values in Christian colleges. It is not too helpful, however, in specifically dealing with the question of integrating Christian truth in the various disciplines. It was also not too clear on exactly defining the Christian values. Only generalizations were given. Just how Christian values directly affected teaching and learning in the disciplines was not made clear.

10. <u>Academic Freedom</u>. In some circles it is contended that academic freedom becomes an impossibility in Christian colleges. Among Christian educators, however, the attitude is just the opposite. Christians have the greatest possible freedom to pursue truth wherever it is found because wherever truth is found there God is found.

Freedom of speech, however, should not be confused with academic freedom. Freedom of speech is the freedom to express one's opinions, whereas academic freedom is freedom to fully discover truth according to the rules of truth. Academic freedom lays responsibility on the teacher to guide and develop minds according to the demands of truth, not personal opinion. This demands complete integrity on the part of the teacher. All teachers in Christian schools should be honest enough to honor the request of the school administration to support the committed position of the Christian college.

11. <u>The Challenge</u>. Christian higher education cannot afford to be compartmentalized. It takes far more than church-relationship, required courses in religion, compulsory chapel, and a student Christian association to make a college thoroughly Christian. Some of these things have their places in the scheme of things, but an adequate philosophy of Christian education must go far deeper.

A Christian theory of education is an exposition of the idea that Christianity is a worldwide and life view, not simply a series of unrelated doctrines. Christianity includes all of life. Every real fact of knowledge and every facet of the universe find their places and their ultimate answers within Christianity. It is a system of truth enveloping the entire world within its grasp.

But where is the Christian college professor to gain Christian perspectives? The answer is several-fold. First, and closely related to the matter of recruiting, if the prospective Christian college professor is challenged sufficiently early in his college career, the curricular considerations at the undergraduate level must include biblical and theological studies. If he is sufficiently fortunate to be a graduate of a Christian college which is motivated by a Christian philosophy of higher education, he will have received a broad foundation in a college which does not merely <u>have</u> a religious program but <u>is</u> a religious program. With that kind of undergraduate training for the embryonic teacher, it would be perfectly safe to allow him to move freely in a typical secular university for his graduate training. It behooves the Christian college to look among its own students for those who will have potential value to the profession of teaching in higher education.

A second possible solution would be in the establishment of genuine Christian universities where Christian training could be secured. What would be possible and desirable is a university which would be liberal in the sense that it could permit and encourage the open expression of conviction on ultimate issue by both Christians and others. Many of our greatest secular universities could not be tagged as liberal in this sense, for expression of the Christian faith in a free manner is neither permitted nor encouraged. To be within the limits prescribed by law, religion must have little or <u>no</u> place. To be liberal is not to be neutral on ultimate philosophical and religious questions. To be liberal is to be willing to hear evidence from all points of view and to weigh it accordingly. In such a liberal university, Christian professors would teach along side secular humanists, and they would teach openly and freely, which they do not now in most cases do in our great secular institutions. This type of teaching situation, on the graduate level, would provide a lively ferment of ideas. Students would be confronted with various alternatives on ultimate issues and would be challenged to find a valid reason for

255

their faith. At present, the decision often goes against the Christian theistic position purely by default. The theistic voices are simply never heard.

The totality of the preparation of the college teacher would therefore be thus. In his undergraduate years he would be introduced to the broad fields of general education, and without narrowing his intellectual boundaries to a great degree, he would then begin to specialize in fields of his particular interest. It is hoped that this undergraduate education would be in a distinctively Christian framework. From there he would go into graduate study in a type of program where needlepoint concentration would be considered less important than breadth of understanding and knowledge. Work toward one of the so-called "broad" Ph.D.'s should be encouraged, but this should not be the eventual determinant of his success in the teaching field. This preparation should include proficiency in his chosen and cognate fields, some understanding of other disciplines in the curriculum, and the proper use of materials and methods to make his own teaching more effective.

Above all, he should have a love for the work. No person should inflict himself on college students if he has a distaste for the classroom. With these qualifications, the Christian teacher is in a position to render conspicuous service to the Christian college.

A third possibility is to be found in a plan for in-service training by which faculty members, while carrying on professional duties, will also have an opportunity under the supervision of more experienced colleagues to fill in the blank spots in his training. Following are three suggestions to accomplishing this:

(1) Optional courses for faculty members in Christian theology and the Bible
(2) Faculty forums for discussion of basic questions, educational and social values, relationships within the curriculum, and the nature of the Christian life
(3) Faculty organization along divisional lines to make group meetings possible, to pursue special problems in discussion at this level, and to increase the sense

of Christian unity and Christian obligation among the teachers.

The institution that desires its staff to grow professionally will utilize many such devices -- committee work, departmental studies, divisional projects, the writing of papers to be discussed at faculty meetings, workshops. The Christian institution can use the same tested educational methods to enrich the in-service training of those persons who come to its faculty ill-trained in the religious aspects and perspectives of the college teaching profession.

Many churches have found that one way to bless the world is not to withdraw from it but rather to minister to it. Likewise, if the Christian college is to be used of God most effectively it must relate and minister to the world. Some colleges maintain the status quo or withdraw from the culture to develop some internal personal emphasis. To be most effective the Christian liberal arts college needs to understand its cultural context, not compromise with it, and work to change it for God's glory. We must be in the world but not of it. We must oppose all anti-Christian forces and work toward turning the kingdoms of this world into the Kingdom of God. This calls for attaining knowledge of and living in a world of science and technology and handling vast resources of knowledge now available. All of this must be worked into a Christian philosophy of life and education which is workable in a twentieth century context. It calls for making God's revelation a reality in personal life and all classroom activities.

D. The Theological Seminary and Educational Practice

1. The Purpose and Needs. For many years a common concept of the purpose of the theological seminary has been to prepare people at the graduate level for Christian ministry, particularly for the pastorate. In this sense the seminary can be thought of as an extension of local church education, for in a very real sense this school is the church in action educating people at the graduate level.

For a long time the curricula in seminaries have followed the pattern of the classical curriculum. By this is meant that emphasis is laid on the personal competence of the minister. Without doubt personal competence is necessary but in recent decades greater emphasis has been placed on preparing ministers to work with people. This has called for a wide expansion in subjects classified in the "practical field." Not only has there been a broader concept of the role of the pastor but also of the nature of Christian ministry where other fields such as counseling, Christian education, music, evangelism and missions, to name a few, are provided for.

The great need in most seminaries is to avoid an exclusively "academic approach" in the teaching of subject matter. Subjects need to be taught, not only for factual knowledge involved, but also for their practical value in life application. This is true both for the practice of ministry as well as in the development of witnessing Christians. Growth in knowledge, grace and life-application should be sought as outcomes of seminary education.

2. The Program. To avoid the pitfalls mentioned above seminary educators need to see the direct relevance that divine revelation has in two important areas of ministry: (1) Christian life-style, and (2) Christian teaching and preaching.

The implications of divine revelation for the development of Christian character are not solely to be found in presenting the propositions of truth biblically and theologically, but primarily as "revelation of life." Doctrines are not mere statements of Christian fact but formulas for belief. Belief is the power of living truth but it is belief that is directly related to life. It is the work of the Holy Spirit to make "written truth" a "living reality." God comes into our lives in a saving and living relationship which frees us to live for and serve Him.

In both Christian teaching and preaching efforts should be made, not only to present the facts of Christian truth, but also to show how such truths are related to life. Instructors needs to show students how to utilize truths which they study in life situations and local church settings. Christian truth not only affects character development but also provides guidelines for Christian living and service. All of life is sacred and should be given to God. Each subject, therefore, should be presented in such a way that God is revealed and at the same time shows the student how to reveal God through the knowledge gained. A great deal of contact with and experience in local church programs will be required to adequately reach these goals.

A study of the history of the seminary curriculum reveals the same two-track problem suffered in liberal arts colleges. Following the university pattern many seminaries have been plagued likewise with the problem of "departmentalitis." Here largely independent cognitive disciplines taught by area specialists have caused them to function in isolation from one another. The pressure to increase subject matter specialities has helped to determine this situation.

The other track has resulted from the tension which exists between the classical-practical emphases in curriculum. This was particularly evident during the 1960's and 1970's. Pressures from ministers on the field to provide practical and useful subjects helped to bring about this development.

One way to correct this matter is to restore theological unity to the curriculum as a whole. It is the contention of this writer that one of the best ways to do this is by making the concept of divine revelation the unifying core of the curriculum. Studies which reflect this approach would lay biblical, theological and philosophical foundations for curriculum construction and the practice of ministry. Upon this base other studies of a more traditional character could be built. As indicated above the implications of a unified approach by means of revelation would also affect organization, administration and instruction.

DATE DUE

Demco, Inc. 38-293